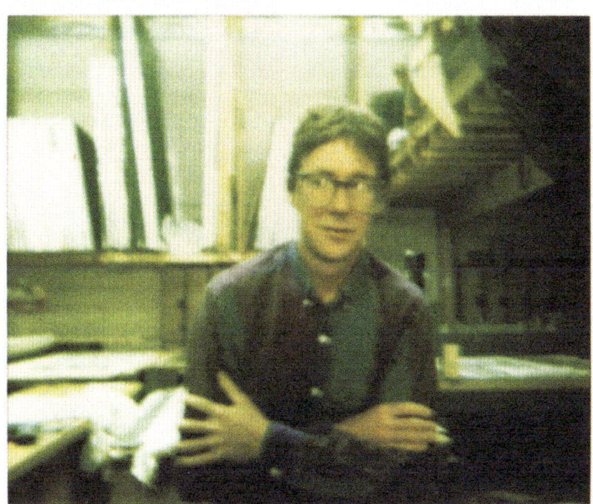

I found this polaroid on my garage floor. It's of the dummy I used in my photographic selfportrait titled No. *Originally it was taken as a working shot to help me visualize the final piece. Now both pictures almost seems equal to each other.*

electrovoices, Joseph Beuys' dead hare and so on all began to refigure an element human and subjective, however weirdly pictured or uttered. If something died, it was minimalist sculpture and its fullest implications for abstract modernism as the end of self-reflexive art, not Charles Ray. If something was born, it was identity politics and the arts of critical representation, not an unmediated savior.

If Ray is pointedly acute about anything referential, it is, for example, a McCracken fibreglass plank which he has knowingly rusticized, a mocking reference to that West Coast artist's mono-diagonals which, buttressing from floor to wall, represented the plasticized, shiny version of minimalism's anonymous silence. Like all of Ray's references, it is very topical, part of the journalistic and critical discourse of contemporary art at that moment[6]. Ray is not having a dialogue with a world outside of art, although the space for that is created; rather he is boring into art's self-serving myths, into its own self-justifications of social relevance. He is questioning art's dogmatic presumptions and pretentions by pricking himself in the process.

In minimalism and its rationally abstract forms, he had intuited a violence which underlay its assumptions and its macho demands on audiences. He understood what Donald Kuspit was later to write, that "the objectlikeness of the Minimalist art objects is sadomasochistic...in that they establish a dominance/submission relationship...there is something predatory about the Minimalist object, with its insidious way of invol-

Artists in the Exhibition

Ai Weiwei
Akasegawa Genpei
Tauba Auerbach
Robert Bechtle
Dike Blair
James Casebere
Maurizio Cattelan
Vija Celmins
John Clem Clarke
Chuck Close
Susan Collis
Thomas Demand
Esteban Pastorino Diaz
Daniel Douke
Keith Edmier
Leandro Erlich
Dan Fischer
Fischli and Weiss
Tom Friedman
Robert Gober
Duane Hanson
Alex Hay
Jasper Johns
Matt Johnson
Jeon Joonho
Edward Kienholz
Isaac Layman
David Lefkowitz
Ron Mueck
Catherine Murphy
Jud Nelson
Ruben Nusz
Kaz Oshiro
Roxy Paine
Evan Penny
Sylvia Plimack Mangold
Robert Rauschenberg
Charles Ray
Gerhard Richter
Ugo Rondinone
Peter Rostovsky
Edward Ruscha
Jonathan Seliger
Paul Sietsema
Rudolf Stingel
Yoshihiro Suda
Sam Taylor-Wood
Paul Thek
Robert Therrien
Mungo Thomson
Rirkrit Tiravanija
Gavin Turk
Andy Warhol
Paul Winstanley
Steve Wolfe

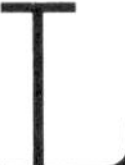

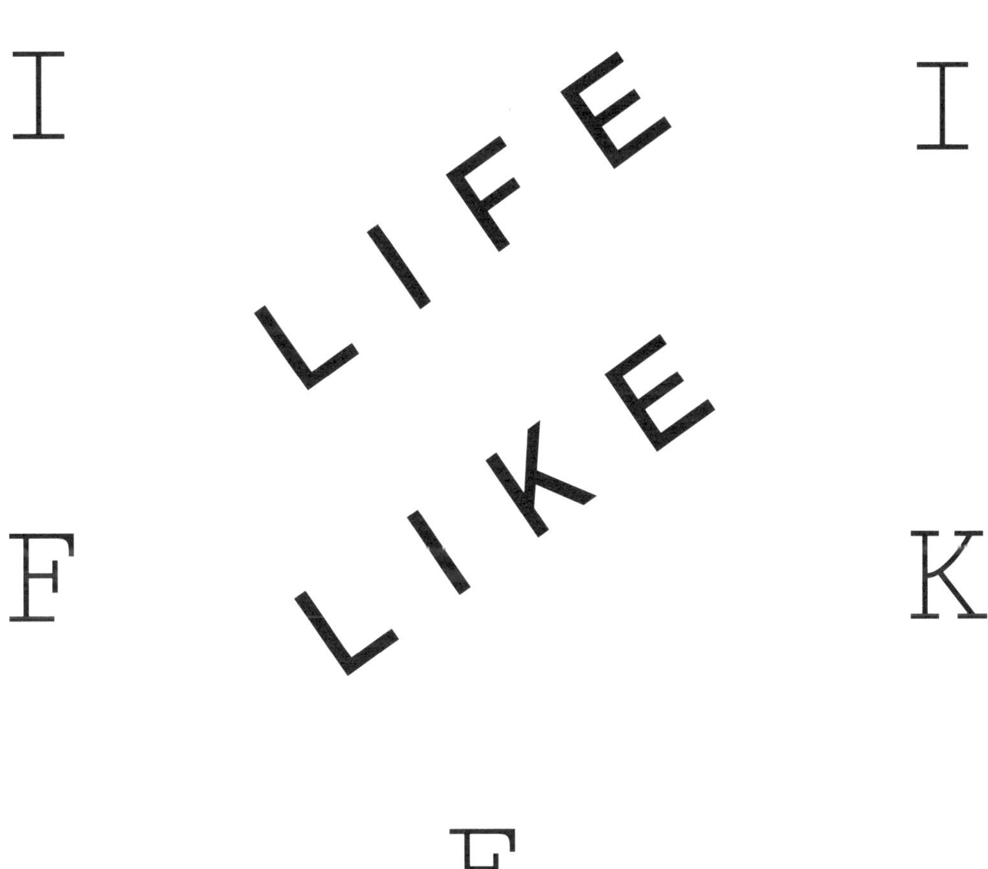

Siri Engberg
with contributions from
Michael Lobel, Josiah McElheny, and Rochelle Steiner

Walker Art Center, Minneapolis

Contents

Previous Lives Sections 1–5

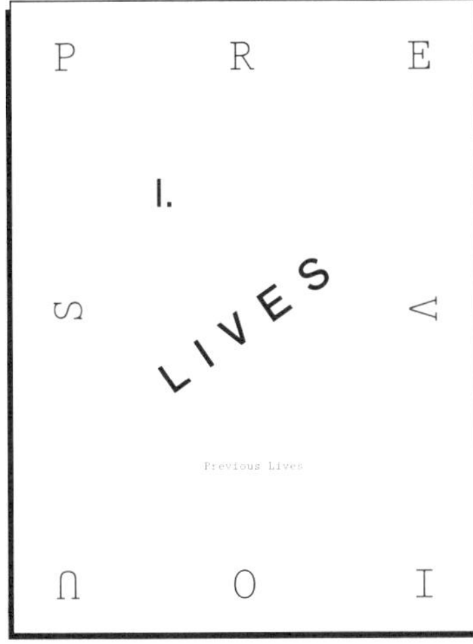

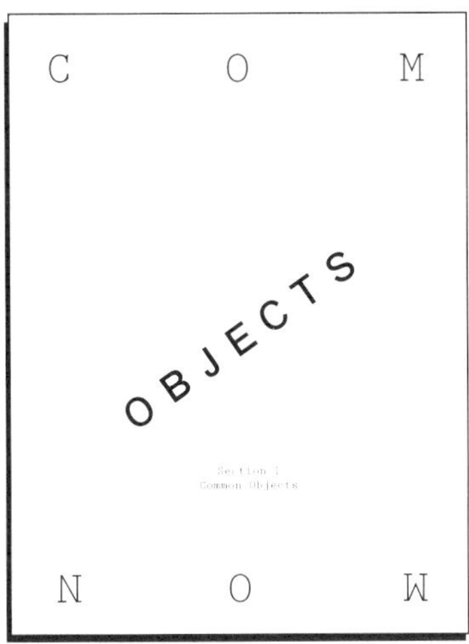

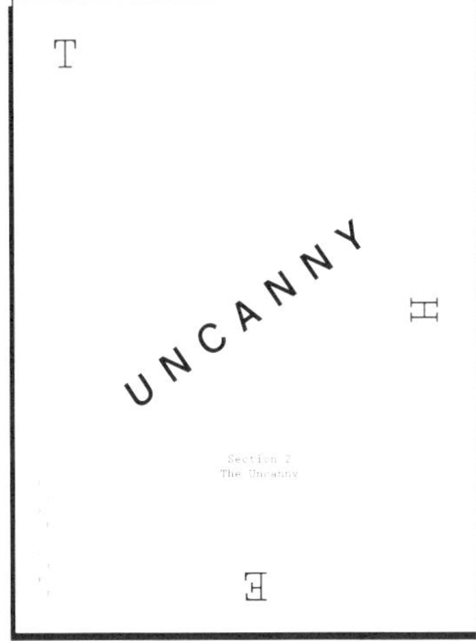

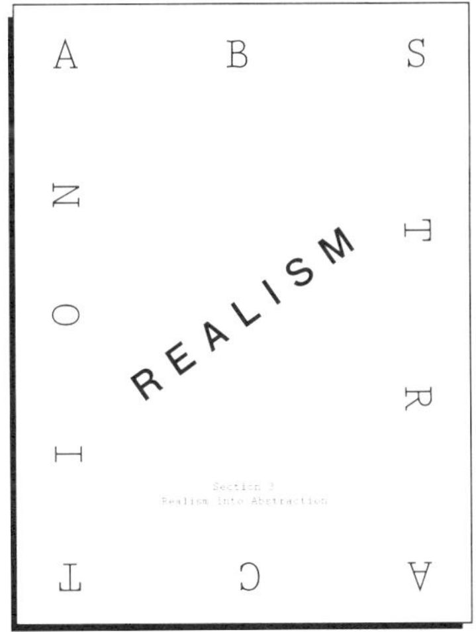

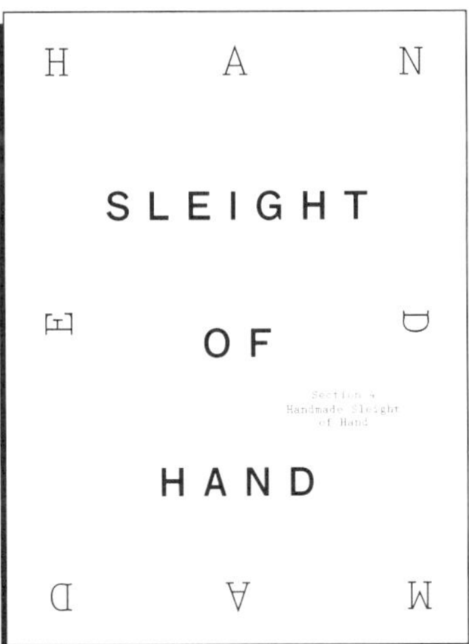

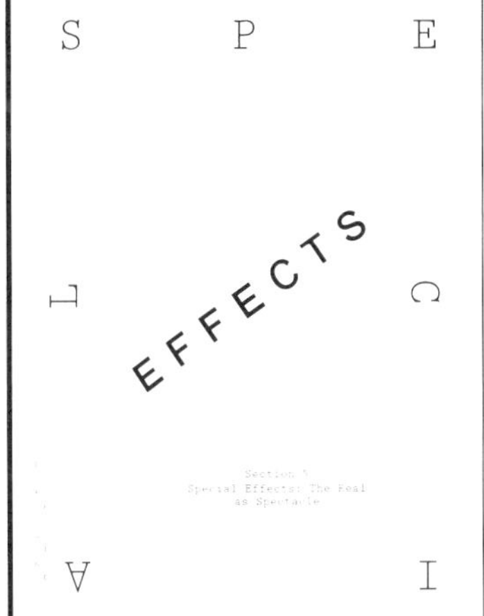

Foreword

What does it mean for an artist to faithfully render something from real life that is likely to go unnoticed because it resembles an ordinary object? Art has long since shed the burden of having to look like anything in particular, as it has seemingly exhausted every genre and ism. Yet the compulsion to strengthen the connective tissue between art and the stuff of the everyday persists. Indeed, in seemingly inverse proportion to the ease of producing packaged goods for the marketplace, many artists are slowing and complicating their own working methods by painstakingly re-creating the generic items that surround us and making them into objects of fixation and desire.

The Walker is pleased to present *Lifelike*, an exhibition that gathers the output of artists who have embraced this practice since the 1960s. From arrestingly realistic paintings based on offhand snapshots to meticulously handcrafted sculptures of unremarkable items, they transform the prosaic into something infused with narrative and metaphor, often mining unsettling terrain. The show surveys more than ninety pieces by an international, multigenerational roster of practitioners and explores the many approaches through which they have pursued the effects of verisimilitude, including painting, sculpture, photography, drawing, video, and three-dimensional environments.

This broad view affirms that this particular type of mimetic realism—informed by the history of Pop Art and Marcel Duchamp's recontextualization of the readymade object in the early twentieth century—remains a significant presence, and that younger artists are continuing to redefine its possibilities. In today's intensely mediated world, attaining the type of trompe l'oeil figuration with which many of those represented in *Lifelike* are engaged is now easily afforded by the digital creation or enhancement of images, which can easily be harnessed to compelling effect. For the most part, however, what binds their oeuvre together is their rejection of the simpler route technology might offer in favor of handmade, labor-intensive fabrication. These are works about time, about noticing what gets lost between the fast-paced moments of day-to-day life.

Lifelike has been organized by Walker visual arts curator Siri Engberg, who has assembled a group of artworks that offer a fascinating account of the persistence of pictorial realism in contemporary art. By presenting recent work (most of it made within the past decade) against a backdrop of projects made by 1960s and 1970s artists who mined the in-between spaces unheralded by Pop or the Photorealists, *Lifelike* is the first exhibition to compellingly posit this sensibility as an art-historical continuum. Engberg's insightful essay in this publication examines this trajectory, exploring the links between artists across generations who have been drawn to this manner of production. She has additionally gathered contributions for the catalogue from artist Josiah McElheny and scholars Michael Lobel and Rochelle Steiner, and I extend thanks to each of them for approaching this topic from new critical angles.

A project of this scope and rich variety would not have been possible without the generosity of the many institutions, galleries, and private lenders, all listed on page 188, who have graciously parted with their works for the exhibition and its national tour. To them, we extend our utmost appreciation for making these loans available to be shared with audiences in this exciting context. We are enormously grateful for the early funding for this endeavor from the Andy Warhol Foundation for the Arts, which has helped support many important Walker projects. We thank the foundation's president, Joel Wachs, and its board of directors for their continued advocacy for the Walker and its ambitious exhibition program.

Significant gifts in support of *Lifelike* have been made by trustee Tom Crosby and his wife, Ellie; trustee Michael Peterman and his partner, David Wilson; and trustee John Thomson, and we are deeply indebted to them for their ongoing commitment to the Walker. *Lifelike* has received key support from the Private Client Reserve at U.S. Bank, whose generous sponsorship has made possible many Walker initiatives. We are thankful to Richard Payne, Michael Boardman, and Heidi Steiger for their support and enthusiasm for this exhibition. The Andrew W. Mellon Foundation, through a grant in support of Walker Art Center publications, provided underwriting for the exhibition's catalogue. We are fortunate to have the partnership of D.A.P./Distributed Art Publishers, Inc., and thank Sharon Gallagher and her staff for their commitment to this publication.

The remarkably dedicated and professional staff at the Walker has made this project a pleasure to present. Many individuals, listed in Engberg's acknowledgments on the following page, have made key contributions, and I echo her gratitude for their stellar efforts. I would also like to add my thanks to chief curator Darsie Alexander, chief of finance and development Christopher Stevens, chief of operations and administration Phillip Bahar, chief of communications and audience engagement Andrew Blauvelt, and chief financial officer and treasurer Mary Polta for conscientiously guiding the Walker in its many endeavors across the artistic disciplines.

We are delighted to be sharing this exhibition with the audiences of our partners on its national tour, and are grateful for the early enthusiasm for the project from director Susan Taylor, New Orleans Museum of Art; director Hugh Davies, Museum of Contemporary Art San Diego; and director Simone Wicha, Blanton Museum of Art, the University of Texas at Austin. We thank all of them for their engagement. Lastly, my great thanks to the artists whose works beguile us with their striking familiarity and unnerve us with their reimagination of the commonplace. It is they who have made this show a reality.

—Olga Viso, Executive Director, Walker Art Center

Acknowledgments

This exhibition has been a process of inquiry into the ways that artists can see the world around us, and what they may notice within the realm of the everyday. It examines a mode of working with realism that presents ordinary subject matter through sometimes extraordinary means, tracing what has been a steady trajectory in contemporary art since the late 1960s, appearing between major movements, and advancing with a quiet persistence that continues in the work of young artists today. For artists who have chosen to use a pictorial form of realism in their work, the angles of approach are vast. What unites the practitioners gathered in *Lifelike*, apart from their interest in achieving likeness, is an adherence to strict process, and an attitude toward allowing "the real" to lead to more conceptual, perhaps even intangible ends.

I wish first and foremost to thank the artists in the exhibition who have allowed their work to be examined in this context. Their positive responses to the project, openness to studio visits and conversation, and generosity with countless requests buoyed the project enormously. Special thanks are due to Ai Weiwei, Vija Celmins, Susan Collis, Keith Edmier, Robert Gober, Kaz Oshiro, Peter Rostovsky, Paul Sietsema, and Mungo Thomson for allowing us to print excerpts from their writings or interviews to provide the "Object Lessons" that punctuate this publication, casting further light on the working processes behind key works in the exhibition. Additional thanks are due to Edmier, who has contributed an insert to this book (found following page 136), a "relic" of the wallpaper custom-made for the installation of the kitchen from his *Bremen Towne* project, and to the Friedrich Petzel Gallery, New York, which helped to realize this special element.

Lifelike would not have been possible without the cooperation of a great many lenders, listed on page 188, who graciously allowed works from their collections to be part of this presentation and tour. I am grateful to them all for their engagement with the exhibition. Numerous gallerists, artist representatives, and staff at museums and private foundations generously helped facilitate loans and many other essential details surrounding the project. My thanks go to James Rondeau and Jackie Maman, the Art Institute of Chicago; Tim Blum, Jeff Poe, and Matt Bangser, Blum and Poe, Los Angeles; Wendy Blazier, the Boca Raton Museum of Art; Joanne Heyler and Vicki Gambill, the Broad Art Foundation, Santa Monica; James Cohan and Jessica Lin Cox, James Cohan Gallery, New York; Sadie Coles and Brinda Roy, Sadie Coles HQ, London; Paula Cooper and Alexis Johnson, Paula Cooper Gallery, Inc., New York; Jeffrey Grove, the Dallas Museum of Art; Lucien Terras, D'Amilio Terras, New York; Esther Dörring, Studio Thomas Demand, Berlin; Kathryn Reasoner and Cynthia Drennan, di Rosa, Napa, California; Frank Elbaz, Galerie Frank Elbaz, Paris; Derek Eller, Derek Eller Gallery, New York; Hudson, Feature, New York; Rosamund Felsen, Rosamund Felsen Gallery , Los Angeles; Laura Satersmoen, the Fisher Collection, San Francisco; Peter Freeman, Blair Brooks, and Matthew Armstrong, Peter Freeman Gallery, New York; Martha Blakey, Gagosian Gallery, New York; Andrew Richards and Catherine Belloy, Marian Goodman Gallery, New York; Joe Houston, Hallmark Art Collection, Kansas City; Sojung Kang, Gallery Hyundai, Seoul; Sean Kelly, Cecile Panzieri, and Jessica Venturi, Sean Kelly Gallery, New York; Ben Barzune, Knoedler and Company, New York; Sho Kuwajima, Gallery Koyanagi, Tokyo; Stephanie Jeanroy, Yvon Lambert, New York; Scott Lawrimore, Lawrimore Projects, Seattle; Elizabeth Leach, Elizabeth Leach Gallery, Portland, Oregon; Michael Govan, the Los Angeles County Museum of Art; Lawrence Luhring and Vanessa Critchell, Luhring Augustine, New York; Matthew Marks, Jacqueline Tran, and Katherine Orsini, Matthew Marks Gallery, New York; Marla Hand, the Mayer Family Collection, Chicago; Renee Conforte McKee and Karyn Behnke, McKee Gallery, New York; Louis Meisel, Louis K. Meisel Gallery, New York; Elizabeth Armstrong, the Minneapolis Institute of Arts; Kristin Makholm, the Minnesota Museum of American Art, St. Paul; Madeleine Grynsztejn, the Museum of Contemporary Art, Chicago; Paul Schimmel, Museum of Contemporary Art, Los Angeles; Dennis Szakacs, the Orange County Museum of Art, Newport Beach; Friedrich Petzel, Jason Murison, and Seth Kelly, Friedrich Petzel Gallery, New York; Giema Tsakuginov, the Philadelphia Museum of Art; David Hoyland, Seventeen Gallery, London; Tony Shafrazi and George Horner, Tony Shafrazi Gallery, New York; Jack Shainman and Elisabeth Sann, Jack Shainman Gallery, New York; Maureen Mahony, Robert Therrien Studio; Mary-Ellen Powell, the Frederick R. Weisman Art Foundation, Beverly Hills; and Dana Miller, the Whitney Museum of American Art, New York.

This project took root in 2006, and I wish to thank former Walker chief curator Philippe Vergne for his support of my early thinking on the topic, and current Walker executive director Olga Viso and chief curator Darsie Alexander for encouraging its development as an exhibition. They, along with my curatorial colleagues Clara Kim, Elizabeth Carpenter, Bartholomew Ryan, and Eric Crosby made many helpful suggestions along the way. In 2006, curatorial fellow Nancy Meyer did important preliminary research on the topic and potential artists. Her work was continued in 2010 by Camille Washington, who was instrumental in the planning phases of the exhibition, while intern Kristina Lovaas also assisted with early research. Walker curatorial fellow Yesomi

Umolu arrived as the project was fully taking shape, and was instrumental in assisting with all phases of the exhibition's realization. Her valued efforts are evident throughout the exhibition and this publication. Special thanks also go to librarian Rosemary Furtak, and to Michael Peterman, who cheerfully corralled a broad range of bibliographic materials as the project was honed. Department assistant DeAnn Thyse helped keep myriad administrative details surrounding the exhibition in good order.

Outside of the visual arts department, many individuals at the Walker made key contributions to the exhibition. In particular, registrar Jessica Rolland embraced the endeavor with her own brand of meticulousness, and with extraordinary proactivity and patience, carefully tracking an ever-evolving checklist and its many loans. Her watchful eye over the project and its tour, and her care for the works of art themselves was instrumental to the exhibition's success. This publication is the work of designer Andrea Hyde, who conceived of a book that captures the spirit of the wide-ranging approaches of its subject with her signature elegance and creativity. Kathleen McLean and Pamela Johnson made editorial sense of it all with much-appreciated good humor, while chief of communications and audience engagement Andrew Blauvelt, design director Emmet Byrne, and design studio coordinator Dylan Cole provided guidance on the publication. Cameron Wittig, Gene Pittman, and Barb Economon provided essential support with photography for the project, and senior imaging specialist Greg Beckel gave the catalogue's images clarity and beauty. I am grateful for the work of the Walker's exceptional crew, headed by Cameron Zebrun, which installed this exhibition and its many complex elements with sensitivity under the leadership of technician Scott Lewis. Sarah Schultz and her staff in the education and community programs department arranged a host of programs for visitors of all ages in conjunction with the exhibition, and Robin Dowden, Paul Schmelzer, and their colleagues in the department of new media allowed the exhibition to have a lively presence online. Ryan French, Christopher James, Julie Caniglia, and the staff of the marketing and public relations department ensured that *Lifelike* had great reach and audience appeal. I also extend thanks to Christopher Stevens, Marla Stack, Annie Schmidt, and their colleagues in the membership and development department for securing key project support while engaging a range of donors and members through related events.

I echo Olga Viso's thanks to chief of operations and administration Phillip Bahar and chief financial officer Mary Polta, who kept the big picture, financial and otherwise, in mind at all times, as well as her acknowledgment of the funders who made this exhibition possible. The project was bolstered considerably by the early show of support from the Andy Warhol Foundation for the Visual Arts, and I thank Joel Wachs and Pamela Clapp at the foundation for their advocacy and generosity.

We are pleased to be able to feature writings in this publication from contributors Michael Lobel, Josiah McElheny, and Rochelle Steiner, each of whom has engaged with the exhibition's themes from a distinct vantage point, and has added important scholarly discourse around this particular strain of realism in contemporary art. I am grateful for the conversations I had with each as the exhibition took shape. I also extend thanks to the many others who helped my thinking or otherwise engaged with the exhibition, including Elizabeth Armstrong, Dike Blair, Carter (who offhandedly tossed me a title, which stuck), James Casebere, Michael Duncan, Keith Edmier, Matt Johnson, David Lefkowitz, Ruben Nusz, Paul Sietsema, Peter Rostovsky, and Lawrence Wechsler. I am delighted that the exhibition will have a broad audience through its tour, and wish to thank my colleagues who will realize the project at their hosting institutions: director Susan Taylor and curator of modern and contemporary art Miranda Lash, New Orleans Museum of Art; director Hugh Davies and chief curator Kathryn Kanjo at the Museum of Contemporary Art, San Diego; and director Simone Wicha, deputy director for art and programs Annette DiMeo Carlozzi, and manager of exhibitions and publications Collette Crossman at the Blanton Museum of Art, the University of Texas at Austin.

Lastly, I extend great thanks to my family—Marty, Simon, and Eliza Broan—whose support and love make all things possible. This show is for them.

—Siri Engberg, Curator, Walker Art Center

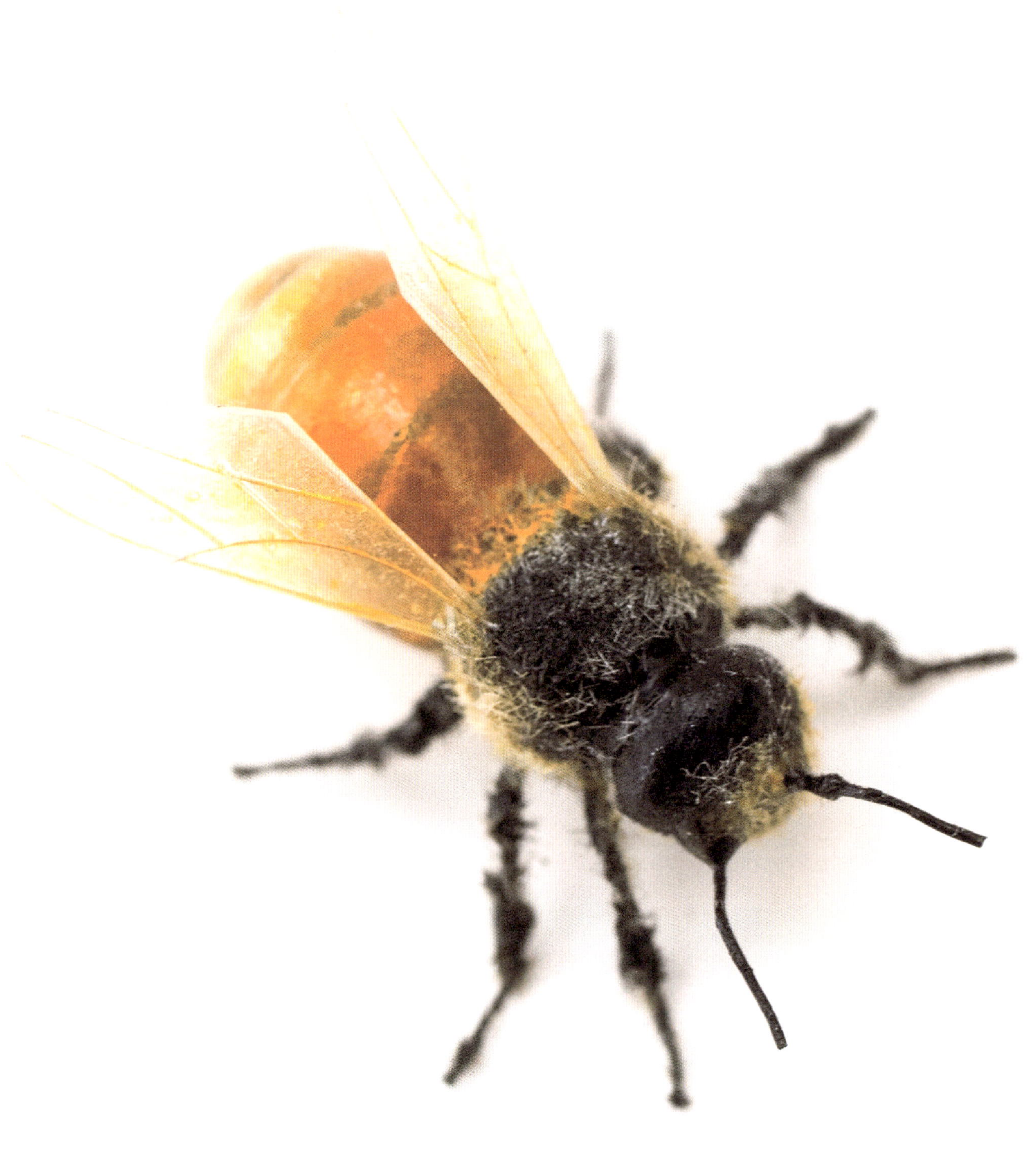

Tom Friedman *Untitled* 2001 clay, wire, fuzz, hair, plastic, paint

P R E

I.

S LIVES V

Previous Lives
Siri Engberg

L I F E L I K E

U O I

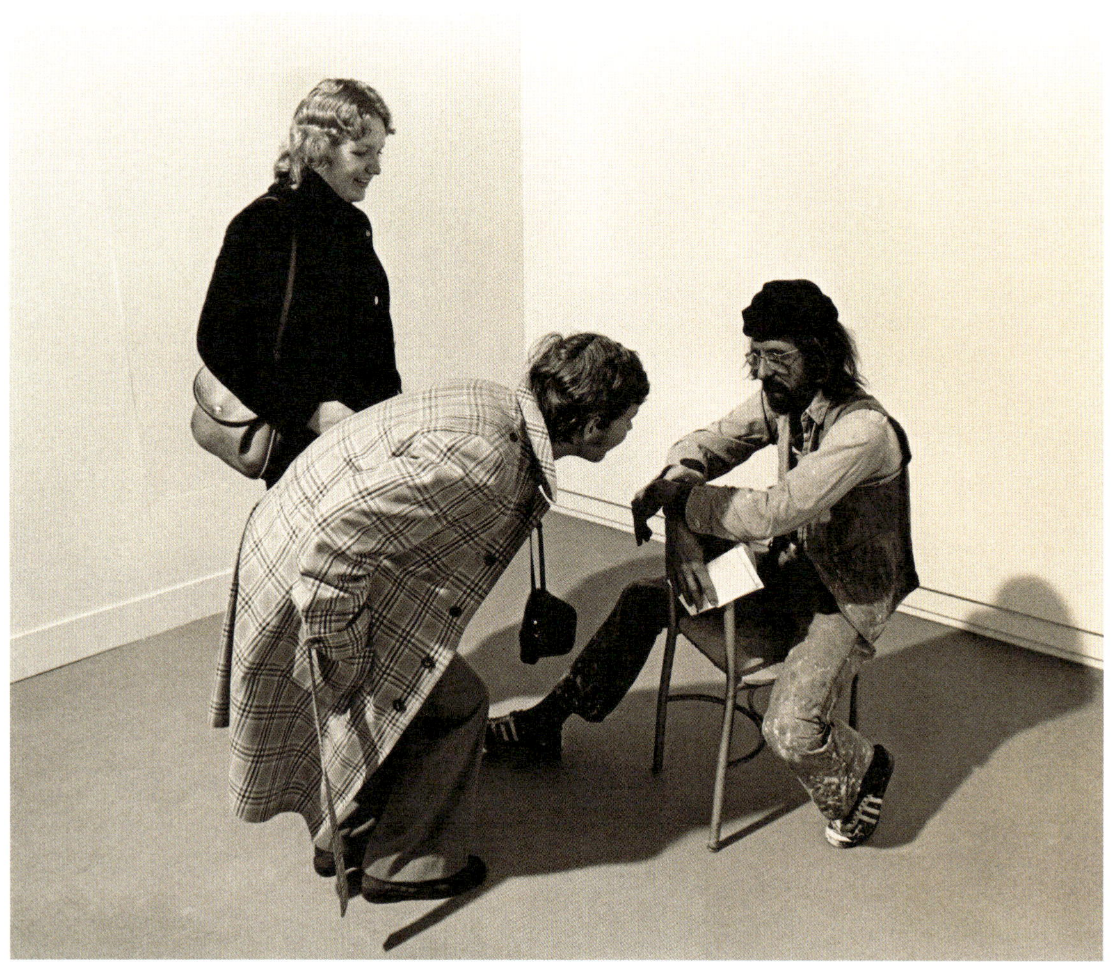

Fig. 1 Installation view of Duane Hanson's *Seated Artist* at documenta 5, Kassel, Germany, 1972

“You always know when you’re seeing an illusion created by a magician. It’s not real and that’s the pleasure in it.”(1) —Chuck Close

Introduction

Illusions have enormous power to captivate and to marshal our attention toward things we might otherwise deem unimportant. When scrutinized through an artist’s hands and eyes, then translated via meticulous, labor-intensive means to a work of art—illusionism as conjured in the studio—ordinary subjects have the potential to be transformed and to take on new meaning. While these renditions might in fact appear quite similar to their source, their past lives as objects, photographs, or fleeting observations are often revealed. This exhibition is an effort to gather a range of contemporary artists working since the 1960s who have at times embraced the practice of painstaking re-creation in their work, fusing it with the subject matter of the generic reality that surrounds us. This impulse toward depicting “the real” has persevered with rich variety, alongside various isms and moments of fashion in the art world, and is as relevant to many artists working today as it was to their post-Pop predecessors.

This persistence is all the more interesting to examine at the current moment, an age in which the quotidian has become ever more amplified by way of genres such as reality television and technologies that allow greater distribution of the real in countless manifestations. Images—both accurate and imprecise—of every conceivable phenomenon and event are captured and exchanged on smartphones. The mundane details of personal lives, conveyed with varying degrees of veracity, are freely shared online in real time. All of this happens at breakneck speed, potentially numbing us to the possibility that one of these images or moments may in

(1) “Vija Celmins Interviewed by Chuck Close,” in *Vija Celmins*, ed. William S. Bartman (Los Angeles: A.R.T. Press, Art Resources Transfer, Inc., 1992), 17.

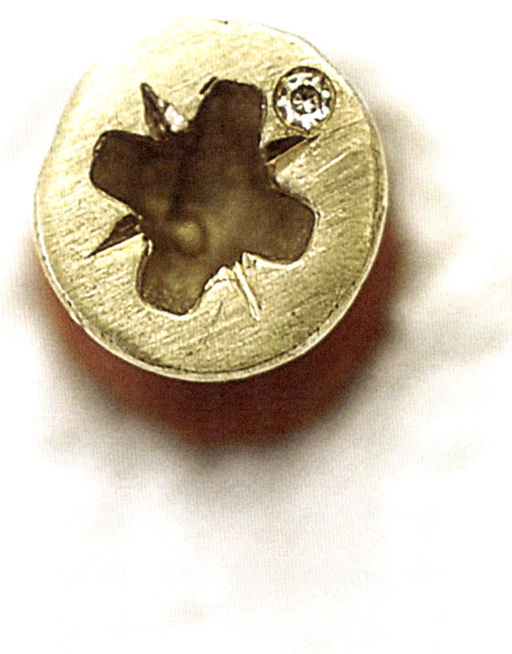

Fig. 2 Susan Collis *Made Good* 2007 18-carat white gold (hallmarked), diamond, coral, silver

fact be remarkable. We have no choice but to be subjective. We have come to accept reality as imperfect.

The works in the exhibition pose a provocative set of questions. What does it mean to be making "realistic" art in an era in which hybrid or dematerialized forms of artistic production are now prevalent? What dialogue does realism have with artists' expanded practice in the twenty-first century as well as the legacies of other postwar movements? How have artists found new means of creating a compelling conceptual framework while still maintaining an essential visual fidelity? Can a use of realism—something rendered with a visually accurate relationship to the observed world—be seen as unconventional in the context of contemporary art?

While their works have been made at various points in time over the past four decades, the artists discussed here share a desire to give us pause for contemplation, often reconstructing images or objects verbatim in order to present what is familiar in a new light: as Magritte famously painted (and pronounced) in 1928, "*Ceci n'est pas une pipe*" (This is not a pipe). These are works that play with verisimilitude and literalness, but also foreground fabrication as the path toward representation. Here, disquieting resemblance becomes a portal through which to consider more abstract ideas. Unexpected materials, shifts in scale, and sly contextual devices variously reveal the manner in which a subject's "authenticity" is manufactured.

This is a story of a particular thread of pictorial realism and its lasting resonance in contemporary art. It is important to acknowledge that the field of possibilities for this tendency is dauntingly large. The artists considered here share a desire to investigate the quieter side of the quotidian, presenting a kind of naturalism underpinned by deliberate craftsmanship and an underlying sense of (sometimes disconcerting) artifice. Some work from photographs; others seek inspiration from the observed world in all of its ordinariness, and the notion that a tangible, perhaps ephemeral object or moment can somehow be brought back to life—reinterpreted through the artist's hand as reclaimed images or post-Duchampian, remade readymades. It is in the encounter with these works that Freud's notion of the uncanny, the tension between familiar and foreign, takes hold as one experiences what artist Josiah McElheny later in this book calls the "hand-formed...perfectly imperfect" physicality of the work. It is in this moment that one's desire for interpretation comes up against the artist's exacting representation. One's sense of something being not quite right erodes the initial assumption of the object as "real," then is replaced by awe and fascination at the compulsive labor of its making.

Interest in the quotidian has long been tethered to realism, from Renaissance trompe l'oeil to seventeenth-century Dutch still lifes, becoming particularly prevalent as the corner of modernism was rounded in the late 1800s, and Édouard Manet, with his unabashedly straightforward portraits and scenes of the contemporary European social landscape, was proclaimed "the painter of modern life," followed by Gustave Courbet, whose astonishingly literal paintings foregrounded the "real." In mid-1800s America, Thomas Eakins' uninflected paintings of urban Philadelphia, and his interest in life viewed through the camera's lens, established him as a singular voice in figurative painting. Edward Hopper, too, fared well in his designation as a realist, though his depictions of urban spaces and rural byways were tinged with the nuance of narrative and imagination. It is no secret, however, that realism—or art that could be characterized as appearing realistic—itself has long suffered from its unfashionable associations with rote technical skill, and is often suppressed in art-historical discourse or discussed with controversy for its identification with populist desire (consider Andrew Wyeth). A number of critics have noted that realism often surfaces at times of crisis—be it the Vietnam era, where this exhibition begins, or our current post-9/11 world—as a reactionary return to conservative modes of art-making or perhaps a fatigue with the abstract or immaterial.(2) Evaluated now, however, its continued relevance for artists across generations, many now working through the lens of conceptualism, continues to be advanced with captivating variety.

(2)
See Dieter Roehlstrate, "Modernism, Postmodernism and Gleam: On the Photorealist Work Ethic," *Afterall* 24 (Summer 2010), http://www.afterall.org/journal/issue.24/modernismpostmodernism.and.gleamon.the.photorealist.work.ethic.

C O M

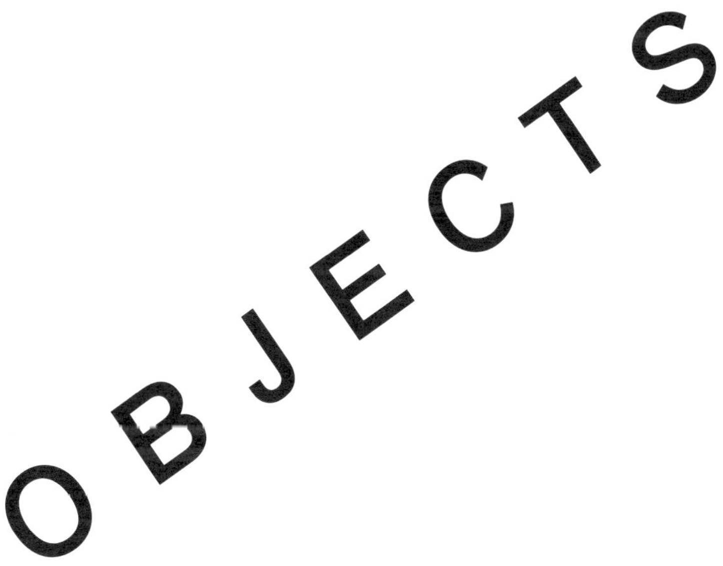

Section 1
Common Objects

N O M

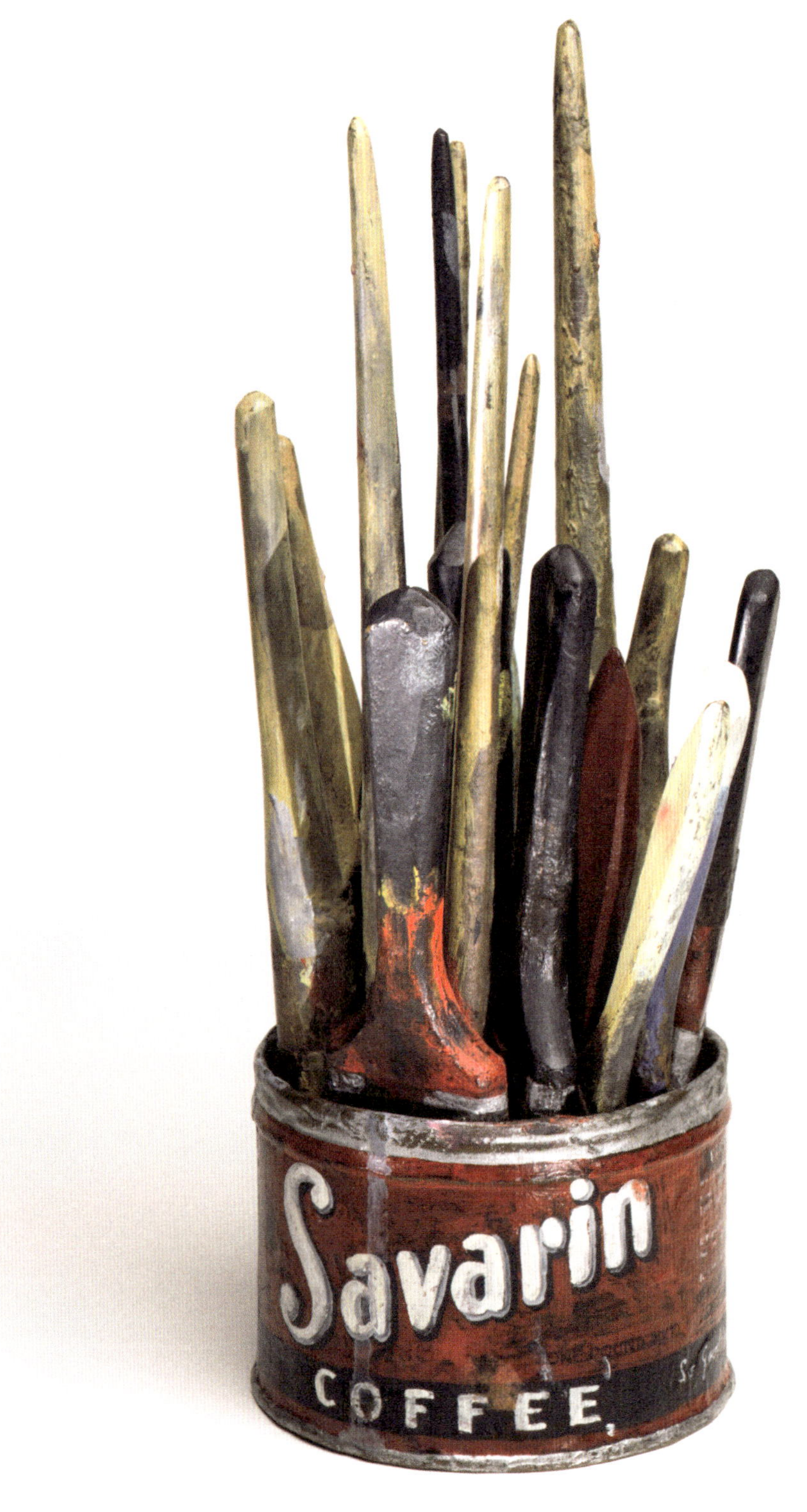

Fig. 3 Jasper Johns *Painted Bronze (Savarin)* 1960 painted bronze Art ©Jasper Johns/Licensed by VAGA, New York, NY

Common Objects

The emergence of Pop in the early 1960s provided a hearty dose of realism, and a brashly ironic antidote to the bravado of the postwar years of Abstract Expressionism. It also addressed the particulars of a new, consumer-driven world.[3] Andy Warhol's Coca-Cola bottles, Roy Lichtenstein's comic-book imagery, and the brightly painted foodstuffs and household miscellany of Claes Oldenburg cemented a new kind of interest in the everyday and its commodities. At the same time, Fluxus elevated banal actions and subjects to center stage with its interdisciplinary blending of performance, music, object-making, and dissemination of printed matter.

Within this climate and alongside the name-brand flash of Pop, common objects began to appear in a particular form of illusionistic painting and sculpture that emerged more quietly at mid-decade. A divergent group of artists began creating canvases that foregrounded fabrication and process over surface, embracing utterly ordinary subject matter. In so doing, they began to infuse the art of the decade with a new kind of poetic reflection.

It is interesting here to explore the ways in which this strain of thinking began to emerge, and to note that in the United States, the impulse was not just centered in New York, but was decidedly bicoastal. As early as 1962, the first exhibition of Warhol's work to appear on the West Coast was shown at the Ferus Gallery in Los Angeles. That same year, curator Walter Hopps presented *New Painting of Common Objects*, a groundbreaking installation at the Pasadena Art Museum containing work by Warhol, Lichtenstein, and other ascending stars. The exhibition remained latent in the consciousness of a number of West Coast artists for whom the show had been an in-person introduction to Pop, and became an important touchstone for those interested in looking closely at everyday subjects from a more personal—rather than a mass-market—perspective.

In California, this path had been explored at the beginning of the 1960s by Ed Ruscha and Joe Goode (two of the few West Coast artists included in Hopps' show). In his early paintings such as *Actual Size* (1962), which features a life-size can of the processed meat product Spam, Ruscha began to insert realistically rendered objects into the picture plane. Goode's *Milk Bottle* series, begun in 1961, included real bottles, positioned on the floor in front of monochrome canvases of the same color. Vija Celmins' first paintings were exhibited in 1965 and included images of humble objects, painted from life, that populated her studio, such as a fan, space heater, and the steam tray in *Eggs* (1964; plate 2). That same year, Maxwell Hendler began making small, realist oil paintings from direct observation, depicting similarly modest scenes in works such as *Afternoon Television* (1965; fig. 4), which shows its unmoored subject in an otherwise spare room, accompanied by its carefully painted electrical cords. And Robert Bechtle, working in San Francisco, began at this time to paint canvases from photographs, such as *Nancy Sitting* (1964; fig. 5), in which or-

(3)
Early Pop was often packaged as realist, as in shows such as *New Realism* at New York's Sidney Janis Gallery in 1963. For work that emerged in the latter half of the decade, this label was misleading. As Gregory Battcock noted in the introduction to his 1975 anthology *Super Realism*, Pop was preoccupied with presenting "first, recognizable pictures, and only secondly, realism as such." See Gregory Battcock, ed., *Super Realism: A Critical Anthology* (New York: E.P. Dutton and Co., Inc., 1975), xxvi.

dinary objects—crackers, condiments, glassware—steal the scene from the accompanying female figure.

While they emerged concurrently with Pop, these California artists notably shared an interest in subject matter that came not from pop culture but from life, and an inclination to dwell on a fragment of lived experience by isolating a singular object or magnified detail from an observed or photographic source. This distillation was a notion that seemed to stem not as much from traditions of realism as from Duchamp, whose readymades—both the found objects and the later incarnations that were fabricated by others—ushered in a new acceptance of pedestrian subjects. It is not inconsequential that in 1963 the Pasadena Art Museum, again under Hopps, presented the exhibition *By or of Marcel Duchamp or Rrose Sélavy*—the first-ever retrospective of the artist's oeuvre. The show featured 114 works of art, including major loans from Europe and the Philadelphia Museum of Art's Arensberg Collection. Ruscha attended the opening, as did many other artists from the region.

Duchamp's philosophy maintained that any subject—however prosaic—could be worthy of interest, thus the act of singling out objects from the everyday world constituted an artistic gesture in itself. This approach proved liberating, opening doors not only for Pop, but for a broad range of approaches to realism (not to mention conceptual art) that emerged in the mid- to late 1960s. Jasper Johns and Robert Rauschenberg, often cited as key bridges from Abstract Expressionism to Pop, were among the first to look to Duchamp's example. Their work of the late 1950s provided an important attitudinal shift that would influence subsequent artists working in a pictorial mode. Where Rauschenberg incorporated items in the form of found objects, à la Duchamp's readymades, Johns employed a level of illusionism that called into question whether the objects depicted were handmade or not. His small-scale cast sculptures, such as his Ballantine ale or Savarin coffee cans, were carefully painted to look as though they were in fact "real" (fig. 3). Both sought to emulate or elevate that which was discarded, as seen in Johns' use of lightbulbs and worn brooms, or Rauschenberg's fascination with cast-off furniture, tires, mattresses, and other detritus, as well as corrugated cardboard (1971; plate 7), which he would sometimes fabricate as trompe l'oeil constructions.[4]

Warhol's *Brillo Boxes* of 1964 (plate 1), perhaps the artist's most Duchampian gesture, has sparked spirited conversation among art historians and philosophers alike, and is also a touchstone for many artists now making work that hybridizes image and object. While the painted wooden sculptures (Warhol made many versions) boasted a recognizable brand name, they were especially notable in that they came closer to pure mimetic replication than most objects of the Pop era. Philosopher and critic Arthur Danto, revisiting the piece in a much-discussed essay of the late 1990s, reflected on the *Brillo Box* as something "drawn from a kind of underground of familiar imagery so seemingly distant from the aesthetic preoccupations of those nominally interested in art that it came as a shock to see it in an art gallery, while at the

(4)
Rauschenberg's *Cardbird* series first appeared as a unique group of constructions made from found cardboard fragments. He went on to produce limited-edition versions of the *Cardbirds* at Gemini G.E.L. in Los Angeles, in which the corrugated "cardboard" was fabricated from custom-made acid-free paper, and the markings—such as tape, mailing labels, and the like—were printed on the objects, using photolithography to create the illusion of the surface of an actual found box.

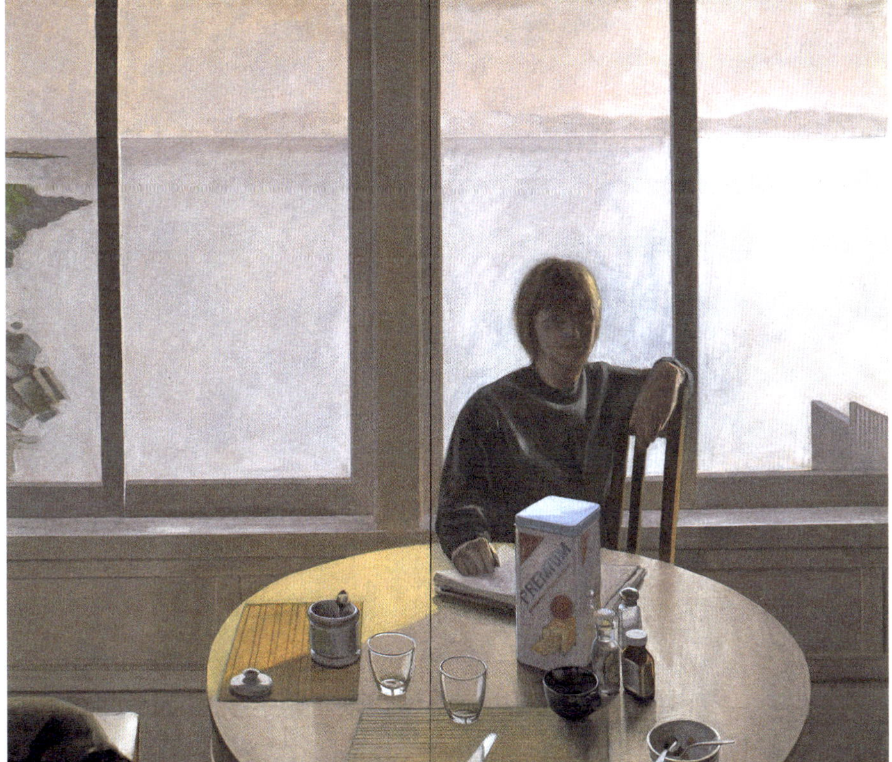

Fig. 4 Maxwell Hendler *Afternoon Television* 1965 oil on wood

Fig. 5 Robert Bechtle *Nancy Sitting* 1964 oil on canvas

same time it was clear that there was nothing in the prevailing conception of art to rule it out."[5] As an apparent clone of the genuine article, Danto argues, this piece signaled a kind of awakening about the possibilities for art, and unleashed a host of philosophical questions, chief among them being whether there is any difference between a real object and an artistic rendition of it, if in fact one cannot perceive the difference. Poet and critic John Yau, considering these questions, reminds us that in writing about the *Brillo Boxes*, Danto had recounted a debacle in 1964 in which a Canadian dealer was trying to import the works. Experts from the National Gallery of Canada were called in for an opinion, and upon reviewing photographs of the piece, they and Canadian customs officials came to the conclusion that these items were not "original sculptures."[6] As a result, the works were subject to additional tax, as they were deemed merchandise, not art. Shortly thereafter, in Japan, the ethics of resemblance pushed the discourse of art back into the real world, when in 1967 Akasegawa Genpei issued fake banknotes as part of his performative practice, leading to his arrest; at issue in his trial was the question of whether he had made real currency, or simply "real" art (plate 5).

Pop in the 1960s, of course, embraced this invitation to scrutinize our culture of consumerism by devouring it, so much so that at the decade's close, the bright and shiny appeared tired. Warhol had moved from Campbell's Soup cans to society portraits and the launch of *Interview* magazine, Oldenburg had turned toward large-scale sculpture, and Minimalism had moved in, establishing a firm hold just as conceptual art was beginning to percolate. There was room for something else. Photorealism, which followed closely on Pop's heels, emerged in the late 1960s, taking upon itself the task of providing a more detached view of contemporary life. The American Photorealists—including Richard Estes, Ralph Goings (fig. 6), and Robert Cottingham—favored a cool form of verisimilitude based on carefully composed photographic sources. Their paintings, sometimes cacophonously populated with visual information, demonstrated an every-square-inch attention to surface and pictorial detail.

Perhaps as a response to the commercial critique posed by Pop artists, the Photorealists became new documentations of modern life on canvas. Their preferred subject matter was the life of the city (Photorealism tended to shy away from the domestic sphere)—its fast pace and its urban architecture, automobiles, and industrial signage. Rarely did the images contain people. These were paintings grounded in the notion of the photographic gaze; they were edited, cropped, and illuminated by light, be it sunlight, neon, or incandescent. Techniques borrowed from commercial art, such as overhead projection and airbrushing, helped to establish a field of vision, eliminate brushstrokes, and facilitate the sensation of the image's areas of focus and nonfocus. This mode of working, both in painting and sculpture, which had many names—among them photorealism, hyperrealism, radical realism, and superrealism—began to take hold around 1966, and had its peak in 1972 when Documenta 5 focused on these artists specifically (fig. 1).

(5)
Arthur C. Danto, "The Art World Revisited: Comedies of Similarity," in *Beyond the Brillo Box: The Visual Arts in Post-Historical Perspective* (New York: Farrar Straus Giroux, 1992), 40.

(6)
John Yau, "Daniel Douke's Defiance," in *Daniel Douke* (Los Angeles: Peter Mendenhall Gallery, 2008), 7. The Danto review first appeared in *The Nation*, September 13, 2006.

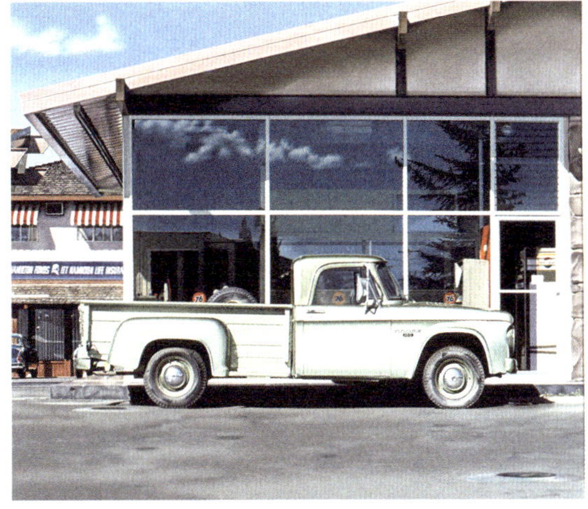

Fig. 6 Ralph Goings *Golden Dodge* 1971 oil on canvas

It began to lose its art-historical luster after this moment, and has had a somewhat conflicted stance ever since. Though underrecognized in academic accounts of postwar art, Photorealism has begun to receive renewed consideration—as seen in a run of exhibitions on the subject in Europe—by a recent generation of scholars and curators as a movement that, despite its populist stigma, was in fact quite significant. Recent twenty-first-century curatorial projects on the influence of photography on painting, the tension between realism and reality, the influence of technology on perception, and the relationship of the hyperreal to surrealism have integrated 1960s and 1970s Photorealism into the dialogue, in a departure from previous considerations, which tended to gather these artists into their own historical subgroup.(7)

With a nod toward Pop's acceptance of the everyday, commercial reality of modern life, Photorealism also made a parallel commentary on the concurrent activities of Minimalism, with its clean-lined precision and removal of the artist's "hand" through systematic, sometimes mechanical methods of creation. As art historian Jean-Claude Lebensztejn has remarked, the movement itself—if it were to be called a movement—suffered from ambiguity, as some took it to be "reactionary," while others saw it as "radical." Photorealism's accessibility and simultaneous linkage with Minimalism and Conceptual Art, he notes, "was behind both its success and its eclipse."(8) In its dogged pursuit of photographic surface quality, Photorealism sought to erase classical distinctions between what was real and what was imitation; visual veracity took precedence over subject matter, which tended toward the formulaic. If Pop gravitated to the recognizable in our culture (brand names, celebrities, eye-grabbing product packaging and commercial illustration), Photorealism embraced archetypal emblems of Americana (cars, dime-store lunch counters, movie marquees) and emulated the slick, reflective facades of glass and metal that accompanied them, not to mention the glossy surface of the photograph itself. As Lebensztejn notes, "In Hyperrealism, you get the impression that the subject matter is very present but of no importance and also that the painting is very present but of no importance. This insignificant pres-

(7)
A selection of international exhibitions with catalogues addressing this and related topics over the past decade include *Hypermental: Rampant Reality, 1950-2000: from Salvador Dalí to Jeff Koons* (organized by Bice Curiger and Christoph Heinrich for the Kunsthaus Zürich and Hamburger Kunsthalle, 2000-2001); *Hyperrealismes USA, 1965-1975* (organized by Jean-Claude Lebensztejn for the Musée d'Art moderne et contemporain, Strasbourg, 2003); *The Painting of Modern Life: 1960s to Now* (organized by Ralph Rugoff for the Hayward Gallery, London, 2007); *Hyper Real: The Passion of the Real in Painting and Photography* (organized by Achim Hochdörfer for the Museum Moderner Kunst Stiftung Ludwig, Vienna, 2010); and *10,000 Lives, the 8th Gwangju Biennale* (organized by Massimiliano Gioni for the Gwangju Biennale Foundation, Gwangju, Korea, 2010).

(8)
Jean-Claude Lebensztejn, "Locus Focus: Jean Pierre Criqui talks with Jean-Claude Lebensztejn," *Artforum* (Summer 2003): 150.

ence—or the insignificance of the presence—is intriguing."(9)

By this time, the camera was emerging for artists as an important tool. The Kodak Instamatic, first introduced in 1963, and other inexpensive models, had become standard accoutrements in the culture at large. Everyone had a camera, everyone took pictures. It was this more casual approach to capturing images that many artists, untrained as photographers, began to embrace as a vehicle through which to document life's minutiae. Their works ushered in a new acceptance of photography as a conceptual tool, rather than simply a documentary one. Ruscha's enormously influential books, such as *Every Building on the Sunset Strip*, *Some Los Angeles Apartments*, and *Various Small Fires and Milk* (fig. 7), which he made throughout the 1960s, were self-published compilations of his own snapshots, matter-of-factly categorized, of Los Angeles ordinariness. Similarly, Sol LeWitt photographed manhole covers, the physical contents of his apartment, and the building outside his studio window and corralled these images-as-information into photobooks.(10) Chuck Close's first self-portrait of 1967 was based on a photographic image the artist made while turning the camera clumsily on himself (fig. 8) after establishing focus on a nearby brick wall. "I never said the camera was truth," he noted in 1970. "[It is rather] a more accurate and more objective way of seeing."(11)

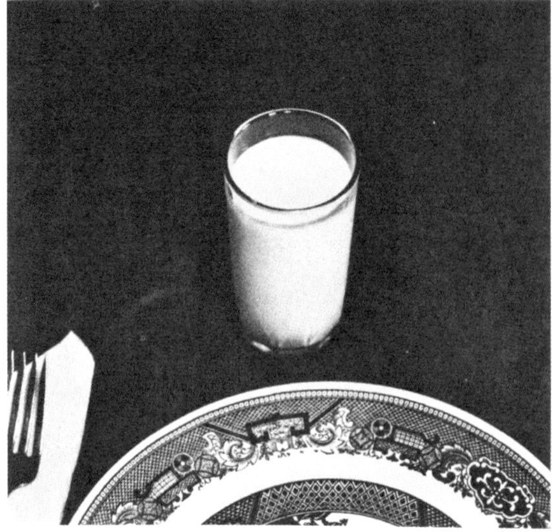

Fig. 7
Ed Ruscha Page from *Various Small Fires and Milk* 1964
artist's book with 16 black-and-white illustrations

It is useful to examine the 1960s work of Close, Celmins, Bechtle, and Sylvia Plimack Mangold in the United States, and of Gerhard Richter and Franz Gertsch in Europe as emblematic of an important shift away from Photorealism. Rather than employing photography as a compositional device that could be controlled, these artists were using photographs, whether their own or borrowed, in the spirit of found objects, ready to be reclaimed through painting. After her first paintings made from life in 1964, Celmins soon turned primarily to photographic sources (mostly newspapers and magazines), sometimes even presenting the clipping itself as an object in the image. "The thing I liked about working with an image that was already in front of me, that I didn't have to make up," she has said, "was that, even though I found it, it had a sort of poetic resonance. I chose it. So, that's already composition."(12)

This intriguing and unlikely convergence of "poetic resonance" located in inconsequential images with the methodical processes in-

(9)
Ibid.

(10)
See Sol LeWitt's influential artist's books, including *Autobiography* (1980) and *Brick Walls* (1977), for these conceptual photographic projects.

(11)
Cindy Nemser, "An Interview with Chuck Close," *Artforum* 8 (January 1970): 51-52.

(12)
Quoted in Franklin Sirmans, *Vija Celmins: Television and Disaster 1964-1966* (Houston and New Haven: Menil Collection and Yale University Press, 2010), 27.

volved in their translation (such as gridding the source photograph as a template) characterized this type of painting as distinct from that of the Photorealists. In general, Photorealism was fashioned with perfect perspective, sharp focus, and a highly attuned sense of classical composition, and yet, despite the virtuosic precision of its brash surfaces, was often cold, vacant, and idealized. The images of Celmins, Richter, Bechtle, Mangold, or Close, by contrast, felt offhanded yet arresting, with an immediacy that spoke to real life, and an ambiguity that left generous room for contemplation.

Celmins' *Freeway* (1966; fig. 9) was the earliest of her canvases to be made not from a found image, but from her own photographs, this one taken while the camera balanced on the steering wheel as her car sped along a Los Angeles thoroughfare. Eerie in its familiarity, the scene looked exactly like a real photograph—not in the way works by Eakins or the Photorealists did, but in the way a photograph snapped by an average person might appear. The painting is small but immersive. The gray highway, the overcast sky, and the anonymous traffic look a bit fuzzy—as if seen through a dirty windshield. But what we also see *is* the windshield, the dashboard, the *objectness* of the car itself. In contrast to the Photorealists, who tended to emulate automobiles, Celmins comments on the tedium of driving this ubiquitous landscape with an accessory to daily life, here shown for what it is—just a car.

Bechtle is an artist whose work was often shown with the Photorealists, but one who, like Celmins, put forth a distinctly different stance about the use of photographic source material. "A photograph," he remarked in 1972, "often gives the feeling of a particular moment in time, and you get the sense of how that is bracketed in with the before and after. I like the kind of photograph that tends to just be. You sense that what came before was exactly the same as what is shown, and that what comes next is going to be exactly the same."[13] *Fosters Freeze* (1970; plate 21) presents a woman and children (the artist's family) captured in a passing moment in a hamburger joint, she wiping her fingers on a napkin, lost in thought, the children bored. It marks a moment of in-betweenness, yet beyond its resemblance to the photographic source, the painting is even more striking in its vivid capture of daily life as it happens. His *'73 Malibu* (1974; plate 17) is one in

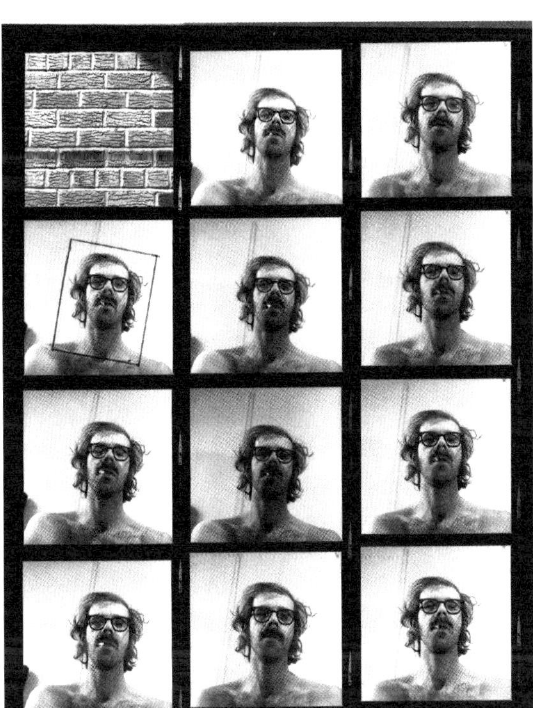

Fig. 8
Chuck Close *Self-Portrait Contact Sheet* 1999
(original contact sheet dated 1967–1968)
Iris print on Somerset Satin watercolor paper

(13)
Robert Bechtle interviewed by Brian O'Doherty, "The Photo-Realists: Twelve Interviews," *Art in America* 60 (November-December 1972): 74. Cited in Janet Bishop, *Robert Bechtle: A Retrospective* (San Francisco: San Francisco Museum of Modern Art, 2005), 88.

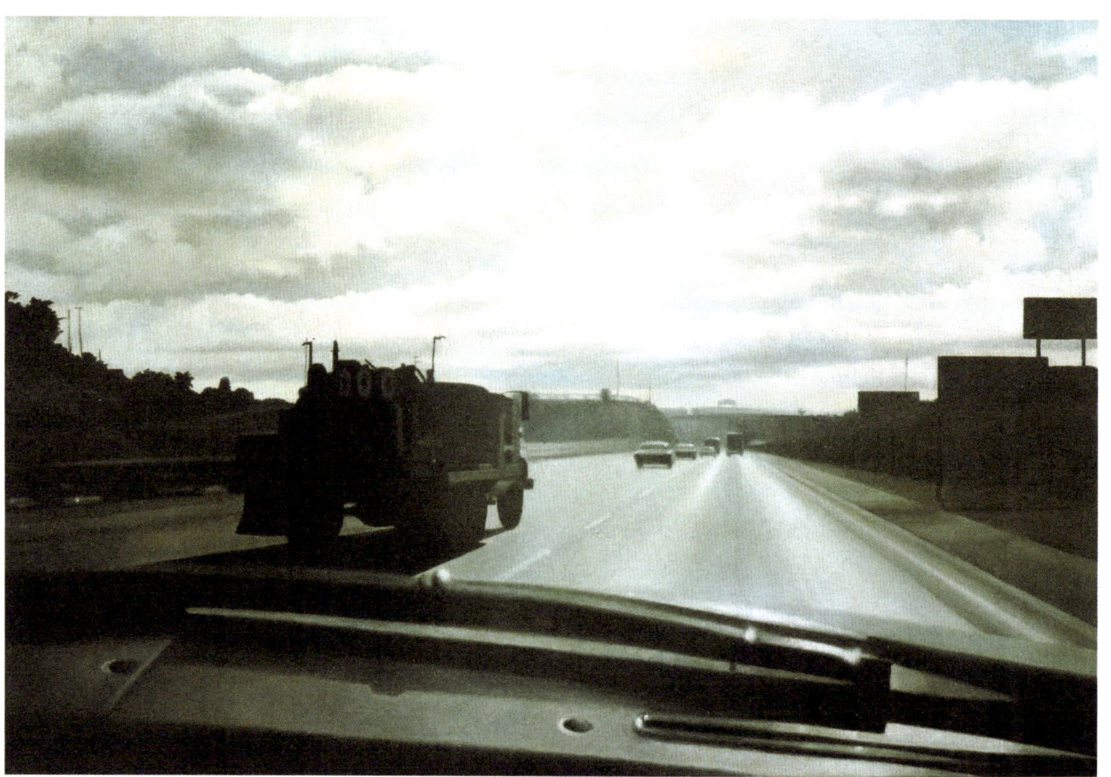

Fig. 9 Vija Celmins *Freeway* 1966 oil on canvas

a series of automobile paintings, an abiding subject matter for Bechtle. His are not the sexy, chrome-trimmed vehicles emulated in advertising (or in many paintings of the Photorealists, for that matter). Rather, they are utilitarian, middle-class cars, parked in driveways or at curbs, awaiting the next errand. When asked to write about Bechtle on the occasion of his 2005 retrospective, artist Charles Ray characterized what he viewed as the "emotional familiarity of Bechtle's painting...a mood or memory that is difficult to describe."[14] This notion that ordinary images have the capacity to affect us in this way is central to the strategy of many of the artists discussed here.

In 1962, Richter began using photographs as part of his painting practice. In selecting his imagery, he was not interested, as art historian and critic Robert Storr has noted, in posing a critique of consumer culture; rather, "his preoccupation was the iconography of the everyday. Implicit in this was the pathos he saw both in the photograph as object and the image it contained, a pathos indelibly marked by use."[15] As part of his larger exploration of painting in its many manifestations, Richter's photographically based canvases were a way for him to hearken back to the medium's mimetic origins, but with a modern twist. His earliest found images ranged from the utterly banal (toilet paper, a ceiling light fixture, a dog) to the provocative. Often, he would smudge or blur his images after faithfully executing them on canvas, a gesture that imbues works such as *Candle* (*Kerze*) (1982; plate 12) with a new layer of resonance, invoking the idea of memory and its power to seize upon pictures.

Celmins admits that some of her subjects—ocean surfaces, spiderwebs—can be seen as "corny images" that undoubtedly have emotional bearing for some people, but she enjoys the idea that she can "neutralize" this reaction, repackaging pictures via her strict working process in a "cold, scientific dressing."[16] Bechtle and Richter have achieved a sense of remove from their subjects by using a projector to transpose their photographic sources to a large scale. With this physical and conceptual distance, Richter noted early in his career, "You no longer apprehend but see and make (without design) what you have not apprehended. And when you don't know what you are making, you don't know, either, what to alter or distort."[17]

This ability to look at painting made from a photograph as a series of tasks to be performed rather than an image to replicate, has long been key to Close's working process. As the 1960s drew to an end, he was one of the few artists working in a realist vein who focused exclusively on portraiture. Never content to be dubbed a Photorealist, he has continually emphasized his affinity for process over subject matter. Working with-

(14)
Charles Ray, "Alameda Gran Torino," in Janet Bishop, *Robert Bechtle: A Retrospective*, 63. Recounting his experience of viewing Bechtle's 1974 painting *Alameda Gran Torino*, Ray writes, "The composition seemed bland—almost found—and yet perfect at the same time. Is it a painting of a car? A photograph? Or an automobile manufacturer's brochure? A glint of light reflecting off the rear bumper caught my eye, and all of a sudden I was lost in the surface of the work. I remember leaving the museum thinking that Bechtle's painting was not photorealist at all."

(15)
Robert Storr, in *Gerhard Richter: Forty Years of Painting*, exh. cat. (New York: Museum of Modern Art, 2002), 36.

(16)
Vija Celmins, interview in *Art21: Art in the Twenty-First Century*, season 2 (2003), http://video.pbs.org/video/1237794459.

(17)
Gerhard Richter, "Notes, 1964-1965," in *Robert Storr*, exh. cat. (New York: Museum of Modern Art, 2002), 35.

in a rigorously proscribed method of transcription from gridded photographic source to canvas or paper, his first works, such as *Big Self-Portrait* (1967-1968; plate 4), demonstrated a strict adherence to the notion of methodically building a surface. And yet, despite the implication of artist as machine, Close often speaks of his work as "handmade" images, sometimes using metaphors that link his practice to craft techniques such as quilting or knitting—processes that also involve repetition and working in units, as he does, square by square and row by row. For *Big Self-Portrait* and other paintings made in the late 1960s, Close used an airbrush, which approximated the source photograph's variable areas of focus. While the veracity of the image is astonishing, vestiges of the penciled grid are faintly visible beneath the veil of acrylic paint, a reminder that this is a work from a photograph that has been reinvented, and has declared itself a painting. This canvas and others like it at the time were based on flat-footed images, shot frontally. By creating them on a disconcertingly vast scale (the picture is nearly 9 x 7 feet), Close brought into even sharper focus his subjects' anonymity and averageness. These were not celebrities or traditional artist's models, but friends, peers, family members. Like Bechtle, Close chose to use his own personal milieu as found subject matter, and in the process, managed to generate a sense of commonality.

In the pre-digital 1970s, photographs—whether made or found—that were the preparatory studies for many of these artists' works were often demarcated with masking tape to indicate the image crop, a technique that allows for the selective elimination of potentially distracting details.(18) Mangold's canvases, while painted from life, have a decidedly photographic approach, one in which this sense of cropping allows for a more abstracted surface. In her case, tape and other tools used to map out the mechanics of the paintings often migrated into the work as an illusionistic element along with other exacting details, as in the wood floorboards that comprise early works such as *August* (1973; plate 18). Her spatial problem-solving is made visible in works such as *In Memory of My Father* (1976; plate 19), in which the ruler, rendered in trompe l'oeil, becomes central to the composition. "The difference between an illusion and an imitation interests me," Mangold remarked in 1978. "On one level it is logical and as I develop that logic, the further logic gets from the translation, the more complex that logic becomes, [and] the more the pursuit of it appears irrational."(19)

Like Mangold, Alex Hay's early paintings often approached a kind of abstraction in their pared-back representation of found objects. *Cash Register Slip* (1966; plate 10) is a hardware store receipt painted from life and presented at an exaggerated scale distinctly at odds with its subject's ephemeral nature. Similar large paintings made at the time depicted sheets of toilet tissue or a page from a yellow legal pad, delicate meditations on the prosaic that recall Agnes Martin's atmospheric grids or Robert Ryman's layered abstract whites. John Clem Clarke, an underrecognized painter

(18)
Close's maquettes, for example, all use masking tape as a means of isolating the area of the photograph to be gridded off for painting.

(19)
Sylvia Plimack Mangold, unpublished manuscript for lecture delivered on the panel Conceptualization of Realism at the annual meeting of the College Art Association, New York, January 26, 1978, 8. Quoted in Ellen D'Oench and Hilarie Faberman, *Sylvia Plimack Mangold: Works on Paper 1968-1991* (Ann Arbor, MI: University of Michigan Press, 1992), 26.

of Hay's era, sought in his series of paintings (1974; plate 16) to emphasize the physical qualities of his visual source material—often faux bois panels of ersatz "plywood" illusionistically painted with woodgrain, knots, and paint spatters—a readymade Abstract Expressionist composition.[20]

As more artists in the late 1960s began to eschew iconic, archetypal subjects in favor of this new attitude toward realistic painting, a handful began to investigate a similar set of parameters when working in three dimensions. Celmins' most notable freestanding works of the era included *Untitled (Comb)* (1970; plate 13) and sculptures of a pencil and an ordinary Pink Pearl eraser (1967; plate 14), all executed as painting directly on constructed wood surfaces. She refers to these as "object paintings," noting, "I think of them as having fallen out of the picture plane. They are not really sculpture."[21]

This is an important distinction, as it foregrounded what was becoming a new way to consider the idea of the still life, cherry-picking an ordinary object from its everyday milieu and reinvesting it with time, new materials, and interest. Hay's normal sculptural works, such as *Paper Bag* (1968; plate 3), focused again on overscaled, humble items—not to monumentalize the ordinary, as Oldenburg was beginning to do at the time, but to make us take notice, through our body's relationship to the rigorously detailed object before us, of the everyday choreography of our lives.[22]

Art historian Norman Bryson, in his investigations into the traditions of still-life painting, has employed the term *rhopography*, a word with roots in classical studies that derives from the Greek *rhopos* (small wares). Applied to subsequent eras, Bryson sees *rhopography* as "the depiction of those things which lack importance, the unassuming material base of life that 'importance' constantly overlooks." Still life, as he illustrates, has long had tremendous "capacity to explore the 'world without importance' for its own sake."[23] The artists of the late 1960s and forward who have espoused this ethos have indeed used still life not as a genre, but as a metaphor, a jumping-off point for a deeper consideration of ways that isolated objects might be suddenly permeated with a sense of humanity and psychological freight.

(20)

In using realistic depiction to illustrate the conscious experience of an object or thing, Mangold, Hay, and Clarke, to use Linda Nochlin's terminology, can all be seen as "pictorial phenomenologists," in large part because of "their choice of unevocative motifs." See Linda Nochlin, "Some Women Realists," *Arts Magazine* (February 1974); reprinted in *Super Realism: A Critical Anthology*, ed. Gregory Battcock (New York: E.P. Dutton and Co., Inc., 1975), 73.

(21)

"Vija Celmins Interviewed by Chuck Close," in *Vija Celmins*, 11.

(22)

Interestingly, Hay's entrance into the New York art world of 1969 caused him to be included in both Pop and Minimalism anthologies. He also performed with Merce Cunningham and Robert Rauschenberg as part of the Judson Dance Theater from 1963.

(23)

Norman Bryson, "Rhopography," in *Looking at the Overlooked: Four Essays on Still Life Painting* (London: Reaktion Books, 1990), 62.

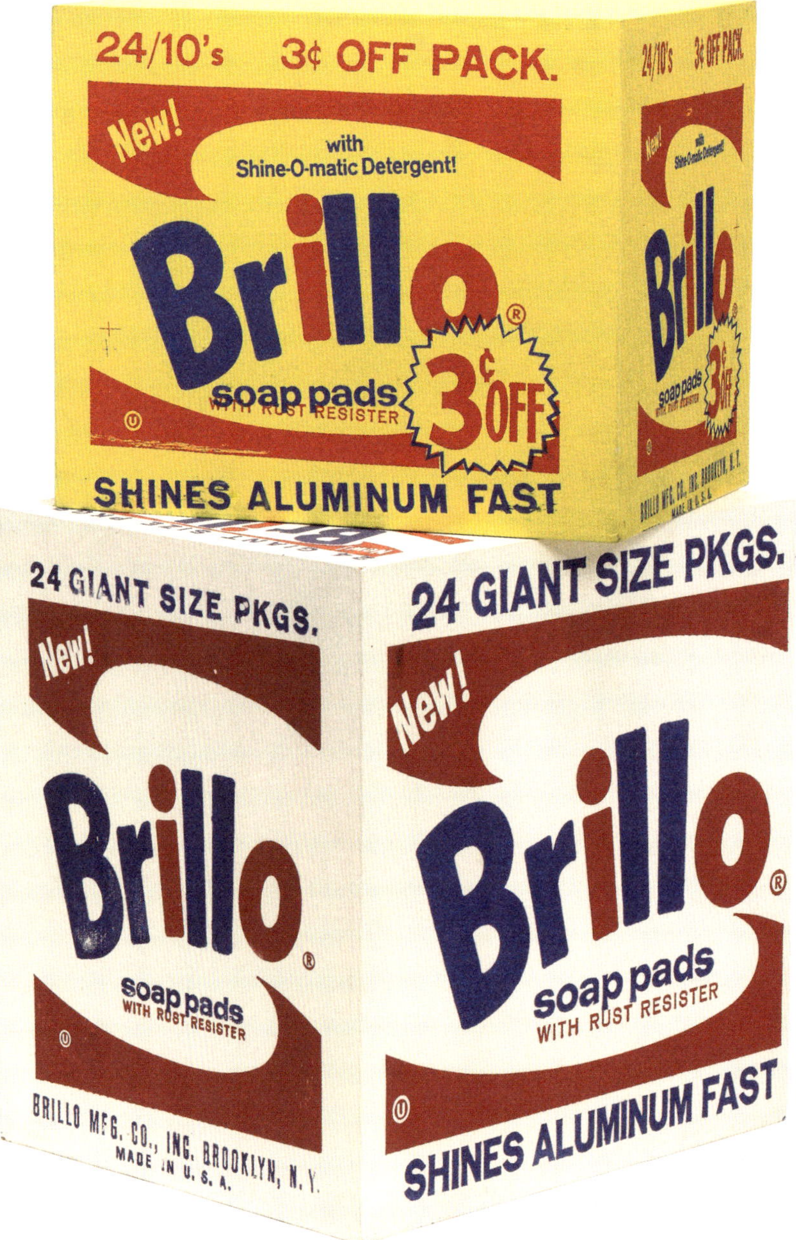

Plate 1. Andy Warhol *White Brillo Box* and *Yellow Brillo Box* 1964 synthetic polymer paint, screenprint on wood

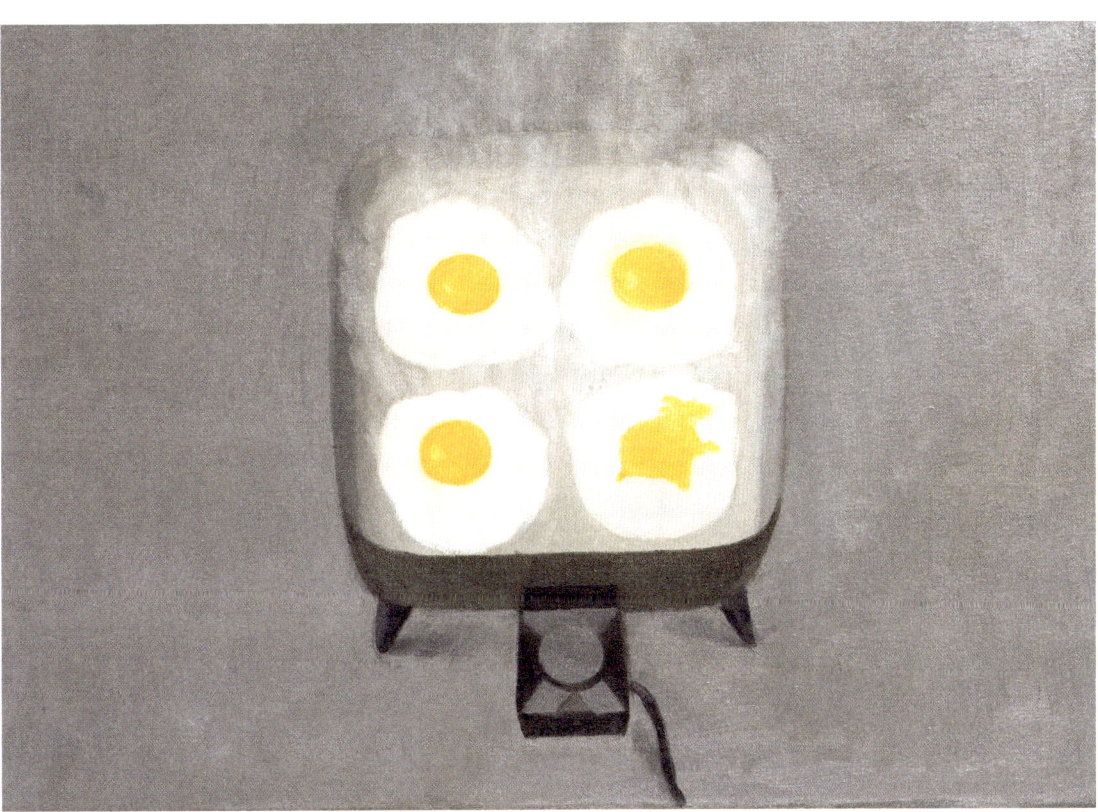

Plate 2. Vija Celmins *Eggs* 1964 oil on canvas

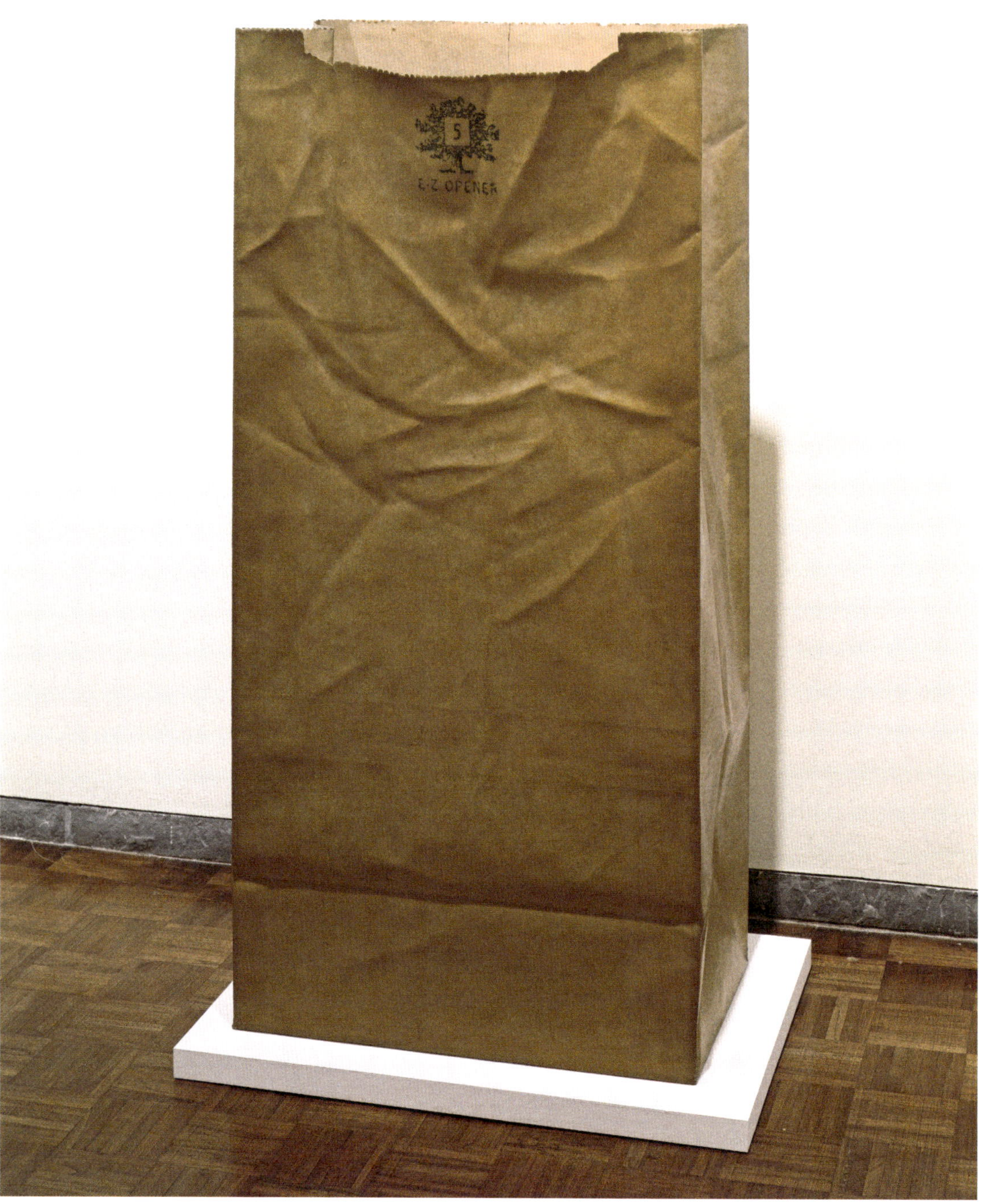

Plate 3. Alex Hay *Paper Bag* 1968 fiberglass, epoxy, spray lacquer and stencil on paper

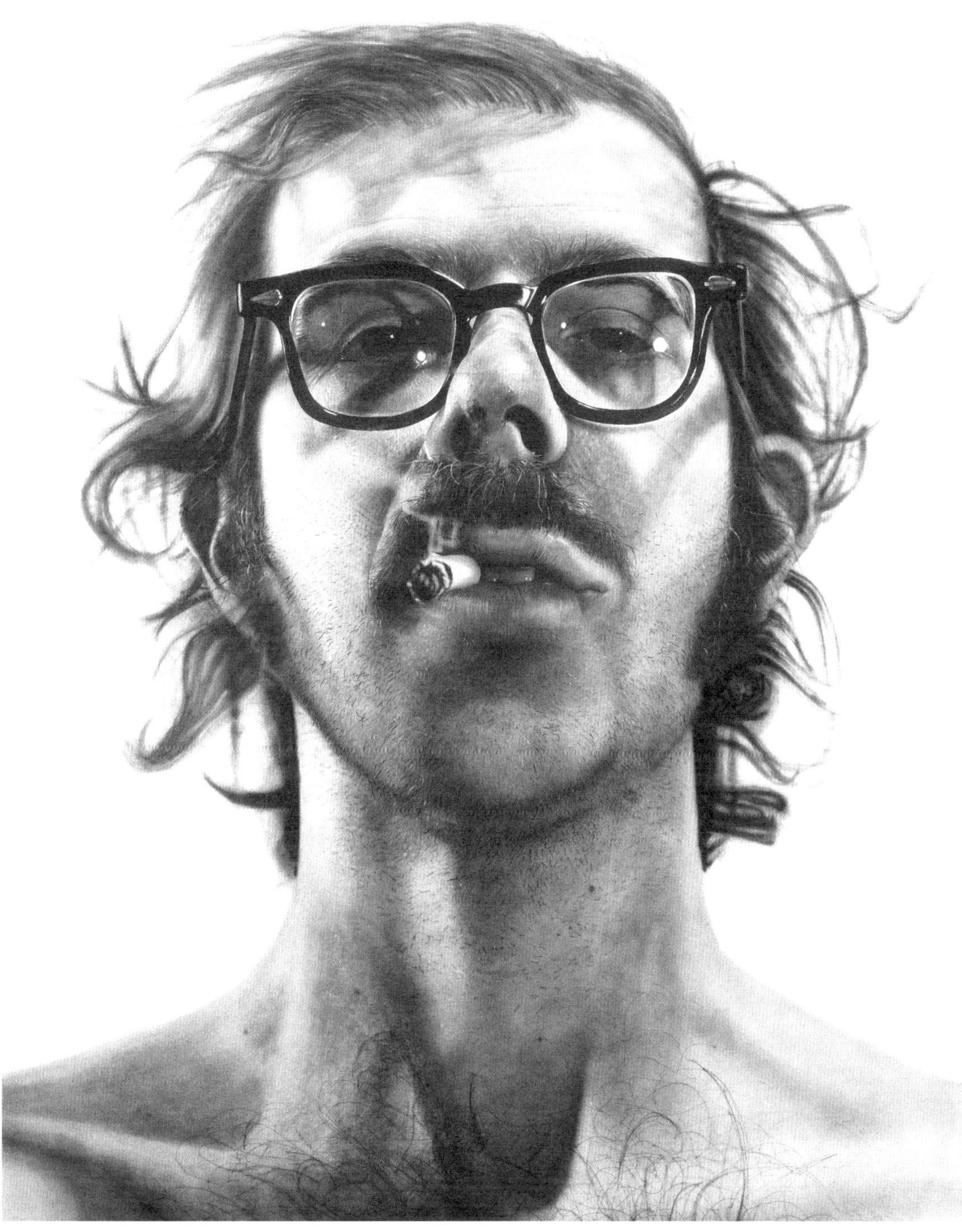

Plate 4. Chuck Close *Big Self-Portrait* 1967–1968 acrylic on canvas

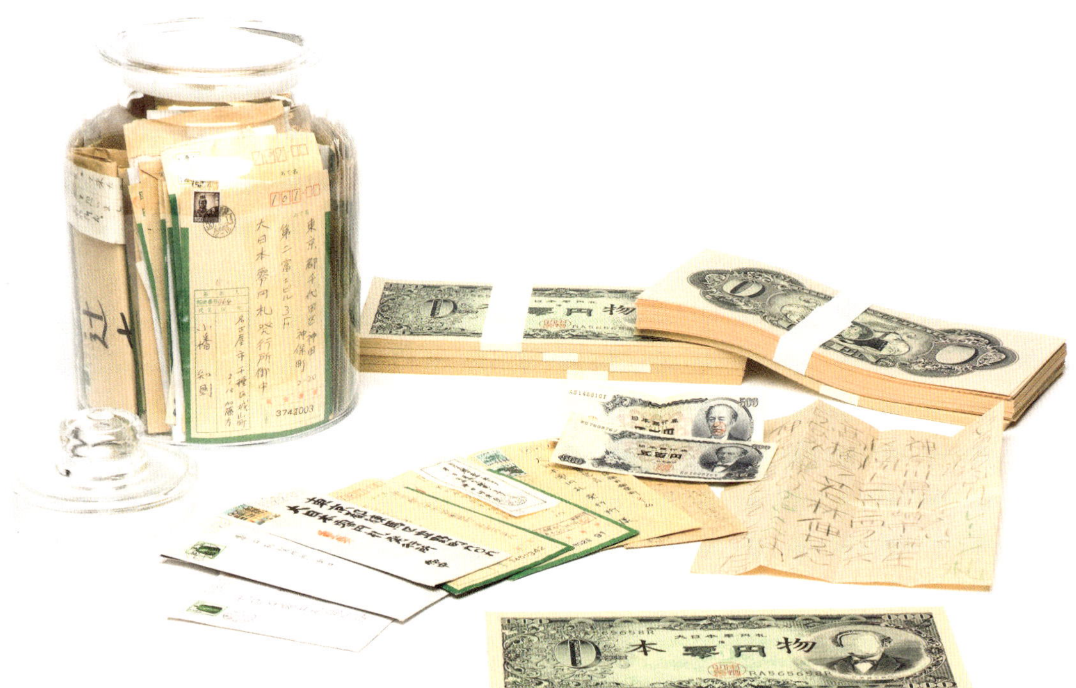

Plate 5. Akasegawa Genpei *"Greater Japan Zero-Yen Notes" and Bottled Money from Exchange* 1967 glass jar, printed material, envelopes, letters, currency

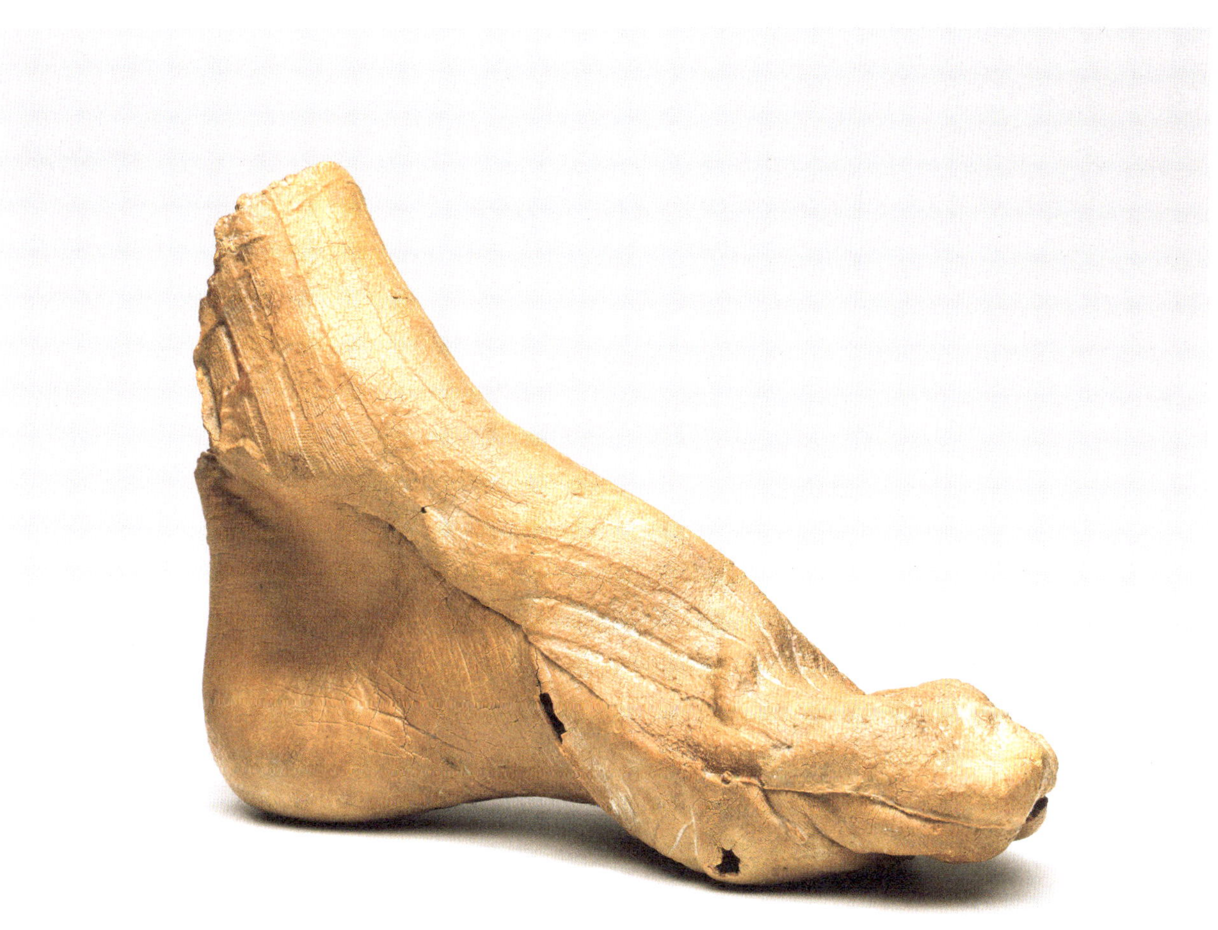

Plate 6. Paul Thek *Untitled (Foot)* circa 1968 latex

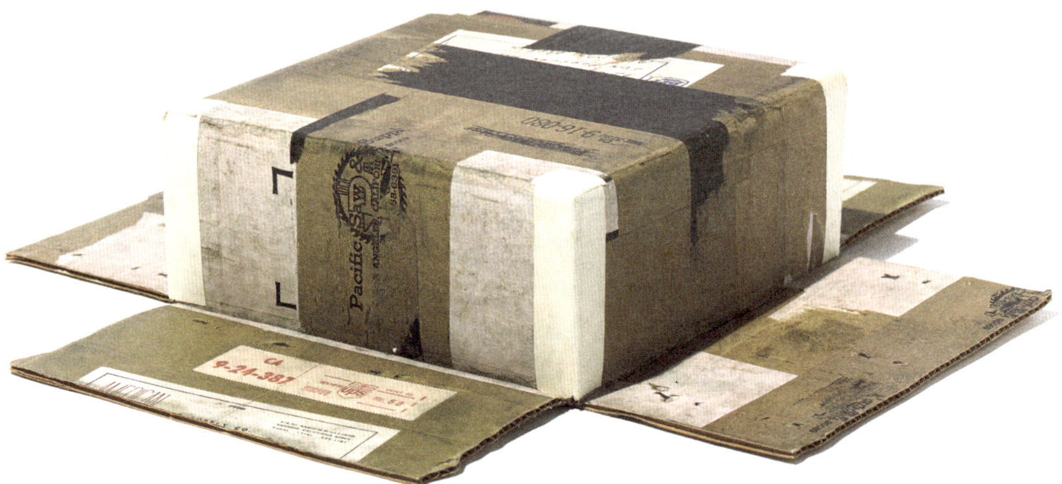

Plate 7. Robert Rauschenberg *Cardbird Box II* 1971 offset printed paper, cardboard, wood Art ©Estate of Robert Rauschenberg/ Licensed by VAGA, New York, NY

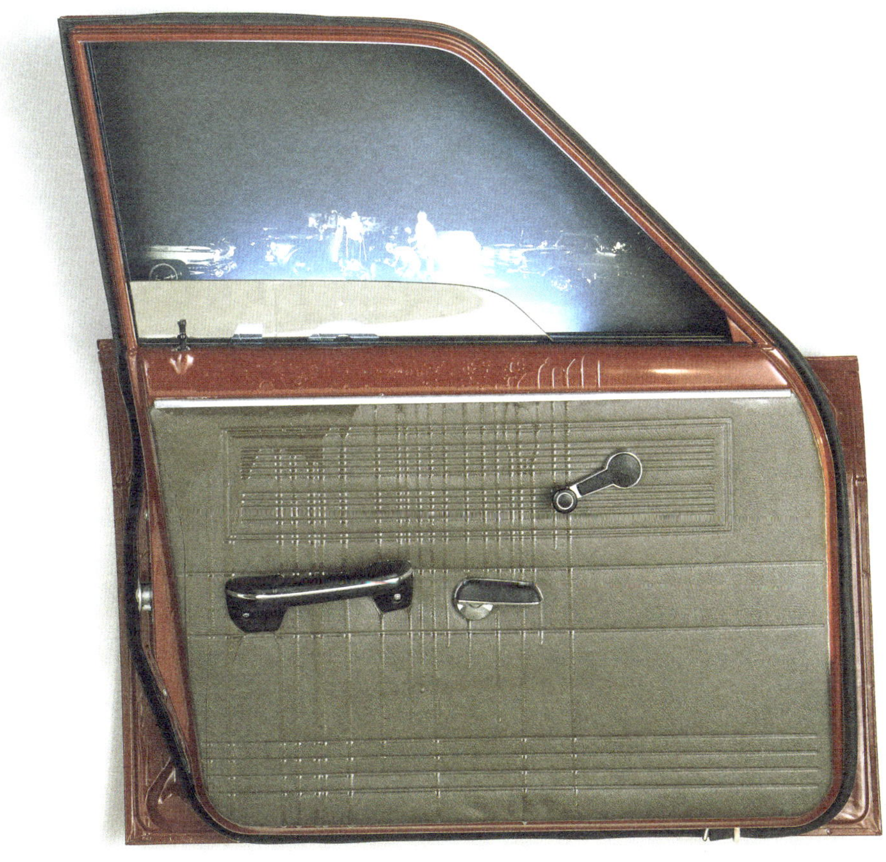

Plate 8. Edward Kienholz *Sawdy* 1971 car door, mirrored window, automotive lacquer, polyester resin, screenprint, fluorescent light, galvanized sheet metal

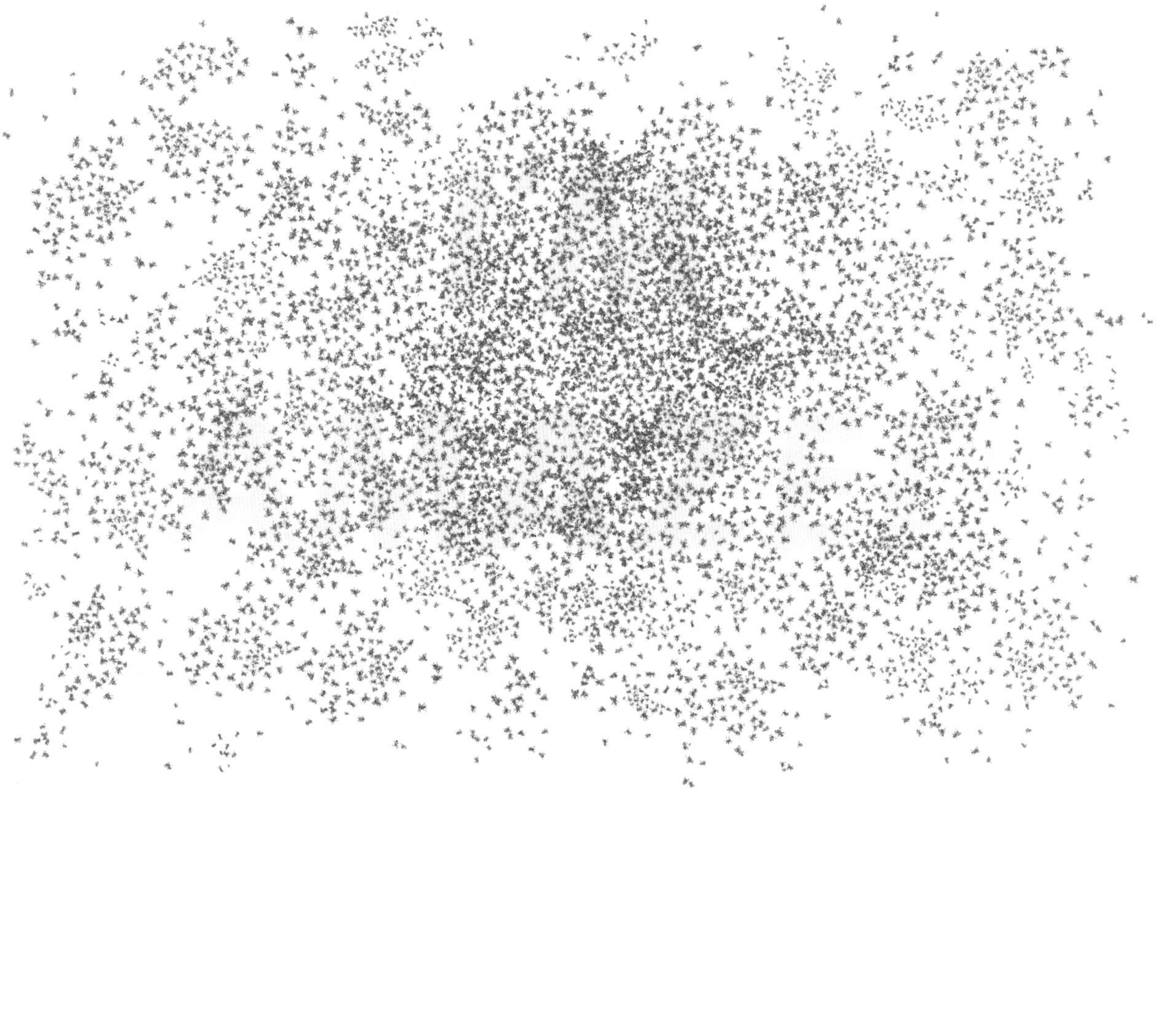

Plate 9. Edward Ruscha *I'm Amazed* 1971 screenprint on paper

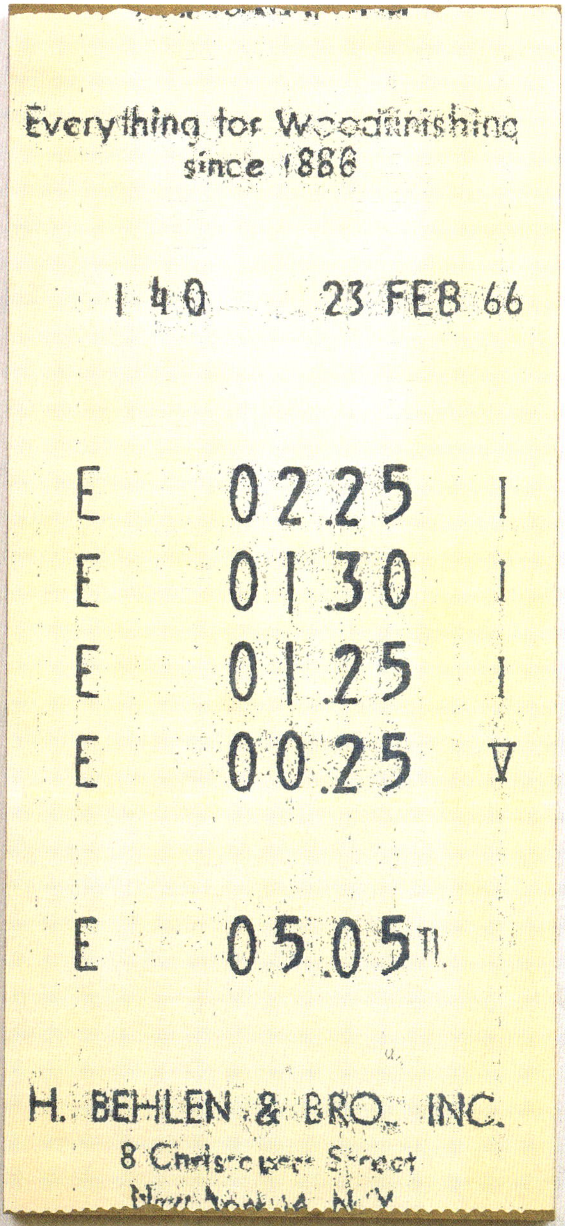

Plate 10. Alex Hay *Cash Register Slip* 1966 spray lacquer and stencil on linen

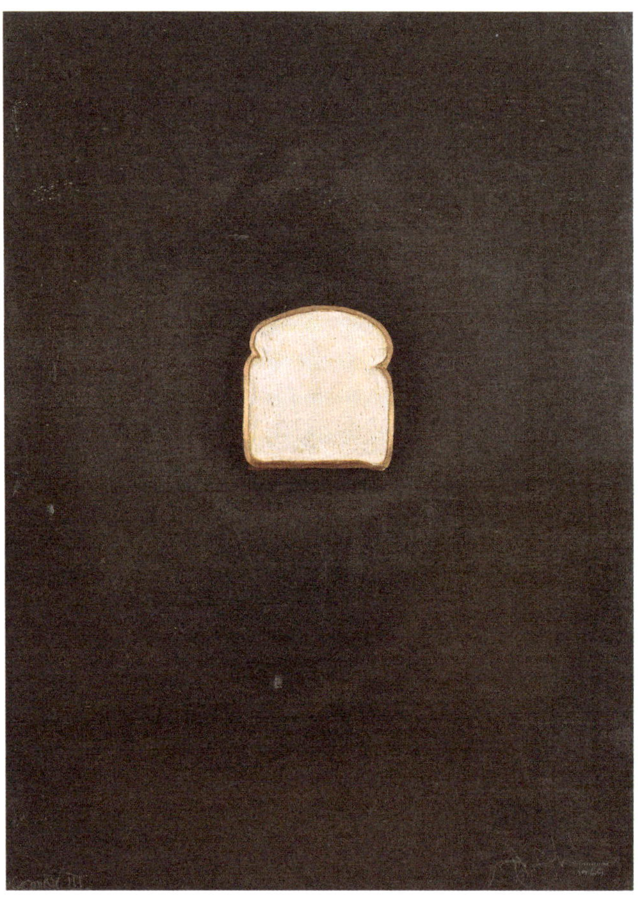

Plate 11. Jasper Johns *Bread* 1969 embossed lead, oil paint, paper

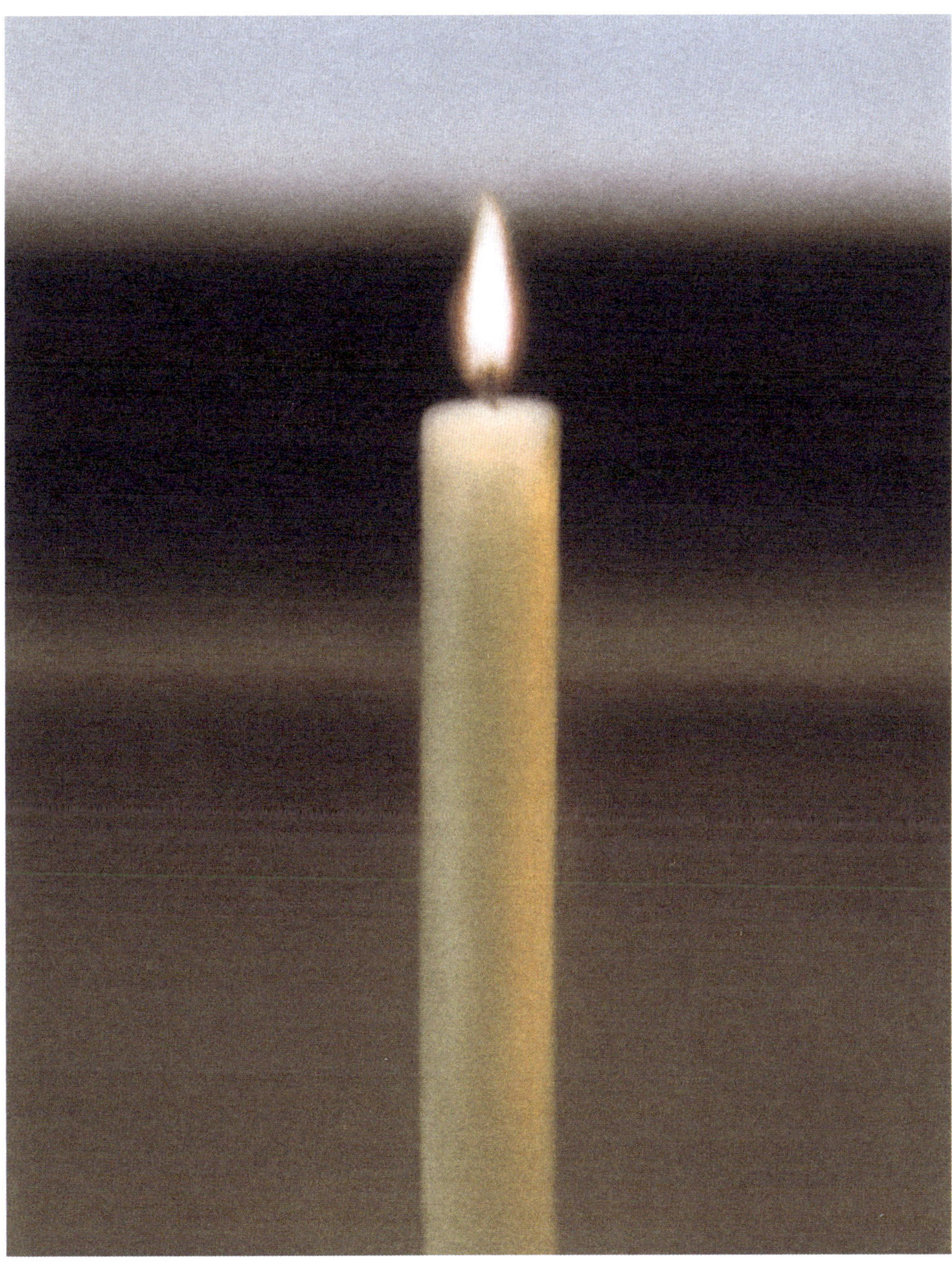

Plate 12. Gerhard Richter *Candle* (*Kerze*) 1982 oil on canvas

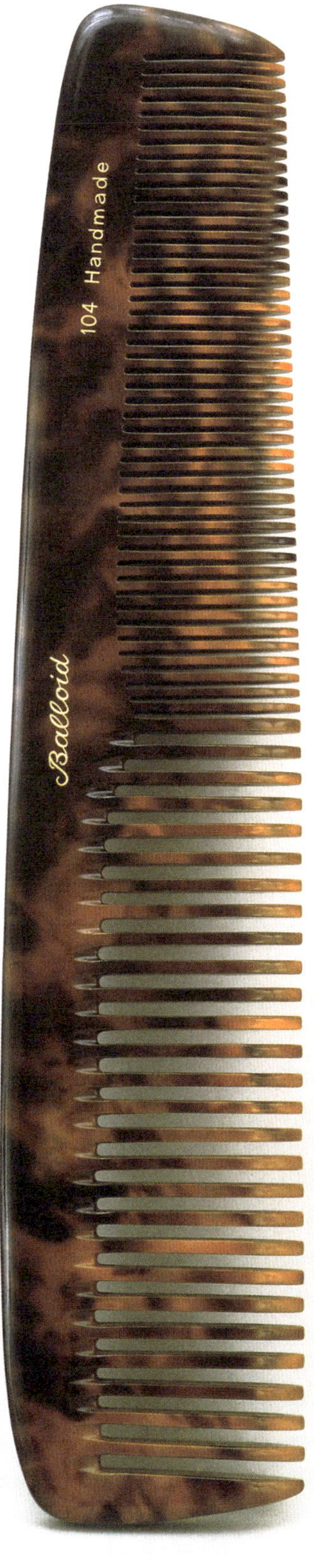
104 Handmade
Balloid

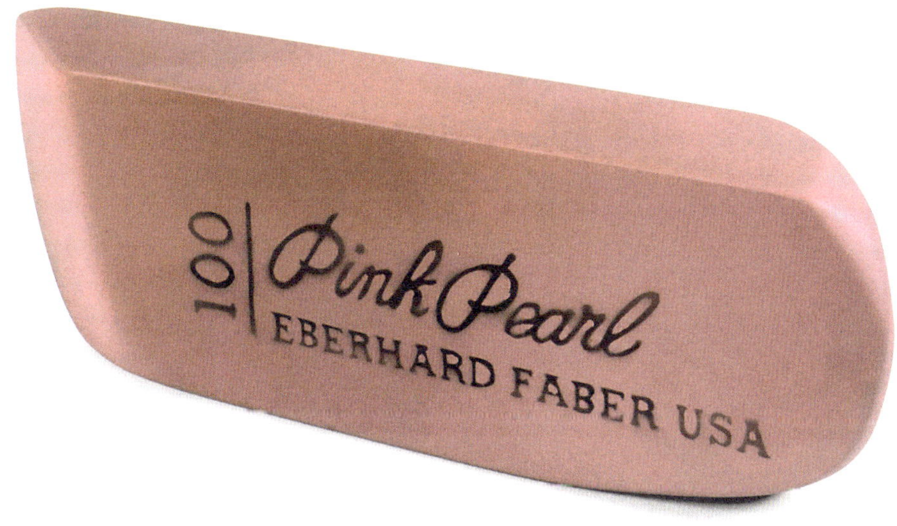

Plate 13. Vija Celmins *Untitled (Comb)* 1970 enamel on wood

Plate 14. Vija Celmins *Eraser* 1967 acrylic on balsa wood

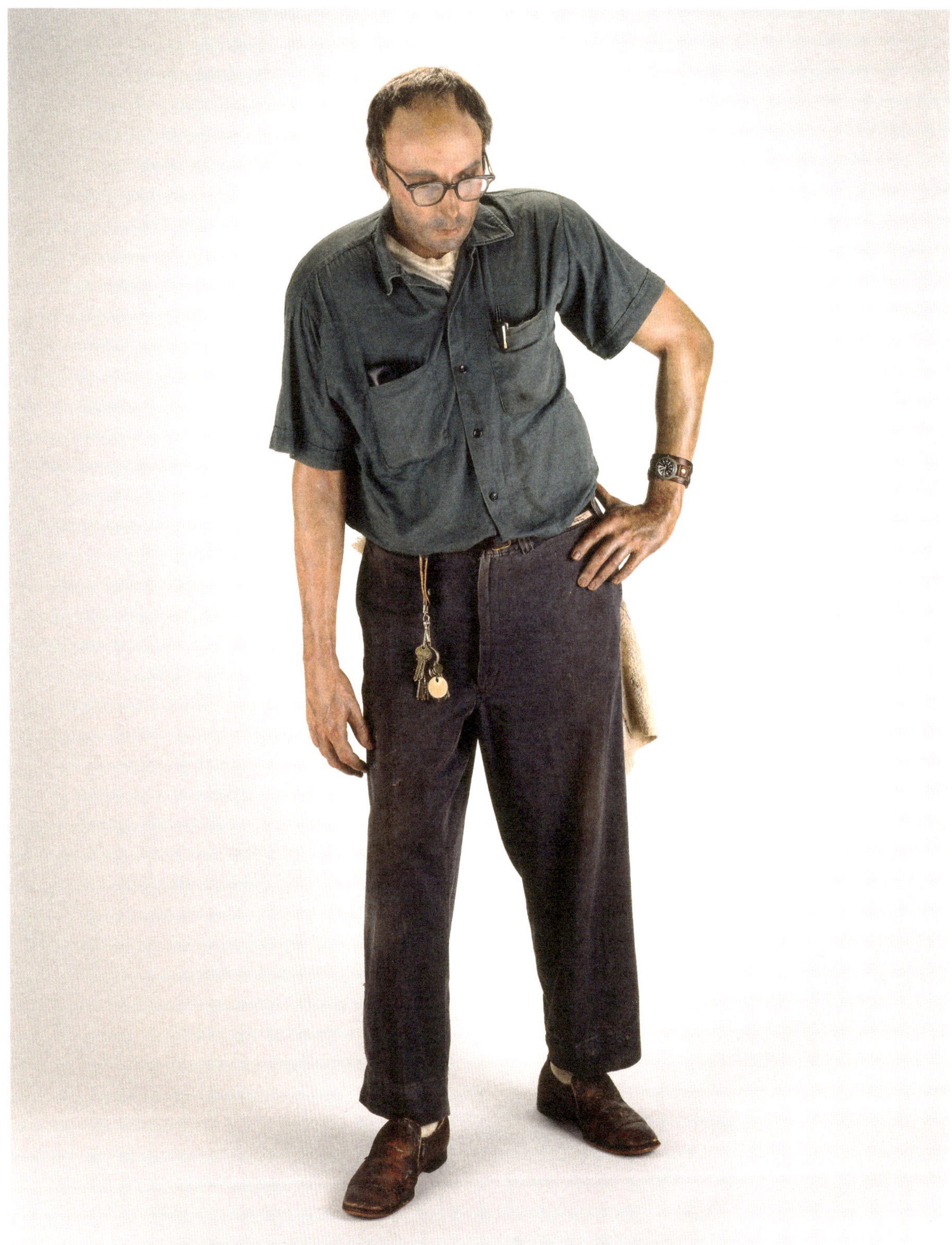

Plate 15. Duane Hanson *Janitor* 1973 polyester, fiberglass, mixed media ©Duane Hanson/Licensed by VAGA, New York, NY

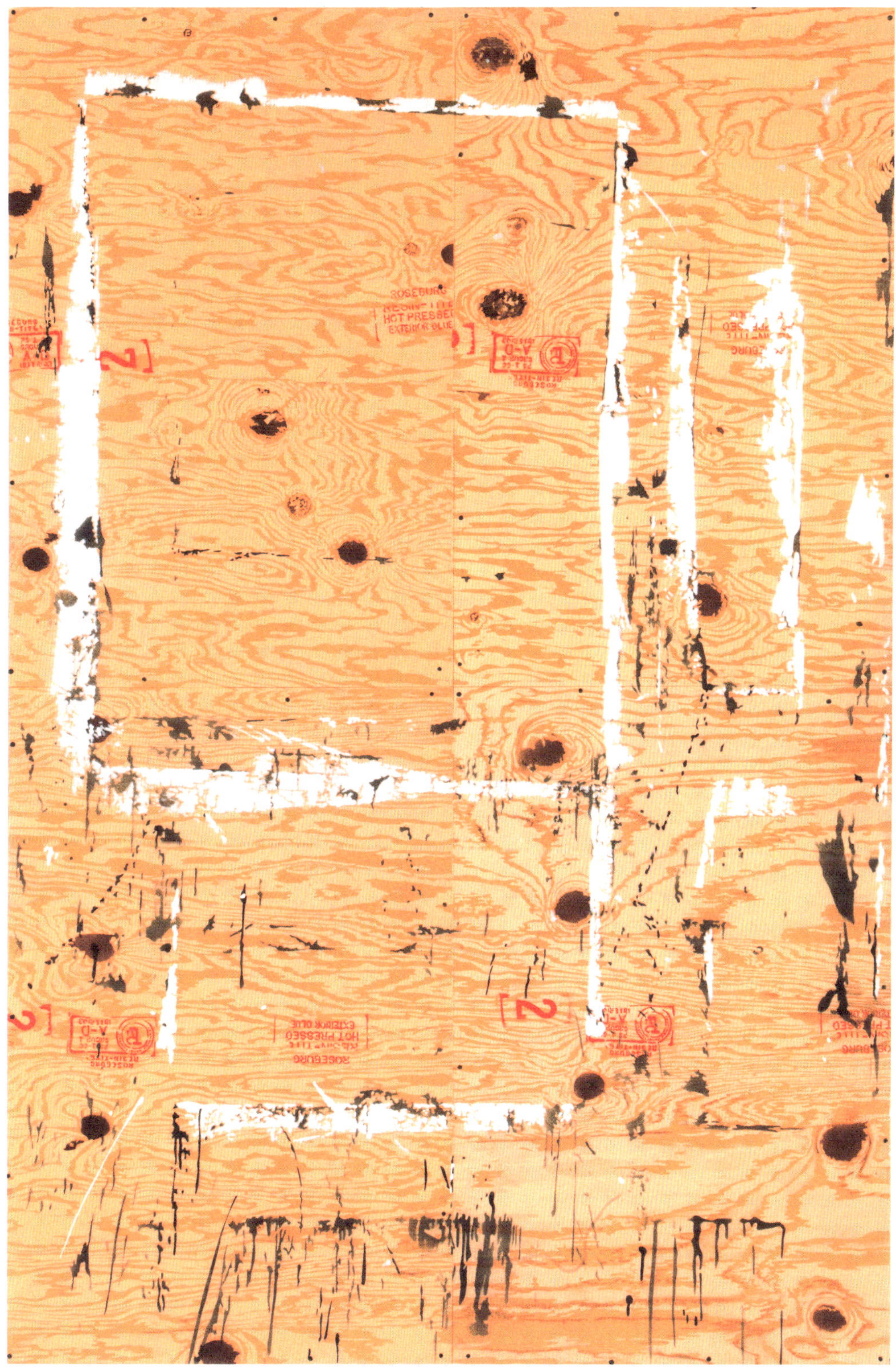

Plate 16. John Clem Clarke *Plywood with Roller Marks, #3* 1974 oil on canvas

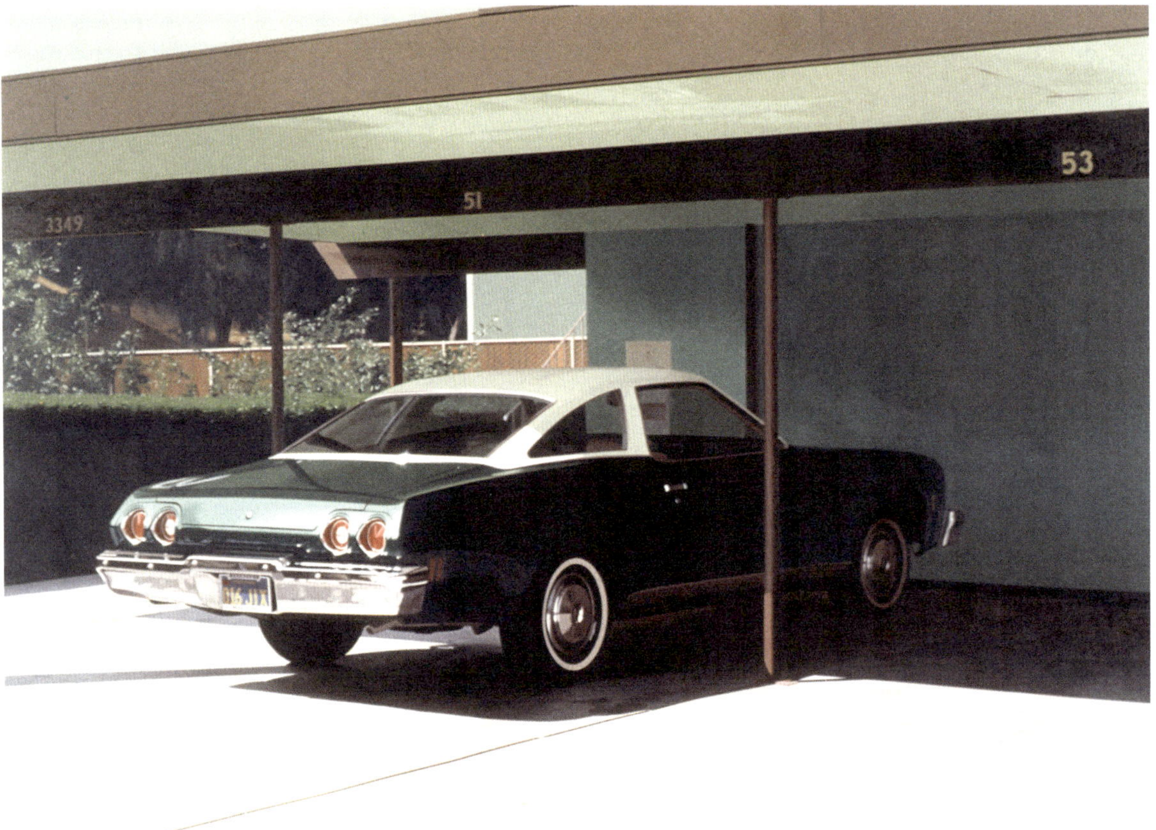

Plate 17. Robert Bechtle *'73 Malibu* 1974 oil on canvas

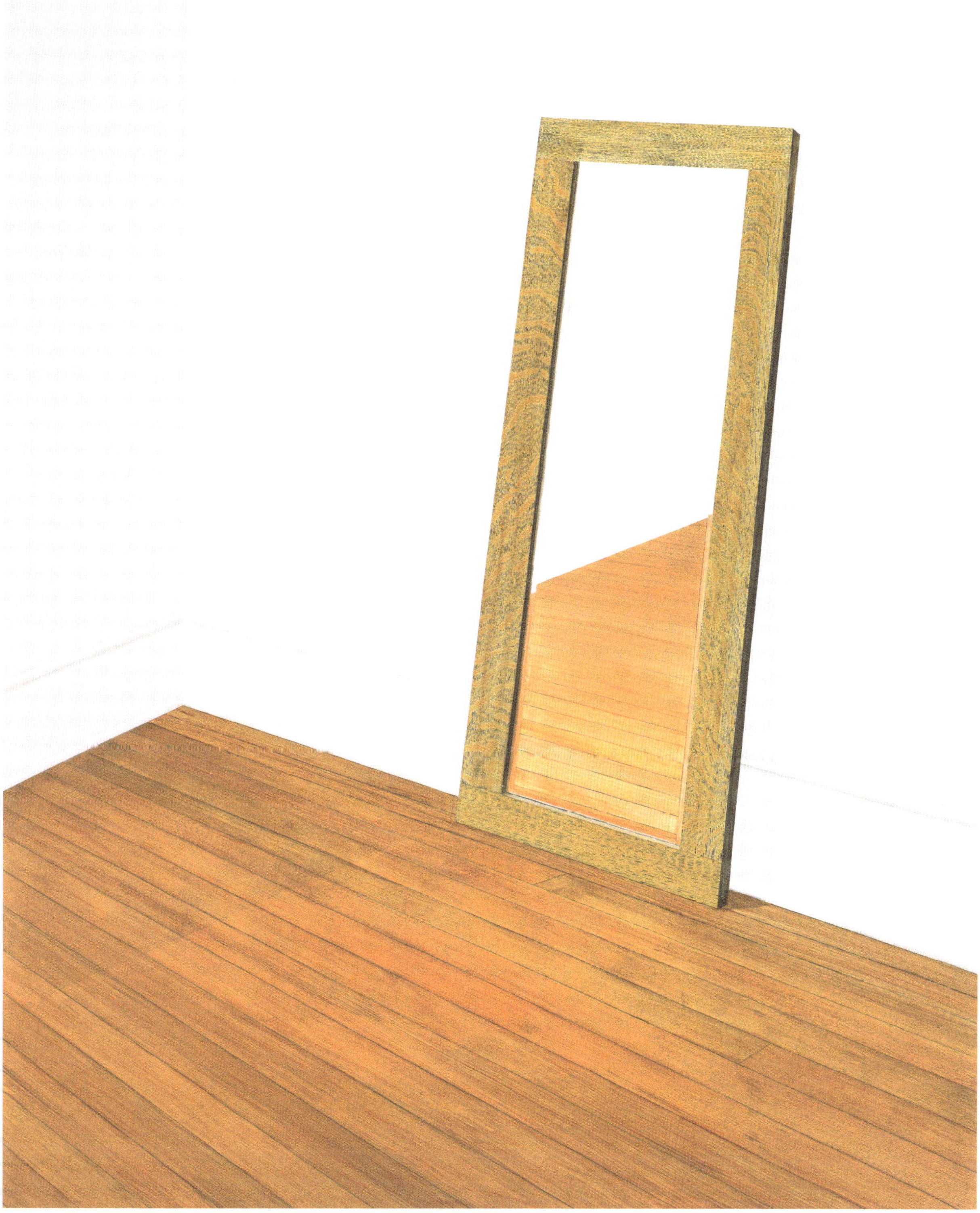

Plate 18. Sylvia Plimack Mangold *August* 1974 acrylic on canvas

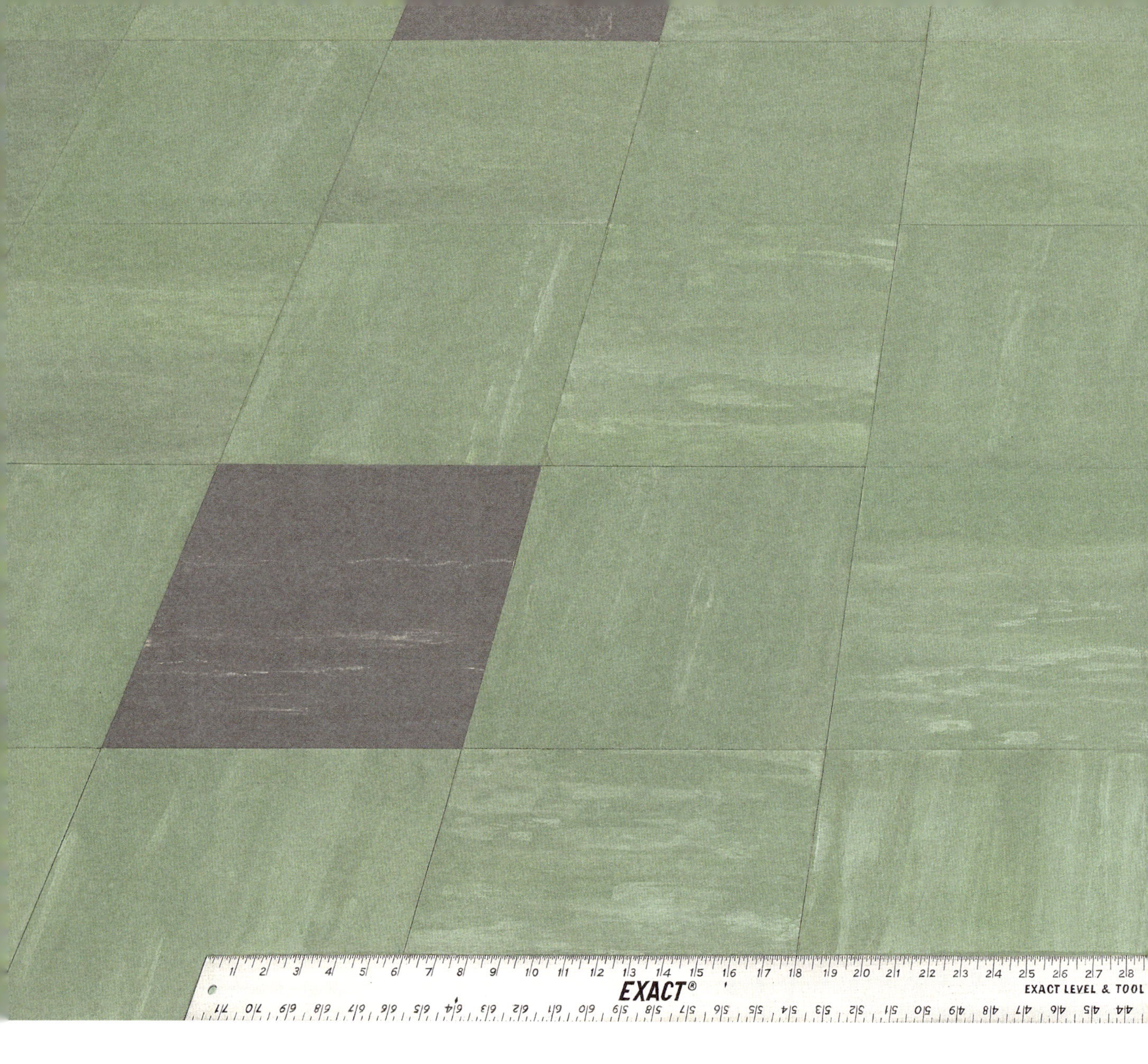

Plate 19. Sylvia Plimack Mangold *In Memory of My Father* 1976 acrylic on canvas

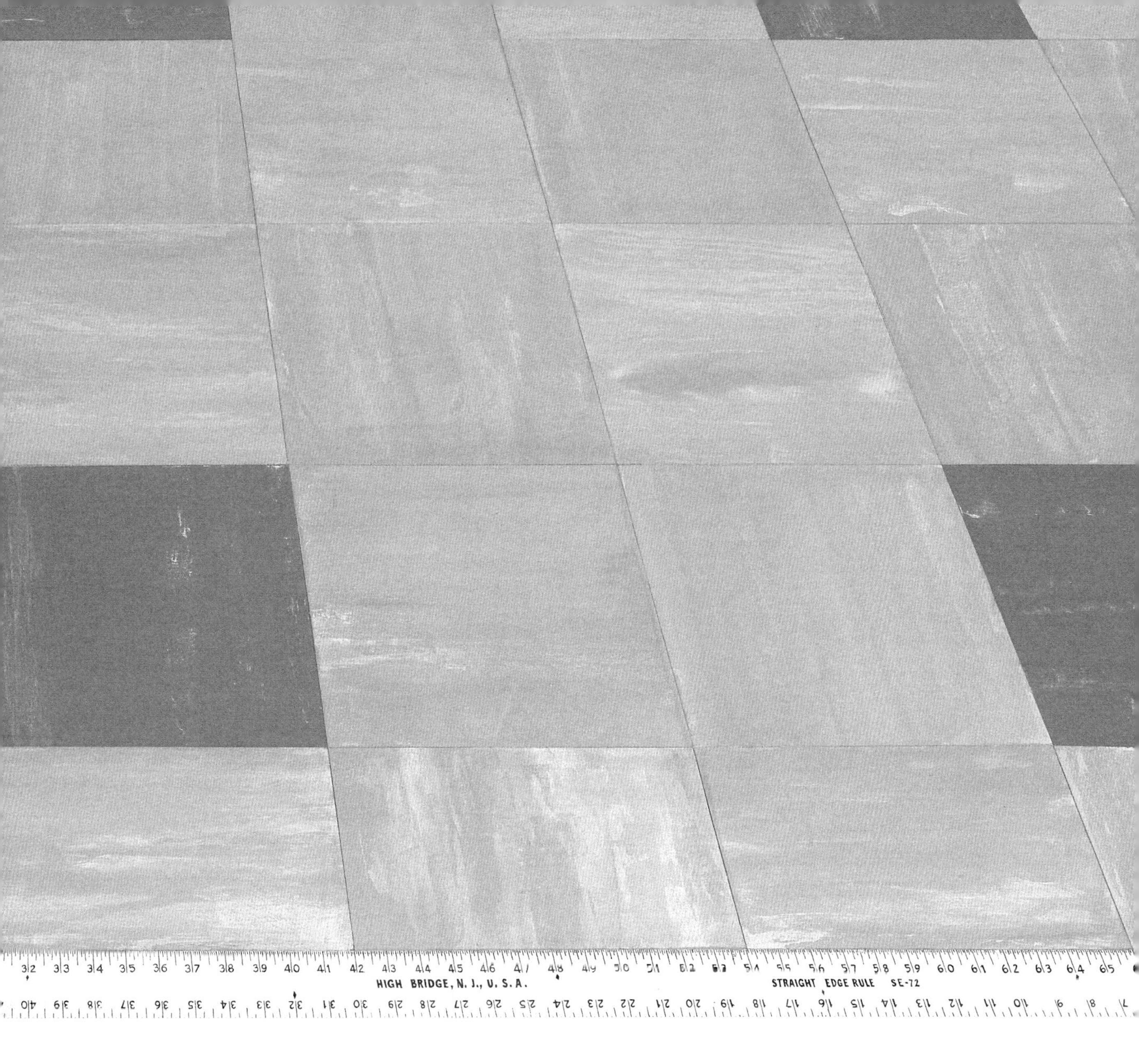
HIGH BRIDGE, N. J., U. S. A.
STRAIGHT EDGE RULE SE-72

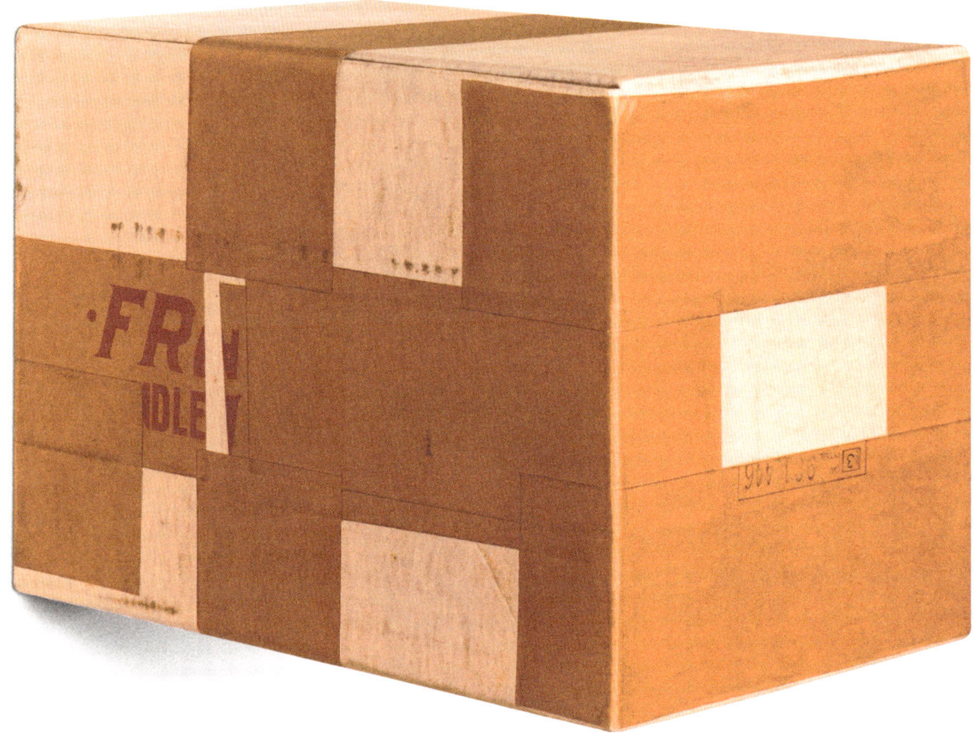

Plate 20. Daniel Douke *Ace* 1979 acrylic on Masonite

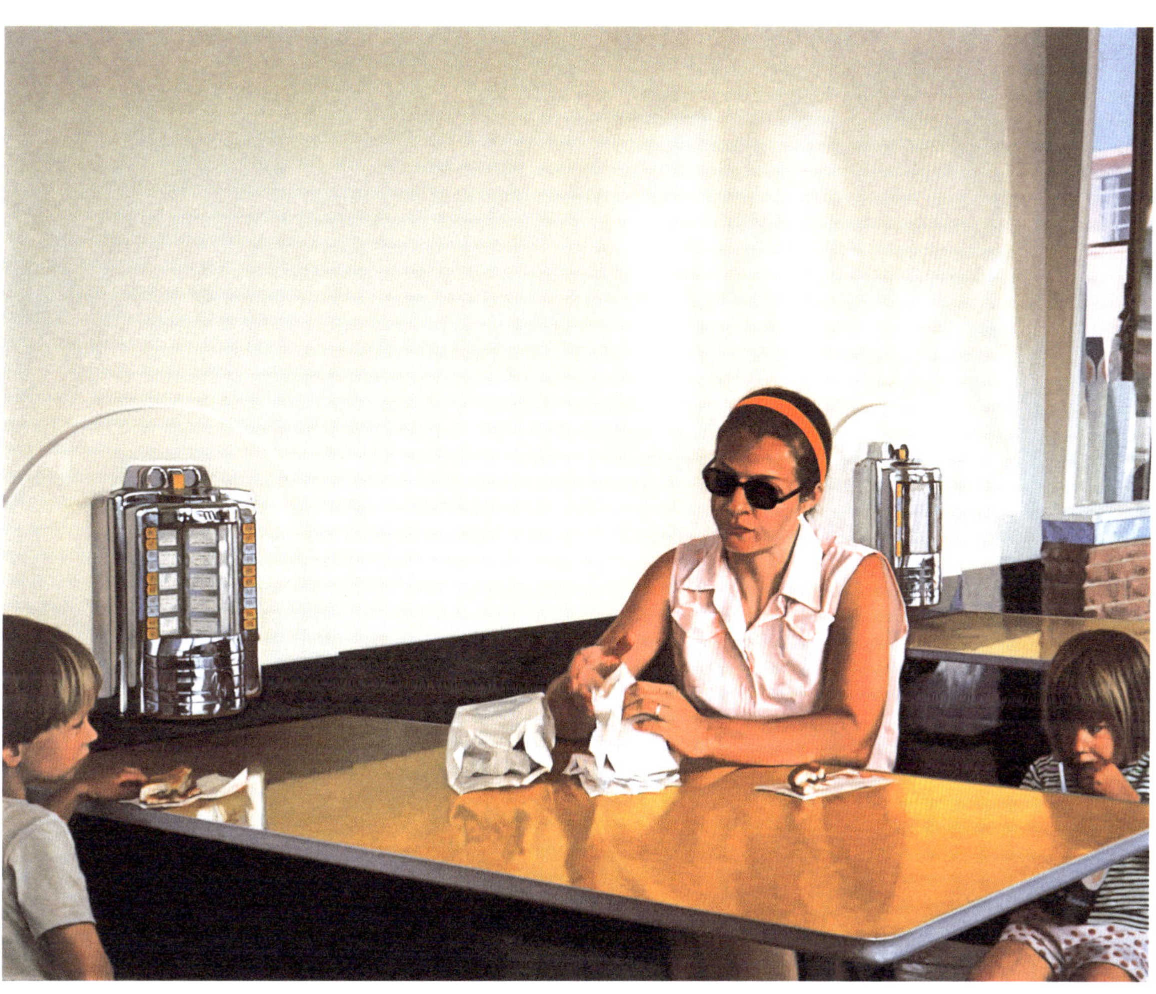

Plate 21. Robert Bechtle *Fosters Freeze* 1970 oil on linen

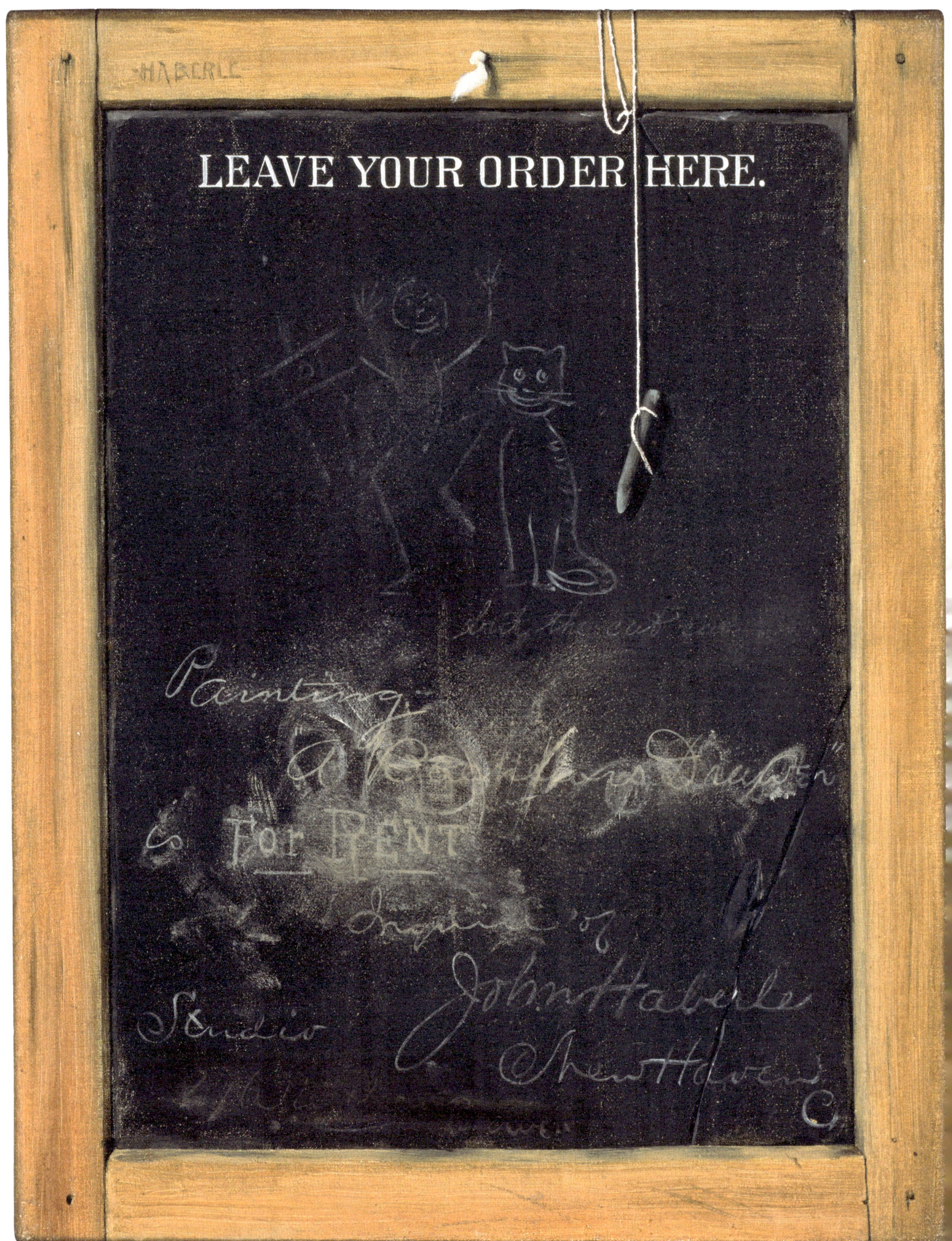

Fig. 10 John Haberle *The Slate* circa 1895 oil on canvas Photo ©2012 Museum of Fine Arts, Boston

T

UNCANNY

H

Section 2
The Uncanny

L I F E L I K E

E

The Uncanny

When in the presence of objects displaying a heightened degree of naturalism, one's reaction can be quite visceral; there is a recognition that the item or situation in question has been removed from context, leaving a viewer to grapple with the encounter in a gallery or museum setting. This is often accompanied by the sense that the astonishing verisimilitude witnessed is somehow underpinned by a kind of artifice, thrown into sharper relief when given uncharacteristic scrutiny. Duane Hanson, who was sometimes shown alongside the Photorealists in the late 1960s and early 1970s, played this sensation to great effect, creating lifelike figures such as *Janitor* (1973; plate 15) that rested disconcertingly in the gallery, seemingly snipped out of the tableaux of daily life and presented as a frozen moment—in the photographic sense as well as the physical. The space of the gallery, for artists working with this type of sculpture, becomes central to the experience of the work. Like Duchamp's readymades, the very existence of these things in this particular space makes one look twice. These are of course not found objects, but fabricated ones, with highly crafted surfaces that beckon a closer inspection, then slyly evidence the artist's hand.

The work of Hanson, John DeAndrea, and others using the figure in a hyperreal manner began to be highly visible around 1970, the same year Japanese roboticist Masahiro Mori published an article entitled "The Uncanny Valley,"(24) which advanced a theory that people would be more receptive to man-made robotic machines that closely resembled humans, but only to a point. There seemed to exist a threshhold, Mori noted, wherein a too-close likeness became eerie, provoking revulsion rather than attraction or empathy. This "valley" between the human and the not-quite-human proved useful for study. If machines were too lifelike, he argued, their effectiveness might be hampered by our skepticism. Since the 1970s, many artists have strived to harness this sense of doubt, inviting a suspension of disbelief until disbelief becomes quite real. In 1993, artist Mike Kelley assembled *The Uncanny*, a genre-bending show-within-a-show as his contribution to the Sonsbeek International Sculpture Exhibition in Arnhem, the Netherlands. Many artists use the uncanny as a means by which to delve into a distinctly psychological archaeology, while others focus on a manipulation of our visual experience in nearly imperceptible ways.

This idea of manipulation proved central to many strains of art-making that would develop within the 1980s, from the so-called "Pictures" artists, including Sherrie Levine, Richard Prince, and Sarah Charlesworth, who used techniques of appropriation, to artists such as Haim Steinbach and Jeff Koons, who promoted a new focus on the presentation of commonplace cultural artifacts in the context of art. Within this milieu, however, emerged a group of artists who were keen to use strategies of trompe l'oeil in the service of a larger discussion about contemporary life and its products. This "trick of the eye" technique, which has a history extending to antiquity, developed as an offshoot of still-life painting that focused on explicitly quotidian subjects, and used techniques of illusionism to test one's ability to discern between what seems to be and what *is*. Compared to other forms, it found itself with a somewhat lowly status, because it was typically seen as a demonstration of one's virtuosity

(24) Mori's article was first published in *Energy* 7, no. 4 (1970): 33-35.

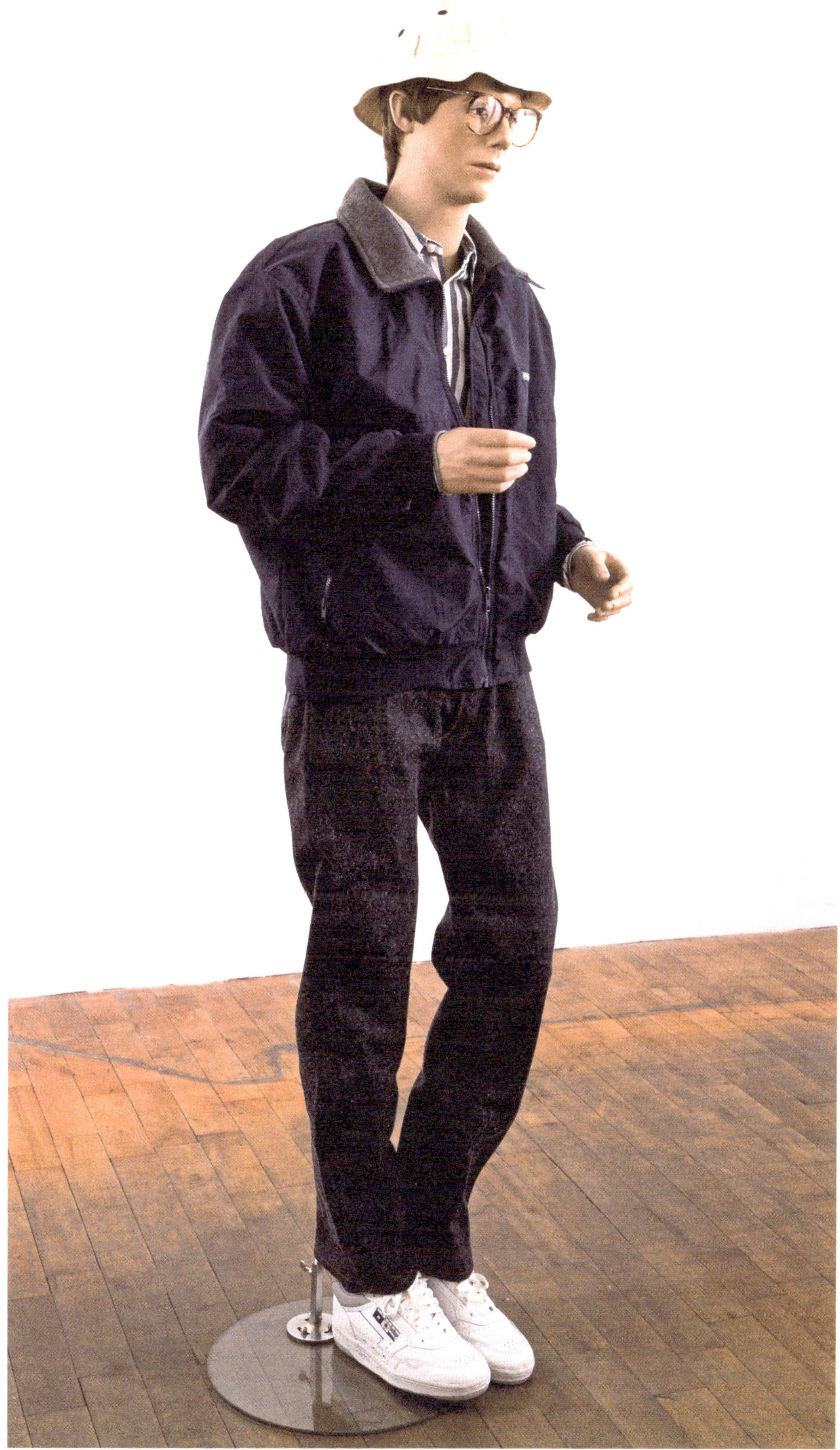

Fig. 11 Charles Ray *Self-Portrait* 1990 mixed media

as a painter, and not much more.[25] But still it persisted, finding a welcome audience from cabinets of curiosities to museum halls. Americans John F. Peto and John Haberle (fig. 10) were masters of the practice at the turn of the century. In Europe, it had become a central strategy in the works of Surrealists Magritte and Salvador Dalí, and had even featured prominently in Duchamp's final oil painting, *Tu m'* of 1918, which contains an illusionistically painted "rip" in the canvas, held together with real safety pins, as well as painted shadows cast from unseen objects. By the 1960s and early 1970s, Johns and Rauschenberg had dipped a toe into these waters, but it was their friend Cy Twombly's "blackboard" paintings, scrawled with abstract, chalklike notations on dark-hued grounds, which at the time came closest to traditional trompe l'oeil.

Trompe l'oeil is above all about bewilderment, and the viewer's growing realization that what was assumed to be true is in fact not, and what was assumed to be real is in fact *art*. Those artists who have been engaged with the practice from the 1980s on have found within its technical confines an area rich for exploration, in a manner increasingly indebted to the heritage of conceptual art. Many artists have used it to play in the space of the encounter—the moment that the viewer is confounded by the object at hand—and to foreground the notion that illusionistic rendering can reflect on itself as well as on its relationship to the viewer. Philosopher Jennifer Anna Gosetti-Ferencei has noted that trompe l'oeils "expose the everyday experience in its perceptual contingency, its dependence upon fallible perception, and its vulnerability to ecstatic reflection." When one is faced with a work of this nature, she offers," the ordinary givenness of everyday reality is disturbed...in the viewer affected by trompe l'oeil doubt has been implanted."[26] It is this doubt, Gosetti-Ferencei says, that gradually leads to the sensation of captivating wonder, or as Danto says, "It is striking that the source of pleasure, in the case of imitations, must be understood as other than real, whatever this is to mean, and the concept is accordingly presupposed available to whomever takes pleasure of this order."[27]

In the 1980s and early 1990s, a group of artists, including Americans Robert Gober, Charles Ray, and Steve Wolfe, Swiss duo Peter Fischli and David Weiss, and British artist Gavin Turk began using strategies of trompe l'oeil in a more conceptual vein, one that also played into a legacy of surrealism. These artists have worked in media ranging from photography to moving images, but continue to keep sculpture at the center of their practice. Their works share an interest in mundane subjects and phenomena awakened from their stupor through the use of meticulous re-creation, often in materials such as polyurethane, wax, and rubber. Realism in these works, however, is not always seamlessly executed. In various ways, each of these practitioners has consciously allowed a suggestion of the process to reveal itself—albeit subtly—so that the "imperfections" of their modeled renditions add to the vague sense of something being off-

(25)
This lasting stigma against the practice might explain some of the reticence of the art-historical canon to fully embrace Photorealism.

(26)
Jennifer Anna Gosetti-Ferencei, "Ecstatic Mimesis in Trompe L'Oeil," in *The Ecstatic Quotidian: Phenomenological Sightings in Modern Art and Literature* (University Park Pennsylvania: The Pennsylvania State University Press), 2007.

(27)
Arthur Danto, "Works of Art and Mere Real Things," in *The Transfiguration of the Commonplace: A Philosophy of Art* (Cambridge: Harvard University Press, 1981), 14.

kilter. While Gober's works often appear as isolated, incongruous fragments, carefully lit and arrayed in the gallery space as if they are on stage, Fischli and Weiss, in works such as *Empty Room* (1995-1996; plate 26), intensify the quality of unease by installing their sculpted and painted objects in ways that at first appear randomly scattered and forgotten, knowingly running the risk that viewers might mistake them for the cast-off objects they painstakingly replicate.

Combining a keen sense of material properties with an ethos of performance, Ray's labor-intensive works (he has referred to his working pace in interviews as "glacial") are highly calculated meditations on perception and meaning. Much of his sculpture has focused on finding strangeness in the familiar through shifts in scale, medium, or working method. He has also regularly made self-portraits, each iteration markedly different from the next, and encroaching on new psychological territory. *No* (1992; plate 22), a self-portrait, relates to several figural sculptures Ray made during the 1990s, including *Male Mannequin* (1990), a department store-like dummy constructed in the guise of an idealized classical male nude but with highly realistic genitals (a facsimile of the artist's own); and *Self-Portrait* (1990), which presents a full-scale physical likeness of the artist fabricated by commercial mannequin-makers and dressed in street clothes (fig. 11). In *No*, these ideas merge and reality stretches. The artist is represented by the model, which in turn is represented by a photograph. The uncanny emerges full force as we struggle to grasp what—if anything—is authentic.(28)

Curator Bruce Ferguson, in an early essay, characterized Ray's practice as "literalizing the real so intensely, so fiercely, and so convincingly that it crosses the boundary back to metaphor and analogy."(29) In acknowledging the expressive possibilities and potential for perceptual slippage that exist within this zone, Ray, Gober, and Fischli and Weiss certainly have a link to Surrealism's early aims. The dreamlike world invoked in Ray's early liquid-filled sculpture *Bath* (1989; plate 23), embedded in the wall so we have the sensation that we are hovering above it, or works such as Gober's *Untitled* installation (fig. 13), where isolated, incongruous elements coexist in real space, point to altered states of perception and the free-for-all that is the unconscious.

What separates these works from the realm of the surreal is that Surrealism's fantastical side is downplayed in favor of a heightened sense of reality within ordinary objects and situations. This approach, and particular distinction from Surrealism, has been characterized by some as Magic Realism, a term introduced into the discourse around literary—and less commonly—visual art in 1925 by German critic Franz Roh, who proposed the notion that an amplified sense of the real could be attained through a celebration of mundane things, and an inquiry into what might lie beneath the surface we at first perceive. He asserted that in art, by turning heightened attention on reality through representational means, by visually clarifying what is assumed to be real, this inquiry could become spiritual, transcendent, and thus propel us back into the world of our imaginations.(30)

(28)
It is interesting to note that Ray's photograph *Yes*, which is sometimes shown as a companion piece to *No*, is a self-portrait that depicts the artist under the influence of LSD.

(29)
Bruce Ferguson, "The Sculpture of Charles Ray," in *Charles Ray* (Malmö, Sweden: Rooseum-Center for Contemporary Art, 1990), 10.

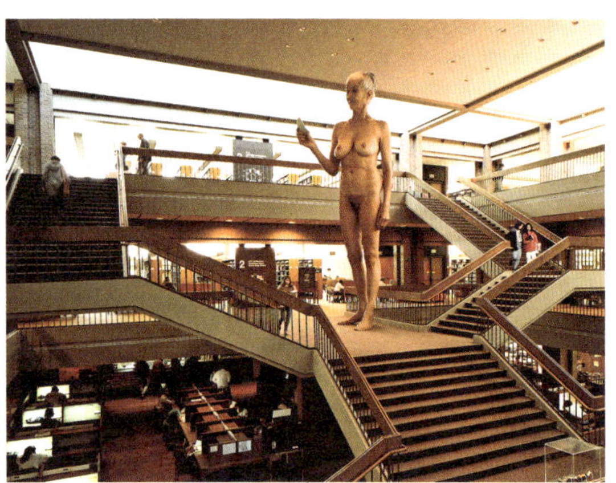

Fig. 12 Jeff Wall *The Giant* 1992 transparency in lightbox

Tapping into this unconscious realm is essential to Gober's practice. He has acknowledged that his process is largely "intuitive," with his subjects evolving on a continuum, flowing free-associatively into one another thematically and materially, and often reappearing at intervals throughout his oeuvre. In some of his works, such as *Untitled* (1997; plate 24) from 1997, his disparate elements blend into a singular visual experience. *Untitled* presents what is ostensibly a child's plastic chair, on which rests a box of tissues—a ubiquitous daycare center tableau—until one notices the mysterious drain (to nowhere) embedded in the floor below, or the handpainted floral pattern on the tissue box, or the slightly odd, marshmallowlike patina of the chair. The work—an example of Gober's "psychological furniture," which included an X-shaped playpen and rakishly slanted crib, a stool sprouting breasts and a bird's nest—is in fact made from cast plastic, painted bronze, paper, silver-plated steel, and wood—the penultimate remade readymade, pulsing with an air of the ominous.

In discussing what she calls "the repertory of the uncanny," Rosalind Krauss reminds us of Freud's musings on this phenomenon as it manifests through doubling, doll-like figures, or mirror images, and his assertion that the experience of a copy is a disorienting one. "The relation between the copy and the original," Krauss writes, "is that of a false resemblance, for while the two might seem alike to outward appearances, there is a fundamental dissimilarity at their core." The uncanny sensation, she writes, "stems from the recognition that these doubles are at one and the same time the extreme opposite of oneself and yet the same as oneself, which is to say both alive and dead."(31)

Ron Mueck, who came to visual art from a background in special effects, dramatically mines this potential with his sculptures of human figures, often extraordinarily out of scale and context, and captivatingly strange. Like Jeff Wall's photographic sleight of hand in early staged works such as *The Giant* (fig. 12), Mueck derives psychological impact by manipulating context. We are immediately forced to confront his figures' astonishing physicality—often their nakedness—in our space. The form in *Crouching Boy in Mirror* (1999-2000; plate 28) is lifelike, yet smaller than life. He peers into a mirror, propped against the wall that tilts upward to capture the viewer in its reflection. In Freud's discussions of the uncanny, the experience of mirror images contributes to a sensation of discomfort with the familiar. In Mueck's tableau, the mirror becomes another painterly representation of the boy. When we view his reflection, he appears all the more "real" to us, yet we who share his space in the picture plane feel disconcertingly out of place.

(30) Franz Roh, "Magical Realism: Post-Expressionism," reprinted in *Magical Realism: Theory, History, Community*, Lois Parkinson Zamora and Wendy B. Faris, eds. (Durham, NC: Duke University Press, 1995), 15-31.

(31) Rosalind Krauss, "The Uncanny," in Rosalind E. Krauss and Yve-Alain Bois, *Formless: A User's Guide* (New York: Zone Books, 1997), 194.

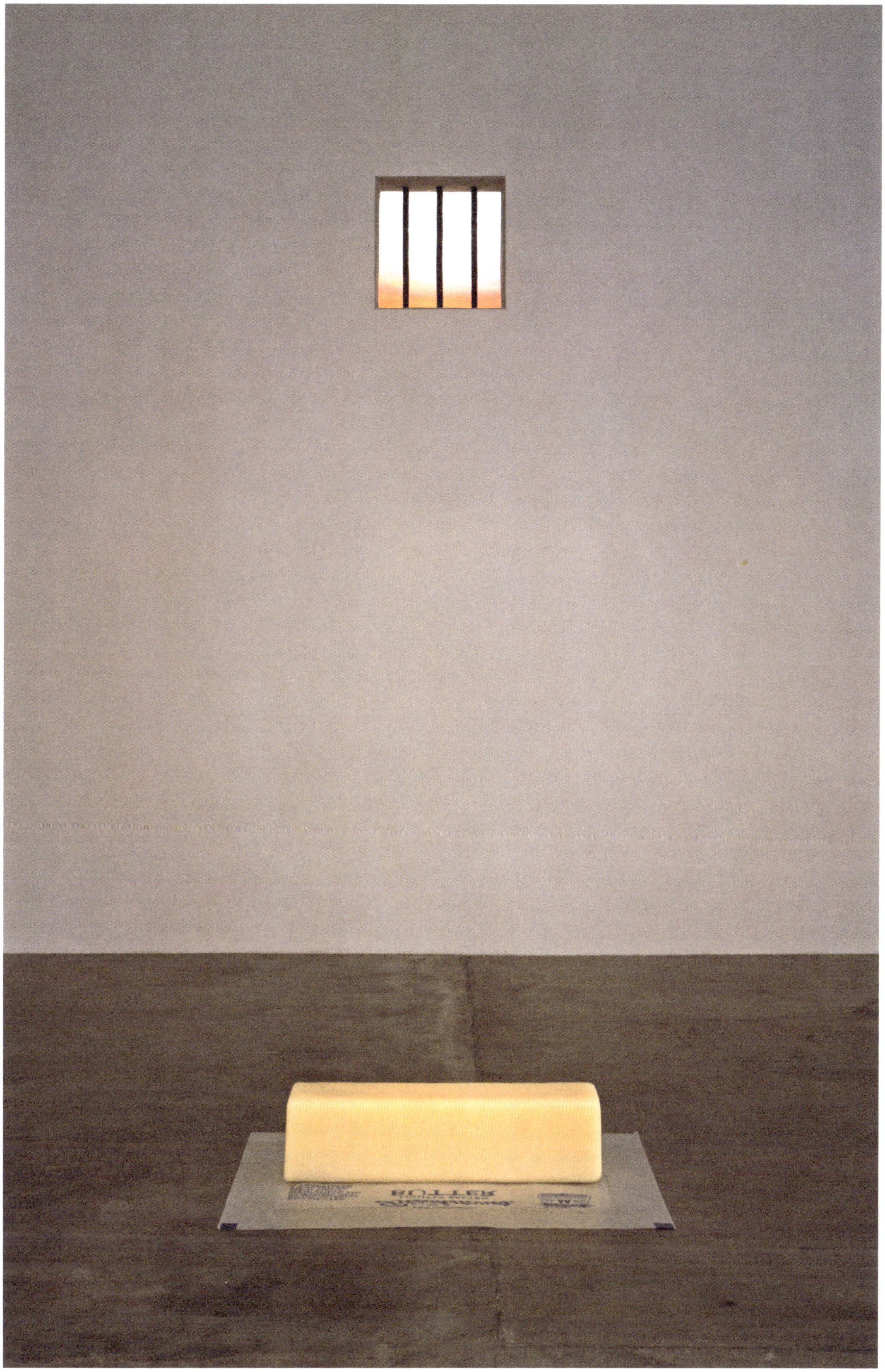

Fig. 13 Robert Gober *Untitled* 2003 window: plywood, iron, plaster, latex paint, lights butter: beeswax, wood, glassine, ink

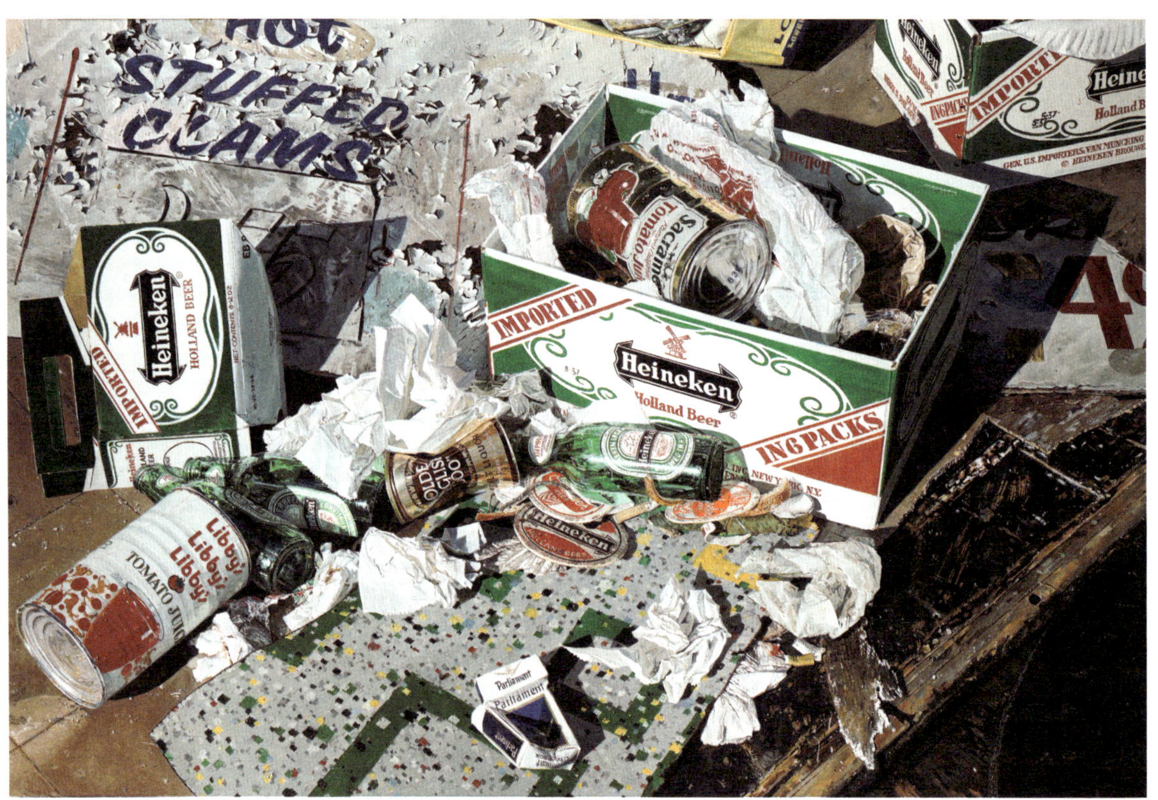

Fig. 14 Idelle Weber *Heineken* 1976 oil on linen

This line of sculptural thinking has been continued in recent years by artists such as Turk, whose works have often depicted abject items of the urban underbelly. *Nomad* (2001; plate 27) appears to be a nylon sleeping bag, spread across the gallery floor. It is curved, however, in the shape of a human form, and although there is no physical evidence of a body within, the piece, like Turk's disarmingly realistic sculptures of discarded apple cores, Styrofoam cups, or piles of black trash bags, invokes the life of the street where disenfranchised, unnoticed people and objects intermingle. Cast in bronze and painted, Turk's sleeping bag and other "throwaways" are made precious and permanent. Their sensibility recalls the 1970s Photorealist paintings of Idelle Weber, whose subject matter often focused not on the bright and shiny city scenes of her male peers, but on found, urban still lifes such as the garbage overflowing in corner trash cans and gutters (fig. 14).

In works involving the moving image, some artists have conjured the uncanny through a process of not only translation from one medium to another as well as transformation, as seen in Sam Taylor-Wood's work *Still Life* (2001; plate 32), a video that at first appears to be not a film but a lightboxlike photograph of the most traditional and academic sort of still life—a basket of fruit on a wooden table. At second glance, however, the image has changed, almost imperceptibly. Slowly, it becomes clear that this is a vanitas, as the fruit shrivels and cultivates haloes of mold before puddling into a decomposed mass. Remaining static, however, is a ballpoint pen—resting casually but resolutely on the table's edge, a reminder of the studio and the artifice constructed in tandem with this natural phenomenon.

Others have played off of this sense of strangeness in their reimagining of found objects. Matt Johnson works with ordinary subjects that he then transforms—via scale, materials, or attitude, often with a dose of illusionism. His sculpture *American Spirit* (2010; plate 29) presents an object that is not inanimate—a handmade package of cigarettes that floats miraculously (via a concealed system of magnets) over its pedestal. It is reminiscent of Ray's 1988 sculpture *Tabletop*, in which a selection of objects slowly rotates on individual axes on a wooden table as a still life in motion.[32] Cigarettes, of course, have a long history in the history of art, from Georges Braque to Robert Motherwell to Oldenburg. *American Spirit*, both in its title and presentation, seems to revere this lineage while invoking a tongue-in-cheek sense of the divine: a holier than thou (all-organic) yet carcinogenic apparition. Likewise, Rirkrit Tiravanija's bowl of "noodles" (2000; plate 35), made in the manner of plastic menu items frequently placed in restaurant windows in Japan and elsewhere, confuses both the average viewer, who takes them to be real (save for the chopsticks hovering in midair), and the art-world insider who assumes they are the edible creations Tiravanija often cooks in gallery settings.

At times, this manipulation of perception operates with artists who use photography—not as a source but as an end in order to make pictures that have an intentionally ambiguous relationship to reality. Richter's edition *9 Objekte* (*9 Objects*) (1969; plate 31) is a series of offset lithographs made from collaged photographic fragments manipulated (pre-Photoshop era) into images presenting impossible constructions

(32) Johnson was a former student of Ray's at the University of California, Los Angeles, where he received his MFA in 2003.

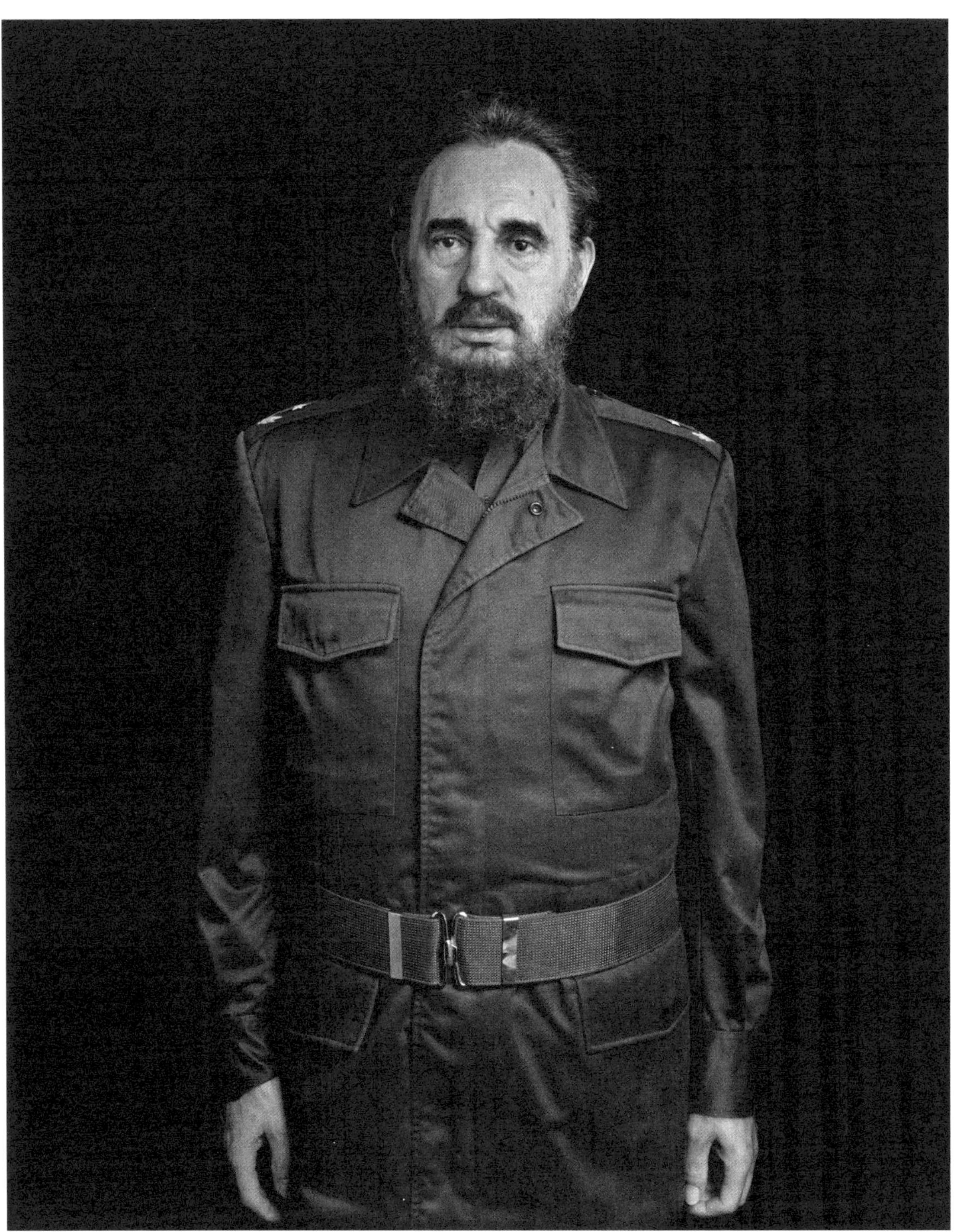

Fig. 15 Hiroshi Sugimoto *Fidel Castro* 1999 gelatin silver print

with edges that fade into one another or don't properly end. Possessing a fuzziness similar to the artist's "blurred" paintings, the images challenge the notion that the camera faithfully records its subject as truth. This practice of constructing scenarios for the camera has been central to James Casebere's practice since the early 1980s. He is known for his fastidiously fabricated models of architecture and landscapes, made from cardboard, Styrofoam, and other basic materials, which he then carefully lights in a studio setup and photographs as large-scale scenes. His recent series based on residential hamlets in Dutchess County, New York, is perhaps his most ambitious body of work to be created from a single, sprawling scale model. Photographed in crisp digital color, the scene is familiar, yet we at once sense an artifice we cannot immediately comprehend. As in all of Casebere's work, humans are conspicuously absent, though in photographs such as *Landscape with Houses (Dutchess County, NY) #8* (2010; plate 63), there are visible signs of "life," such as a bicycle or trash awaiting curbside collection, adding to our disorientation.

Hiroshi Sugimoto, who has used some of these strategies of constructed artifice in his own work, has characterized the phenomenon: "Upon first arriving in New York in 1974, I did the tourist thing. Eventually I visited the Natural History Museum, where I made a curious discovery: the stuffed animals positioned before painted backdrops looked utterly fake, yet by taking a quick peek with one eye closed, all perspective vanished, and suddenly they looked very real. I'd found a way to see the world as a camera does. However fake the subject, once photographed, it's as good as real."(33) Like Ray's self-portrait, Sugimoto's photographs made of figures found in wax museums (fig. 15) embody a near-holographic sense of three-dimensionality within the flatness of the photographic surface.

Conversely, photography sometimes manages to capture the world in a way that appears artificial, even when it is not. The photographs of Esteban Pastorino Diaz (plate 34), which have a visual affinity with the images of Casebere or artists who have also used miniatures as props, such as David Levinthal and Laurie Simmons, are in fact made in a nearly inverse process. Rather than recording fabricated scenes, his images are made with a variety of cameras, some airborne on kites, others attached to moving cars, which capture real panoramas that strangely resemble landscapes built for model trains complete with toy objects and buildings. By investigating ways in which recording the real has the capacity to distort time, or at least our perception of it, Diaz constructs what he has called "a fiction of the extension of the photographic instant."(34)

(33)
Hiroshi Sugimoto, statement on the artist's website, http://www.sugimotohiroshi.com/, September 2011.

(34)
Esteban Pastorino Diaz, artist statement accompanying Fotofest International, the eleventh International Biennial of Photography and Photo-related Art, Houston, Texas, 2006. Fotofest online archives, http://www.fotofest.org/ff2006/exhibitions_diaz.htm.

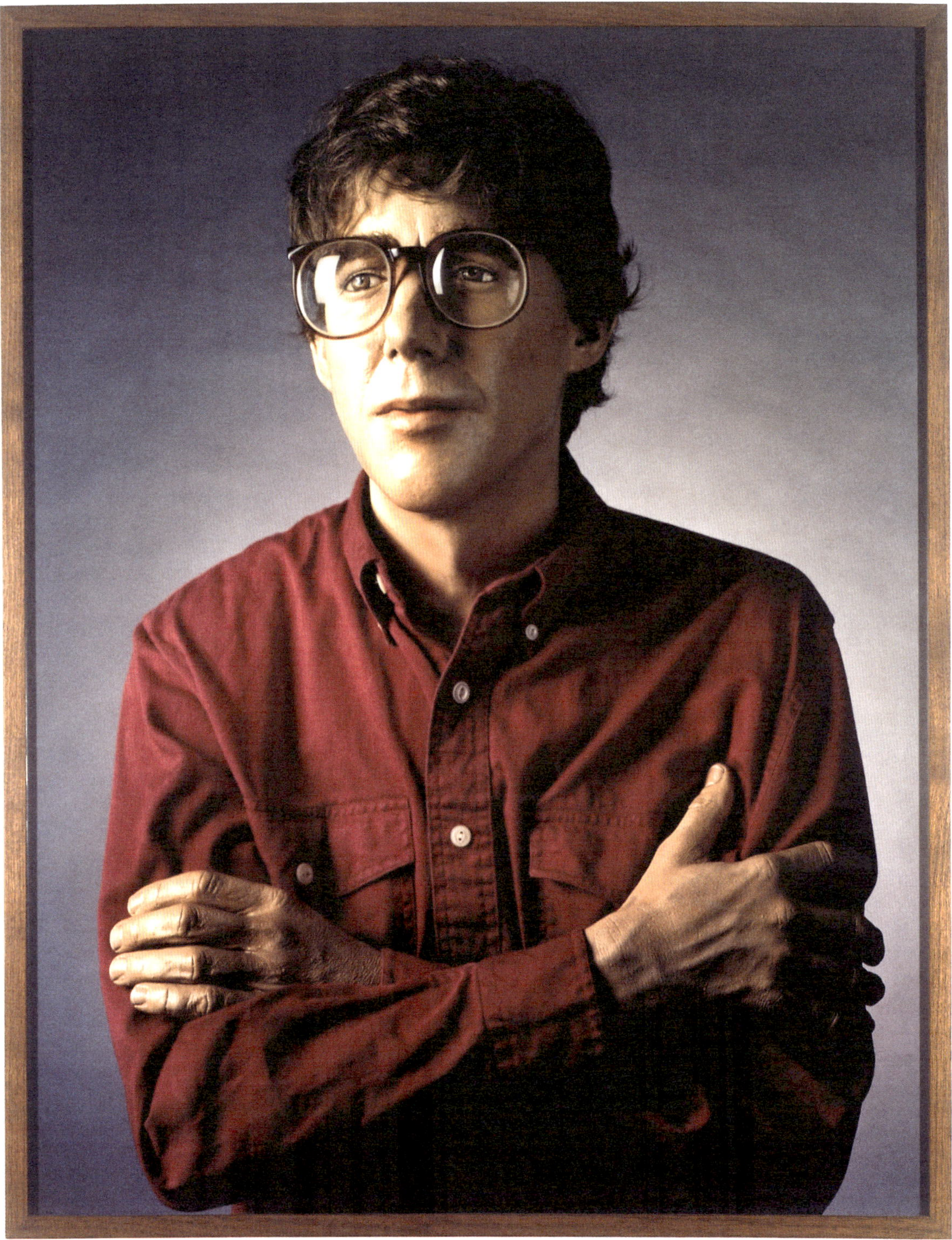

Plate 22. Charles Ray *No* 1991 color photograph in artist's frame

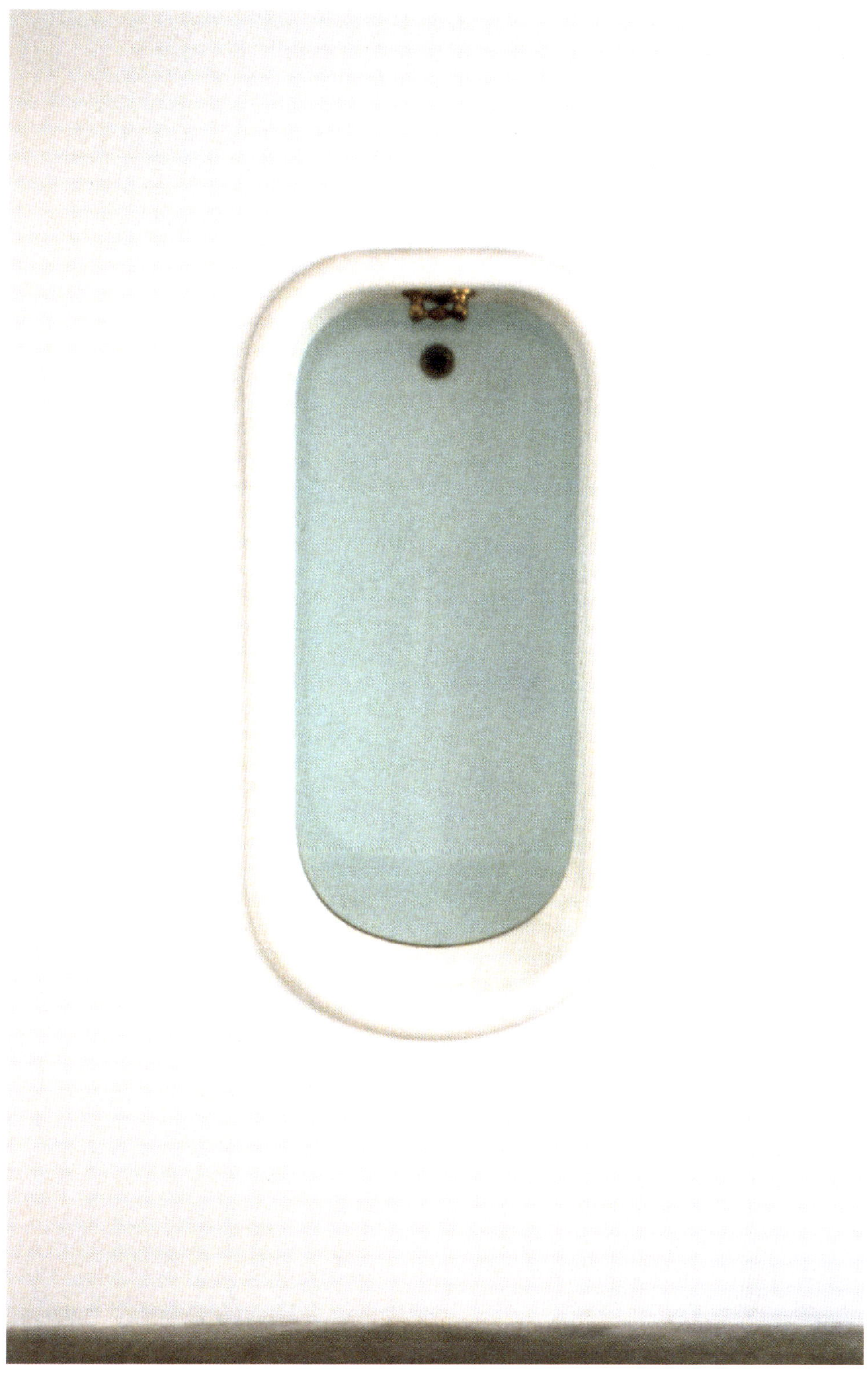

Plate 23. Charles Ray *Bath* 1989 porcelain bathtub, brass, aluminum, water

Robert Gober on Untitled

At the time that I made this sculpture my psychiatrist was a child psychiatrist. The waiting room or hallway was borderline crummy but also wonderful because there were an equal number of adult-size chairs and child-size chairs, evoking an equanimity that frequently moved me.

As is often the case, I didn't realize this sculpture's real life source until well after its completion. I am convinced that for me the visual decisions or ideas happen in oblique, semi-conscious ways. This image or object was the silent companion to my talking cure.

Sometimes the tissues were on a side table or the couch, but the chair, a small wooden one, was always here next to me. In putting the two objects together I thought I was placing adult-size burdens on a child, magnified yet again in the large drain underneath. One time in San Francisco someone asked me what the piece meant. I responded that he should understand what it is physically before worrying about meaning. When you know that the painted tissue box is bronze, you know that it is unnaturally heavy and then the meanings start to flow from the physical thing itself.

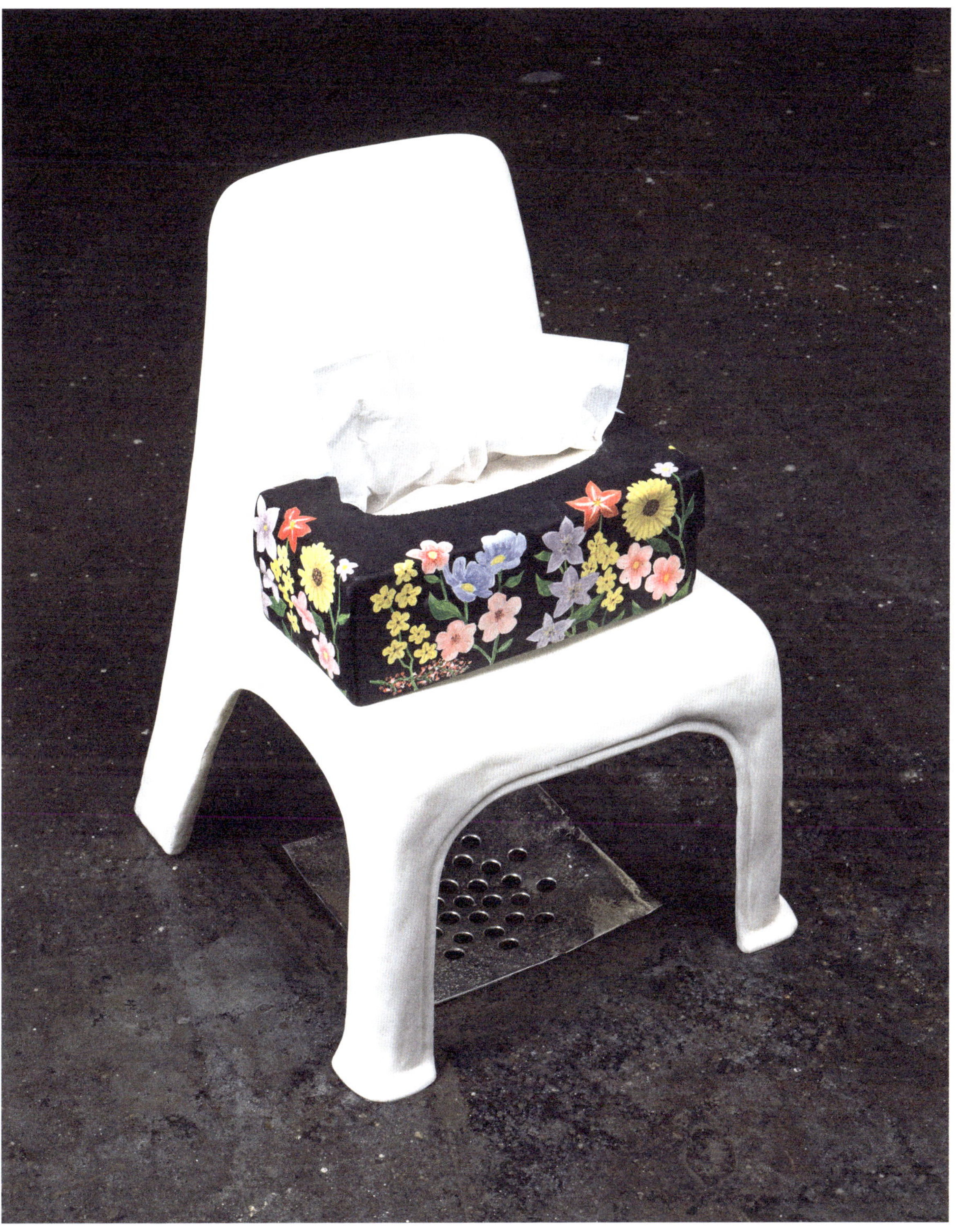

Plate 24. Robert Gober *Untitled* 1997 cast plastic, painted bronze, paper, silver-plated steel, wood

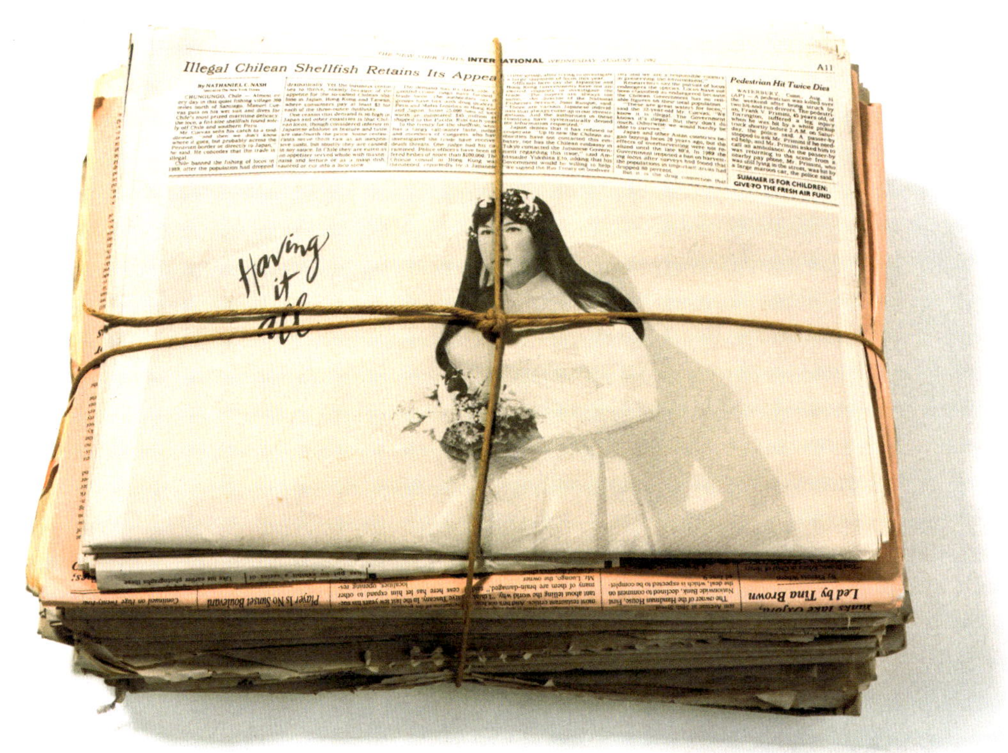

Plate 25. Robert Gober *Newspaper* 1992 photolithograph on paper, twine

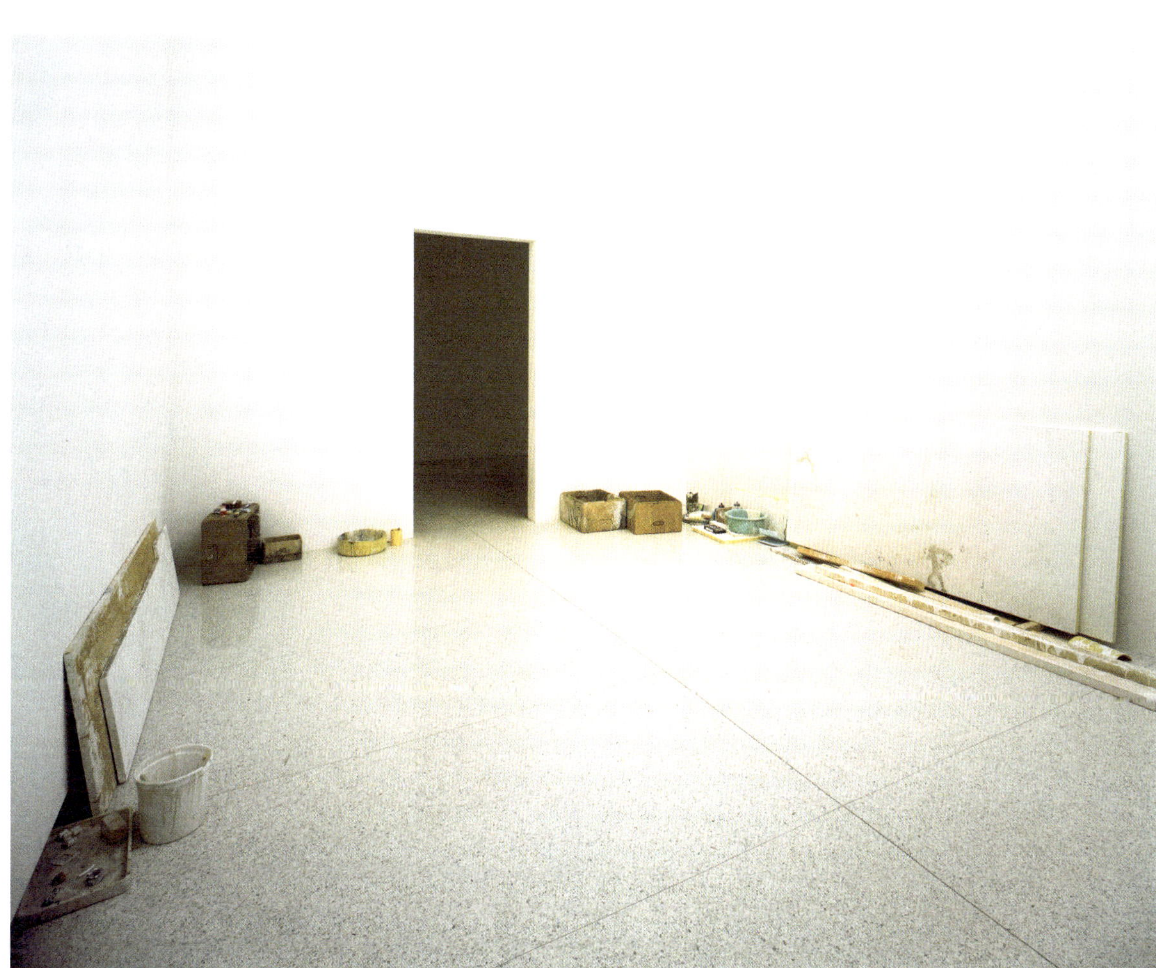

Plate 26. Peter Fischli and David Weiss *Empty Room* 1995–1996 polyurethane, paint

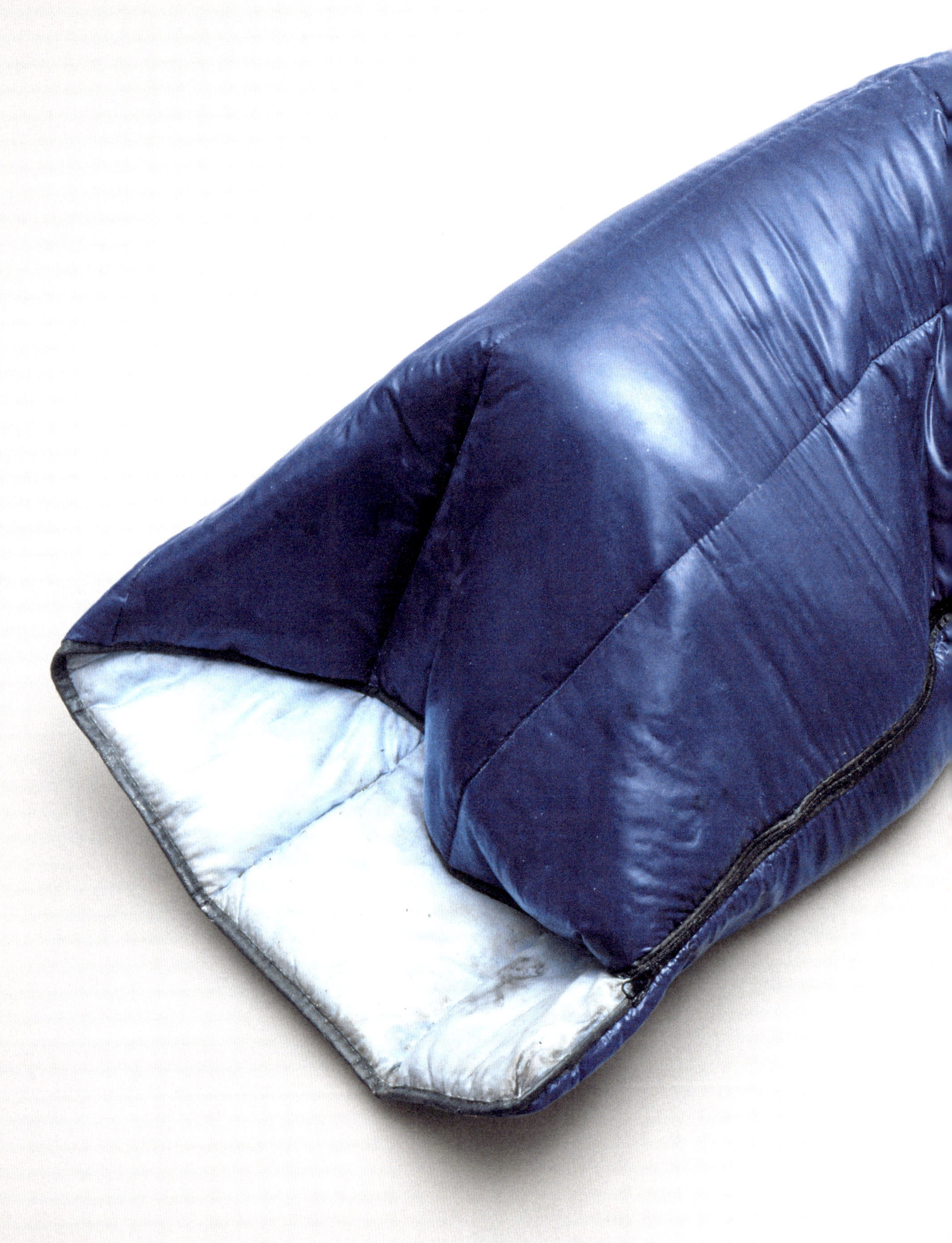

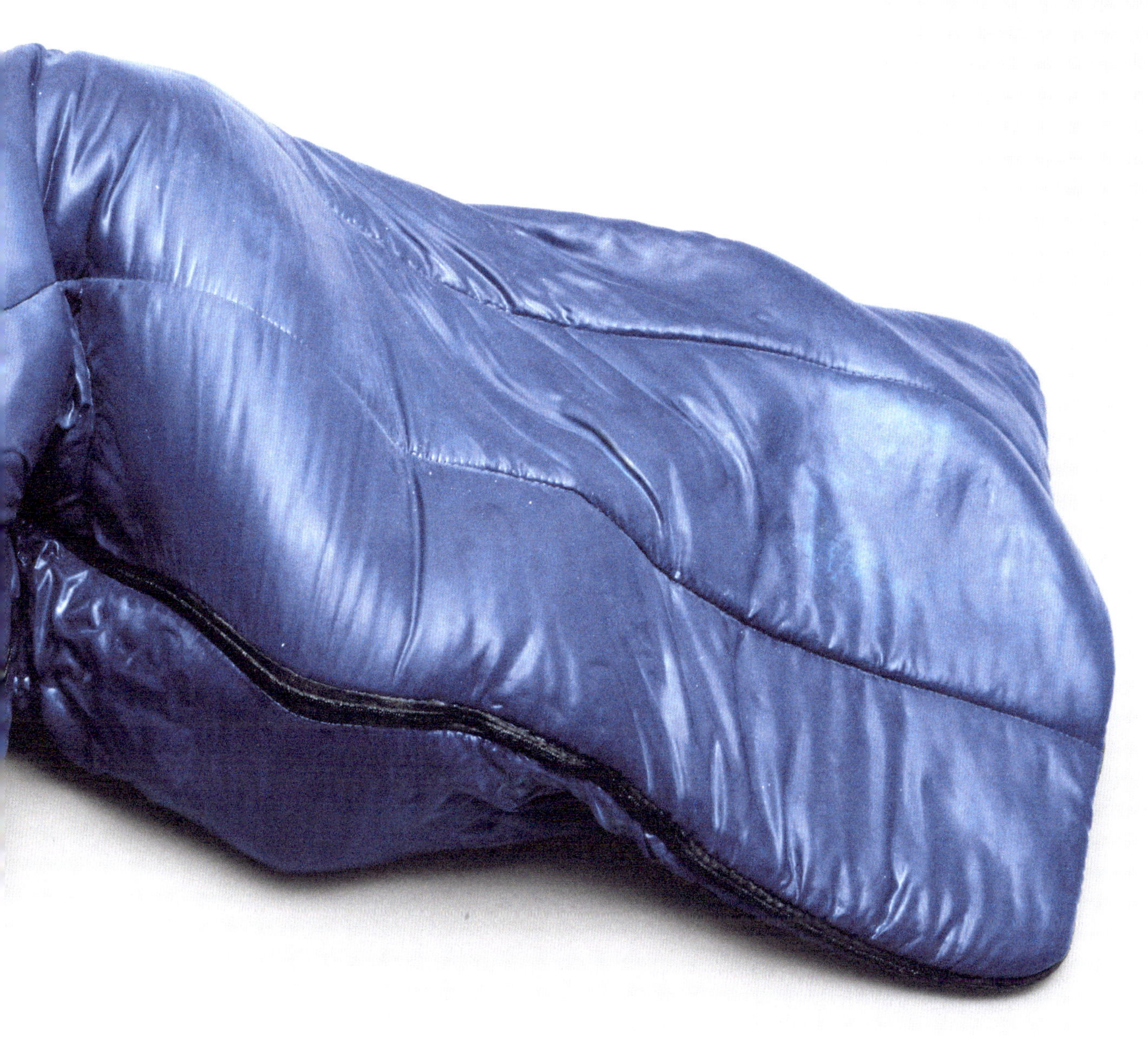

Plate 27. Gavin Turk *Nomad* 2001 painted bronze

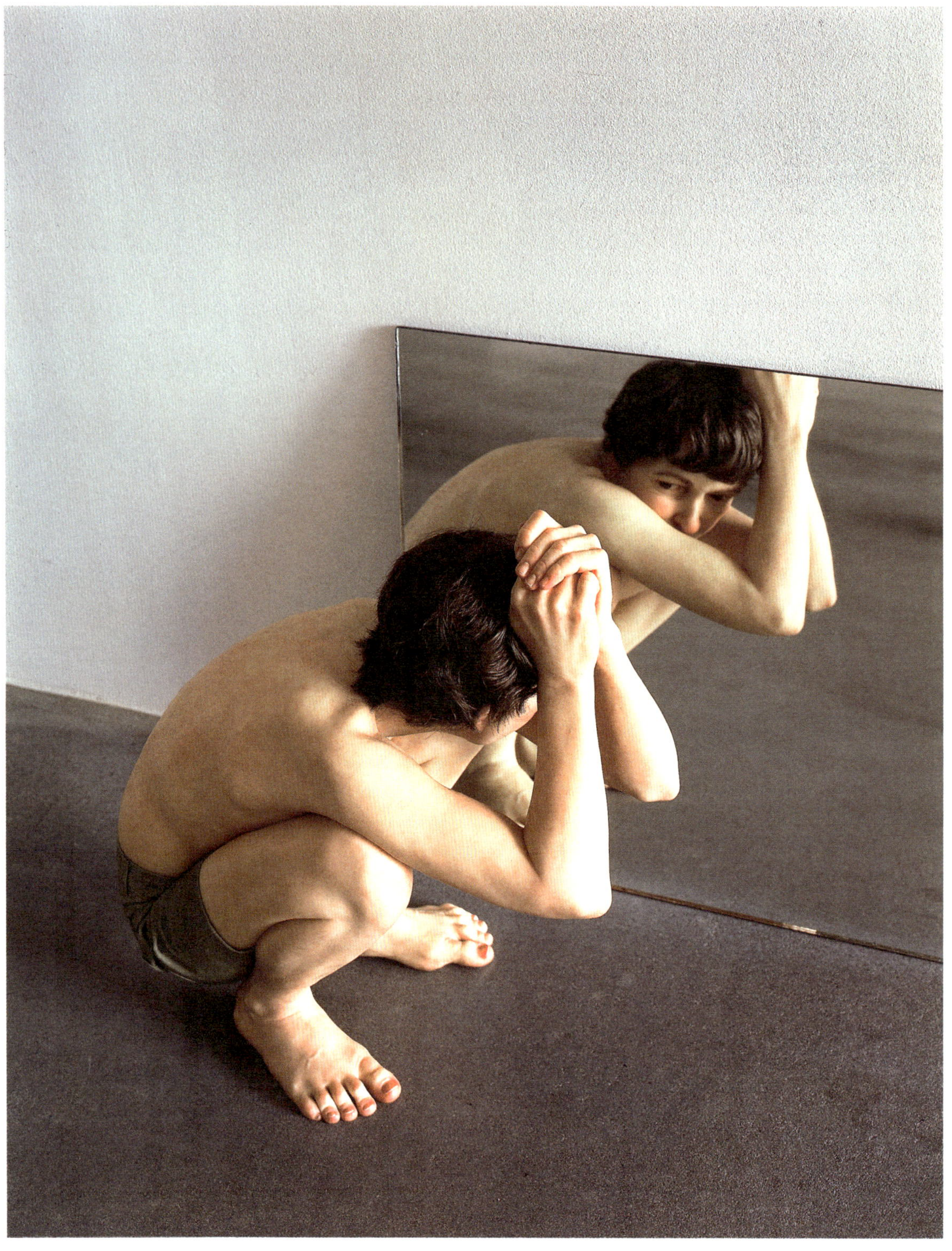

Plate 28. Ron Mueck *Crouching Boy in Mirror* 1999–2000 mixed media

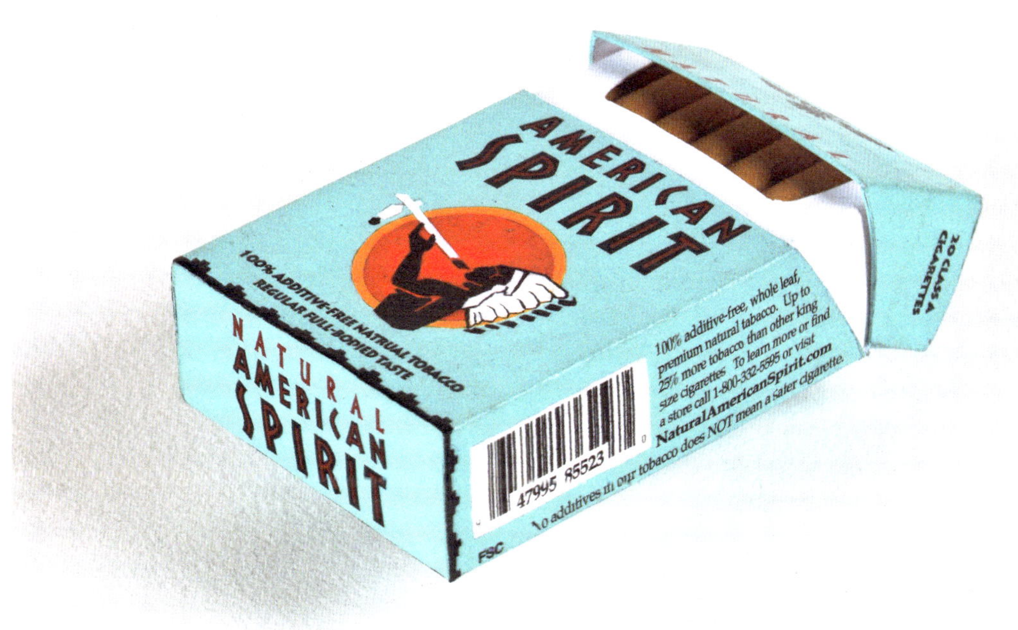

Plate 29. Matt Johnson *American Spirit* 2010 paper, plastic, foam, paint, magnets

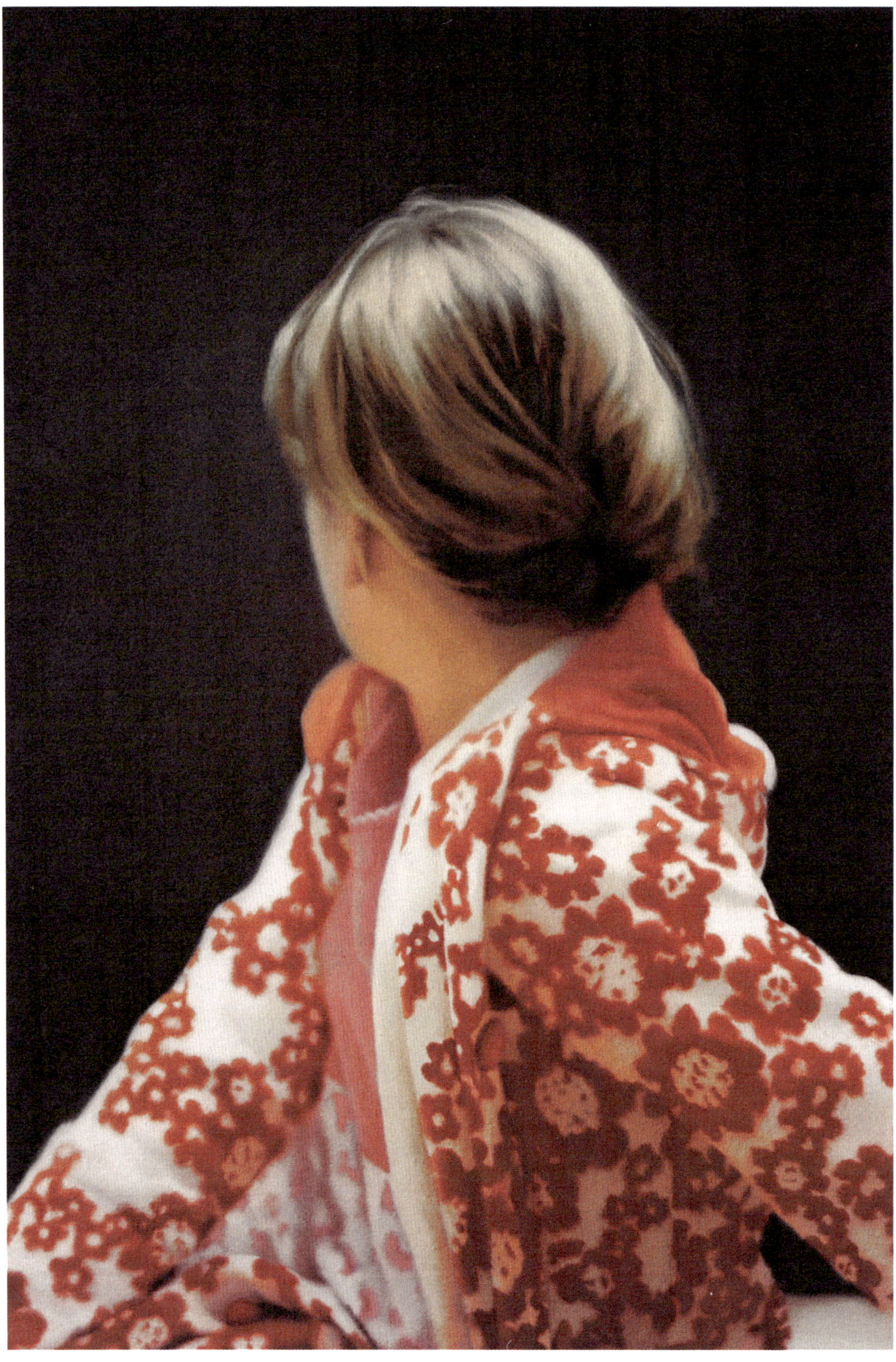

Plate 30. Gerhard Richter *Betty* 1991 offset print on cardboard with nitrocellulose varnish, mounted on plastic, framed behind glass

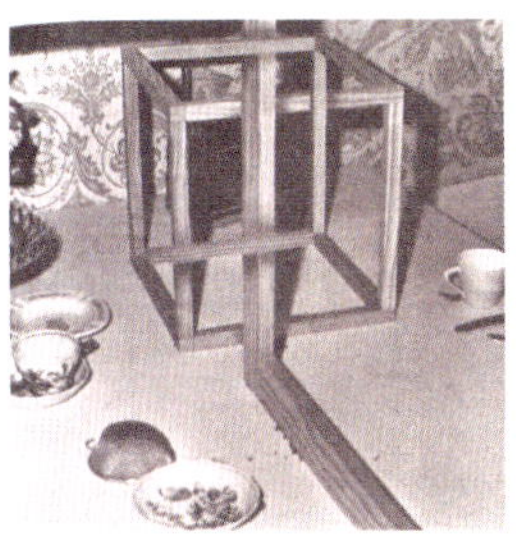
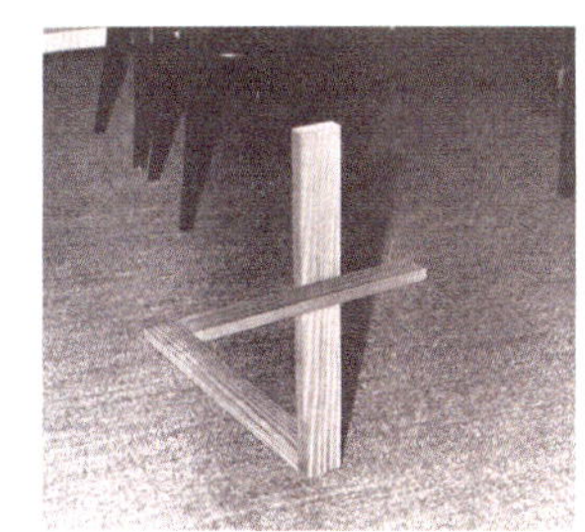
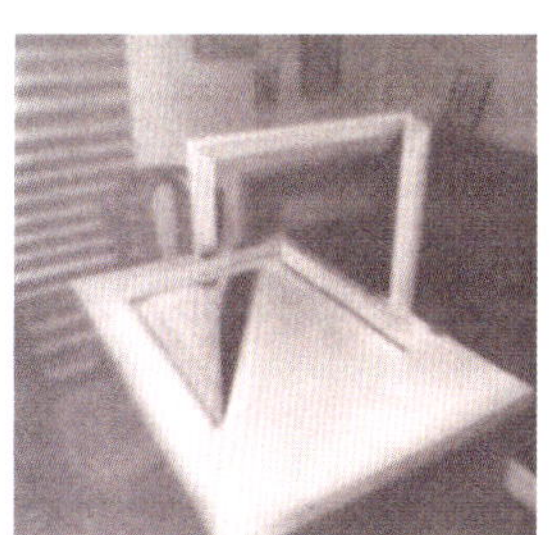
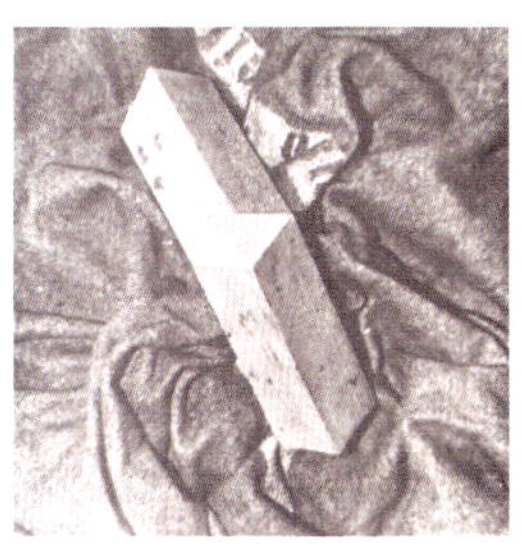
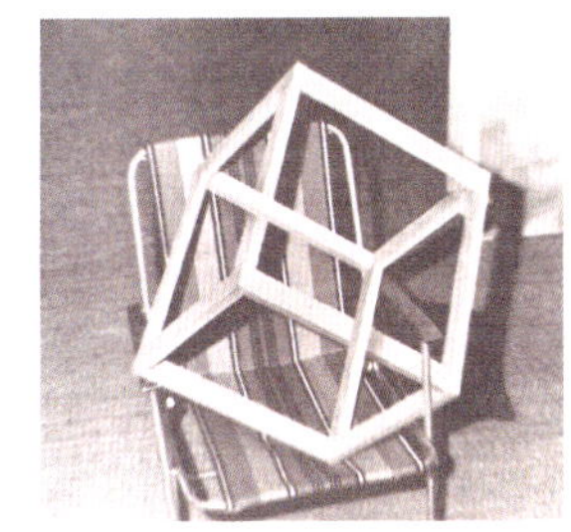
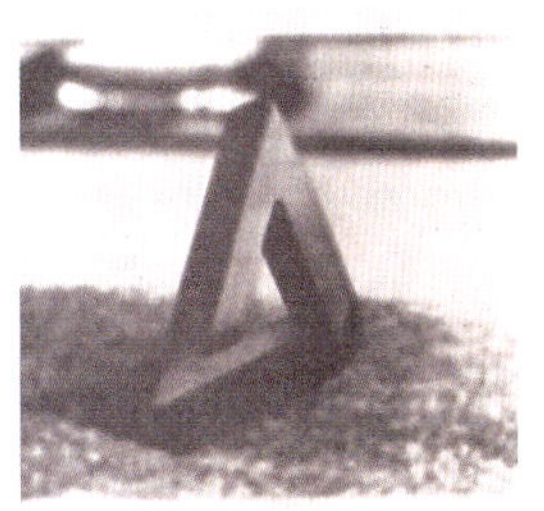
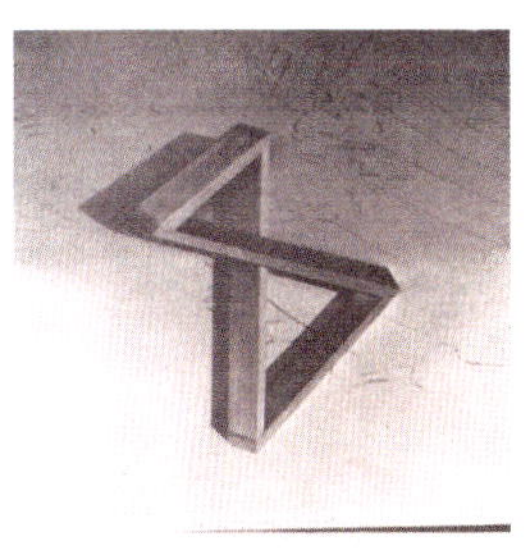
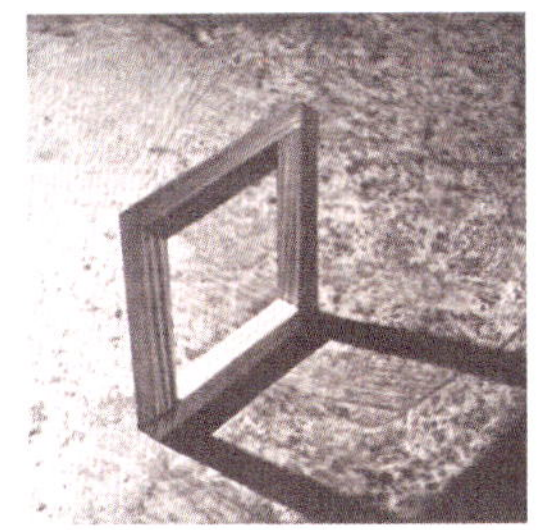
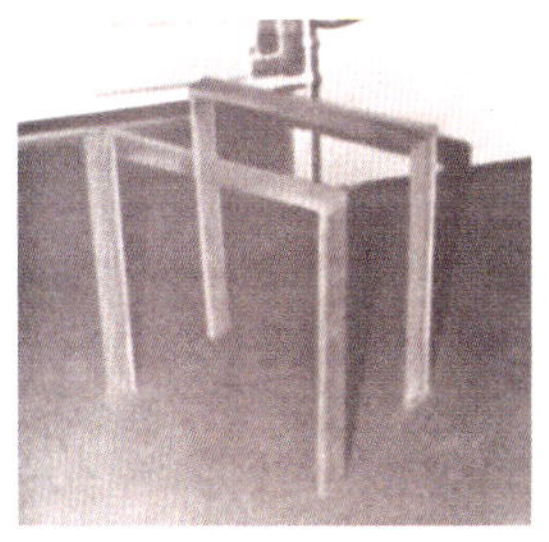

Plate 31. Gerhard Richter *9 Objekte* (*9 Objects*) 1969 portfolio of 9 photolithographs

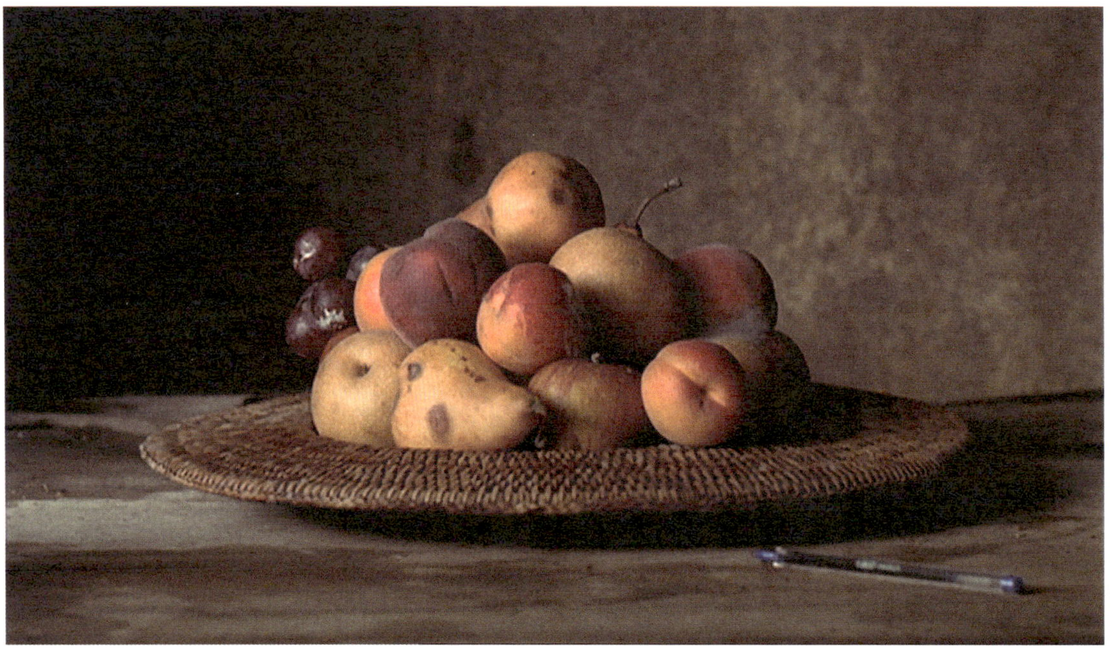

Plate 32. Sam Taylor-Wood *Still Life* 2001 (stills) 35mm film (color, sound) transferred to video

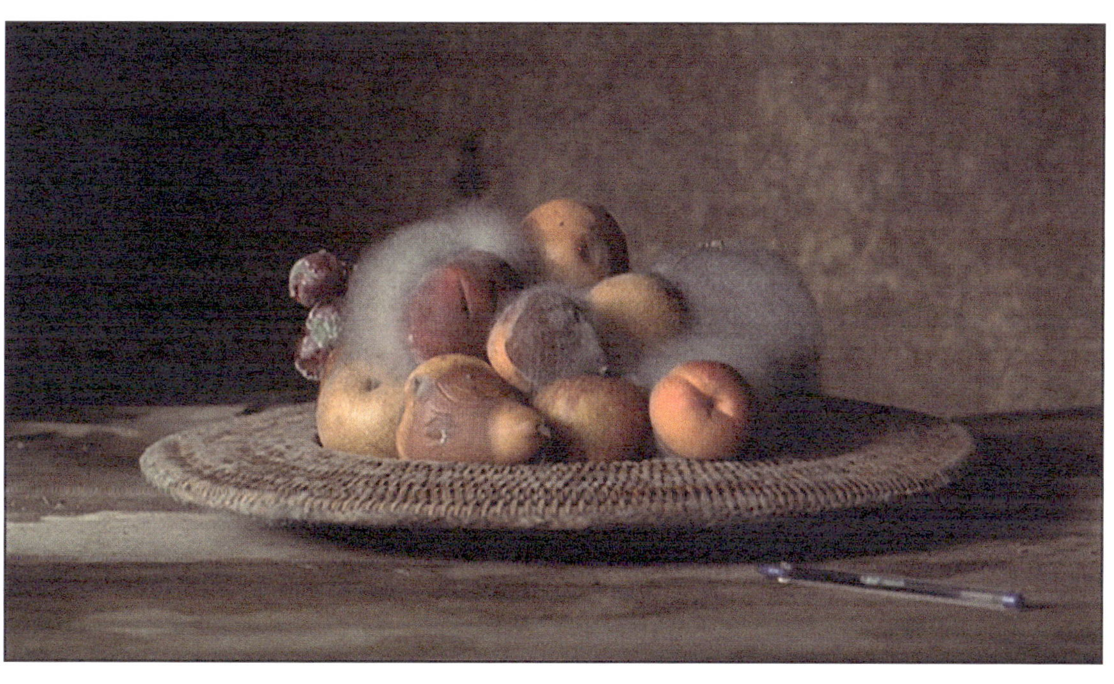

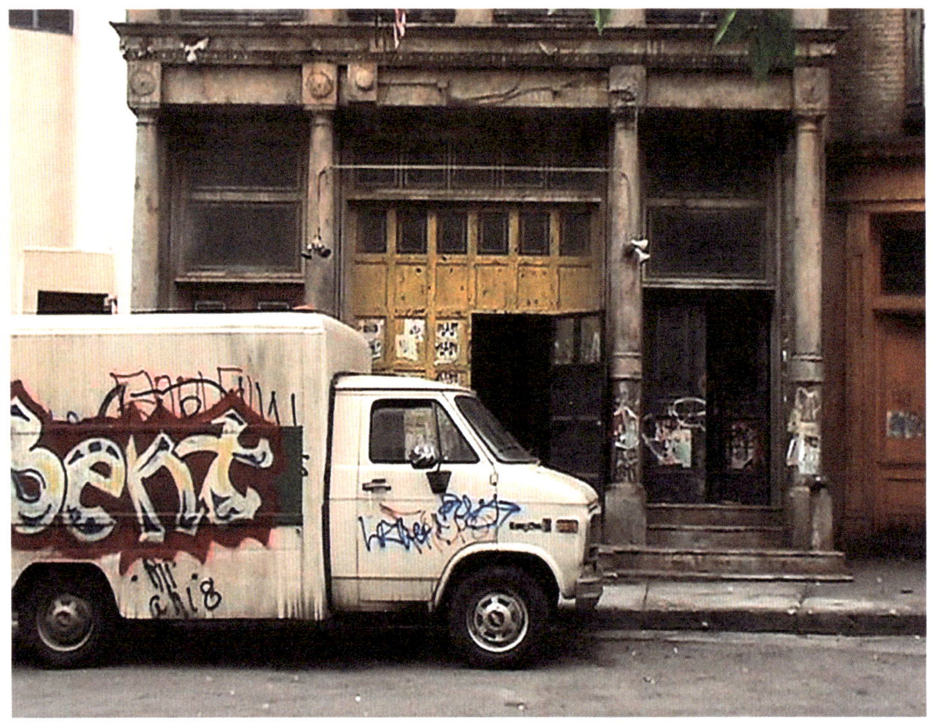

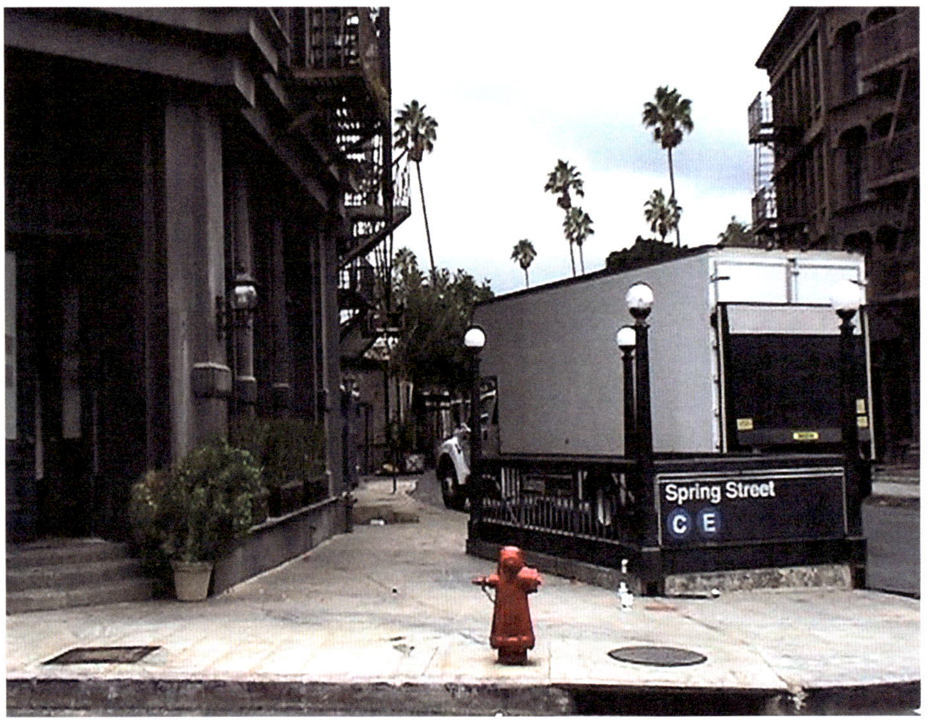

Plate 33. Mungo Thomson *New York, New York, New York, New York* 2004 (stills) 4-channel video installation (color, sound)

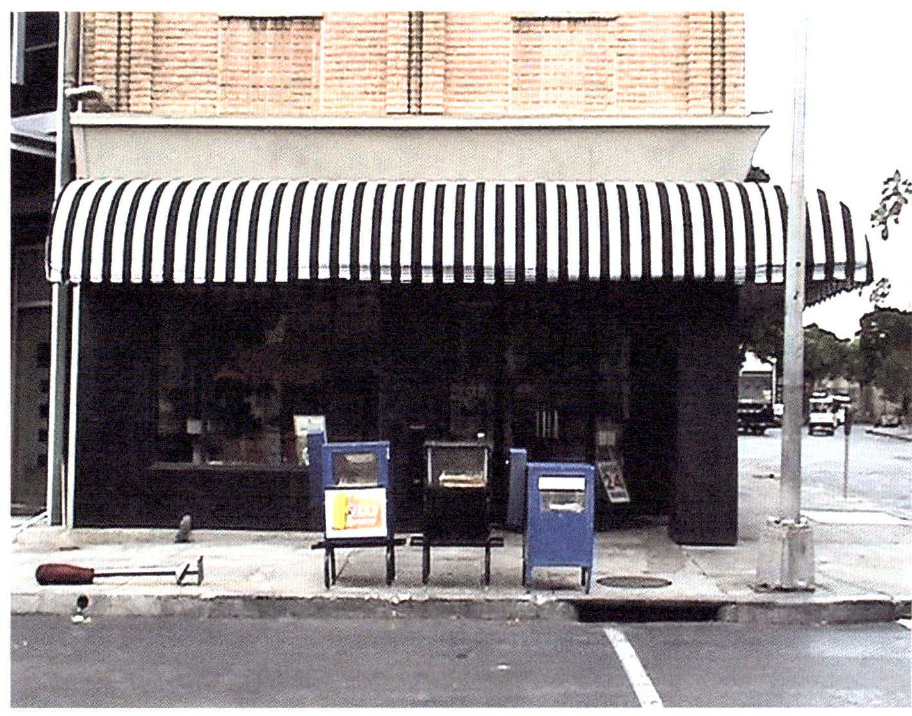

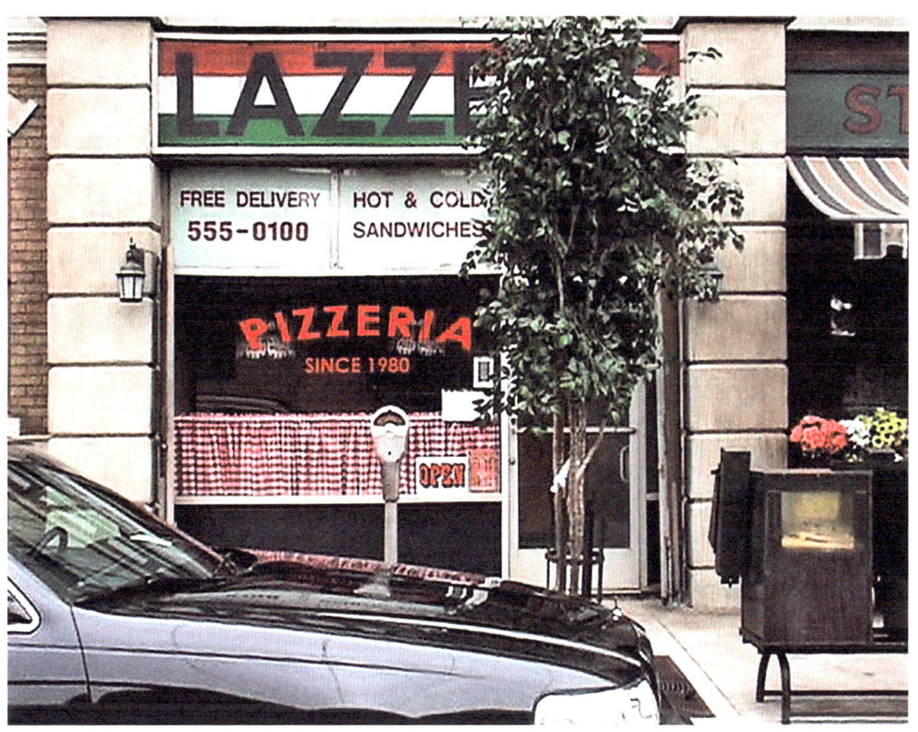
LAZZE
FREE DELIVERY
555-0100
HOT & COLD
SANDWICHES
PIZZERIA
SINCE 1980
OPEN

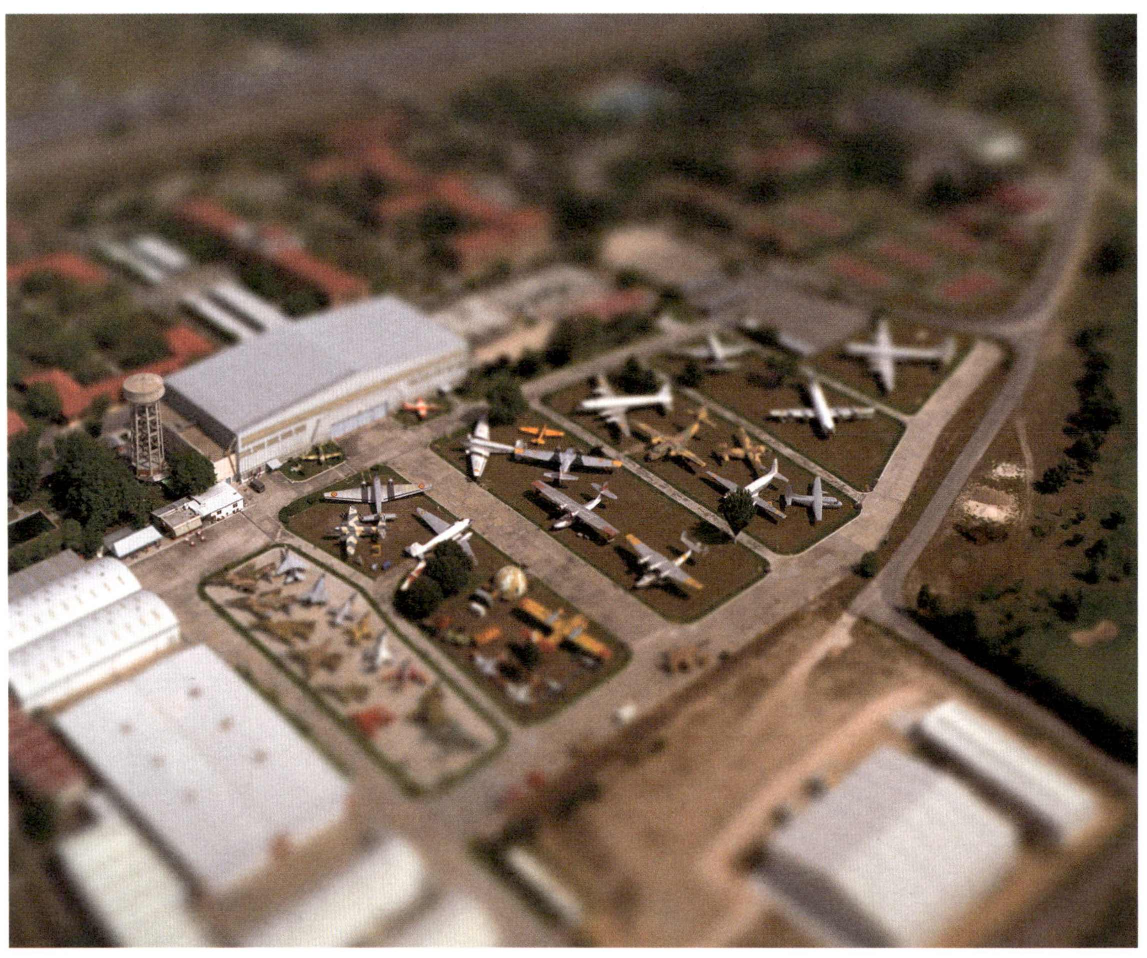

Plate 34. Esteban Pastorino Diaz *Cuatro Vientos* 2006 digital chromogenic print

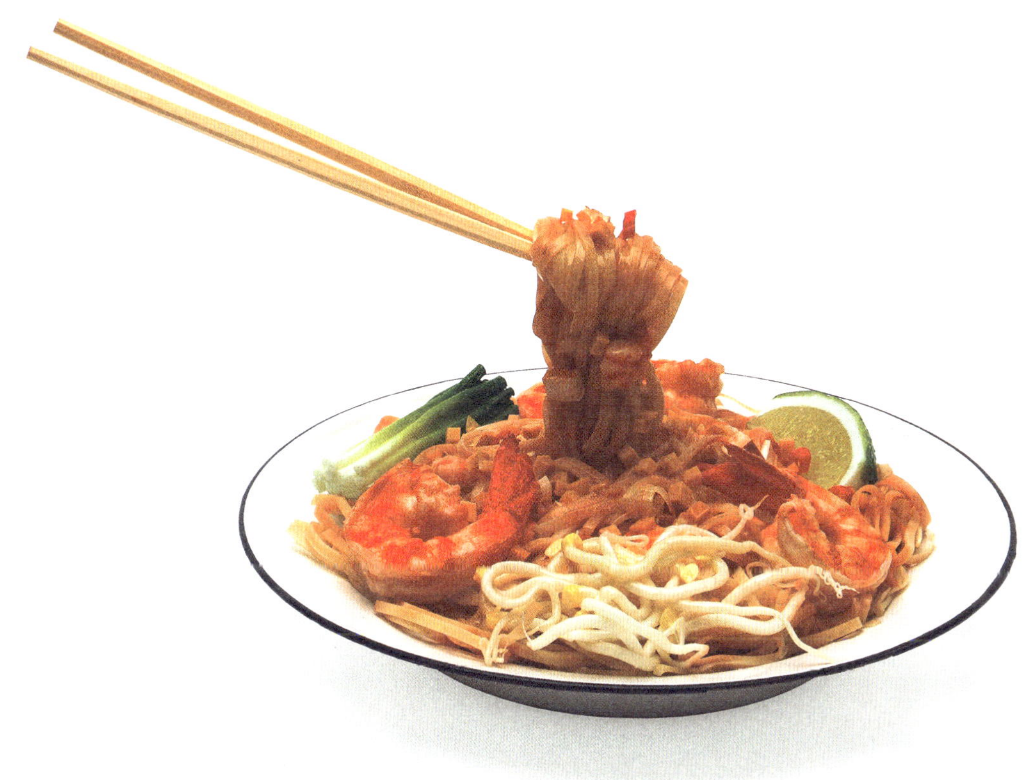

Plate 35. Rirkrit Tiravanija *Young man, if my wife makes it...* 2000 wooden chopsticks, plastic, metal bowl

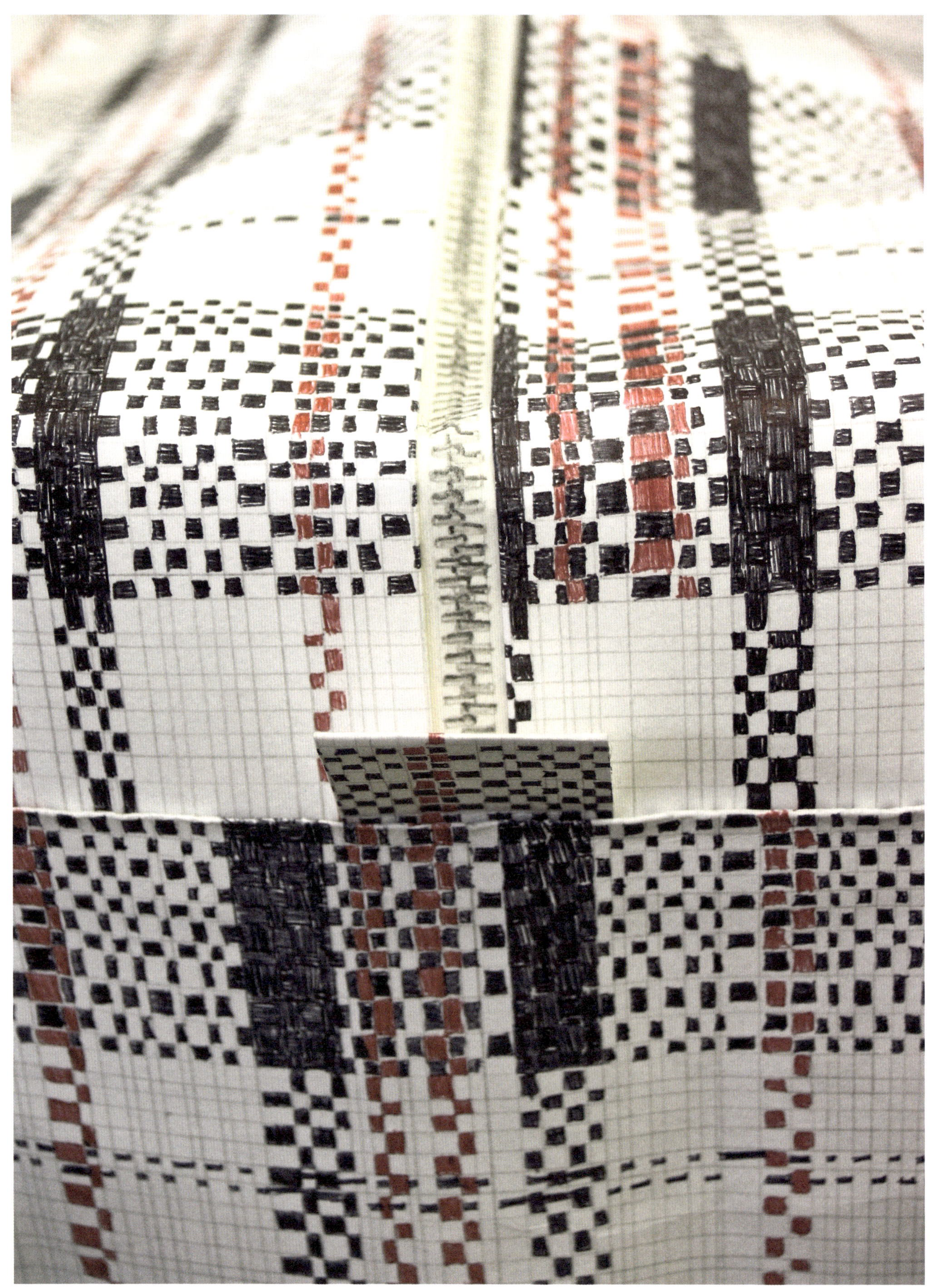

Fig. 16 Susan Collis *Refugee* 2007 (detail) ballpoint pen, pencil and glue on paper

ABSTRACTION

REALISM

Section 3

Realism into Abstraction

Realism into Abstraction

While some artists working within a hyperreal mode posit the real as a given—something that exists in the world that can then be reimagined through replication—others question whether it might be possible to find mystery within the ordinary by taking a closer look. By highlighting aspects of the visually immersive surfaces, textures, hues, or angles of ordinary subjects, a number of artists since the 1960s have viewed realism as a place within which to locate the abstract, playing up the poetic potential of their everyday sources by teasing out intangible qualities. This has often involved a focus on photographic originals, the camera's ability to zoom, and the notion of cropping when selecting imagery. For artists who paint from photographs rather than life, this often becomes a conceptual strategy to signal the possibility of ideas that extend beyond the capacity of the photograph itself.

Painter Peter Rostovsky calls this sensibility, in which artists allude to ephemeral qualities through heightened realism, a "photo-lyrical" tradition, suggesting that the use of photography can be a portal to representing something immaterial. Always working from photographic sources, which he culls from the Internet, Rostovsky is interested in creating a sense of allegory in the vein of Diego Velásquez, John Singer Sargent, and Eakins. *Curtain* (2010; plate 49), with its carefully painted velvet folds, nods to the traditions of drapery in Dutch painting, but it is also a timeless visual symbol of mystery and drama: this image is archetypal, whether the point of reference is the Royal Opera House, the set of a David Lynch film, or the great and powerful Oz. The curtain partitions that which is real (the audience) from that which is constructed (stage, sets, lighting, actors). It also invokes what is perhaps the oldest tale of trompe l'oeil, the contest between classical artists Zeuxis and Parrhasius to determine who painted with the greatest skill. Zeuxis' painting of grapes proved so real that birds were drawn to them. Proof enough of victory for Zeuxis, who then invited Parrhasius to pull aside the curtain on his own painting. When Parrhasius' curtain was revealed to be a deftly painted illusion as well, Zeuxis admitted defeat. Rostovsky's curtain, here portrayed with faithful exactitude, simultaneously summons the mysteries possible in painting itself.

A sense of "zooming," whether out or in, allows pictures like this to straddle the worlds of abstraction and representation. These are works about surface that invite visual immersion and momentary detachment from the real-life subject, for both the artist and the viewer. Catherine Murphy works from life, strictly adhering to the literal qualities of the objects she represents, though her paintings are often composed with an eye toward photographic cropping and editing. Canvases such as *Moiré Chair* (1991; plate 40) evidence pattern, texture, and shadow executed with such intense detail that the whole reads as an abstract field. Yet the painting nonetheless involves subtle narrative, as it suggests a vast world beyond its visual boundaries.

Similarly, the immersive, exquisitely precise imagery in Celmins' starry skies or Richter's cloudscapes become broad meditations on what we do not see. Celmins' 1993 painting *Night Sky #6* (plate 38), one of a series of works focused on this subject, is executed with a full embrace of the all-overness touted by the Abstract Expressionists. Here,

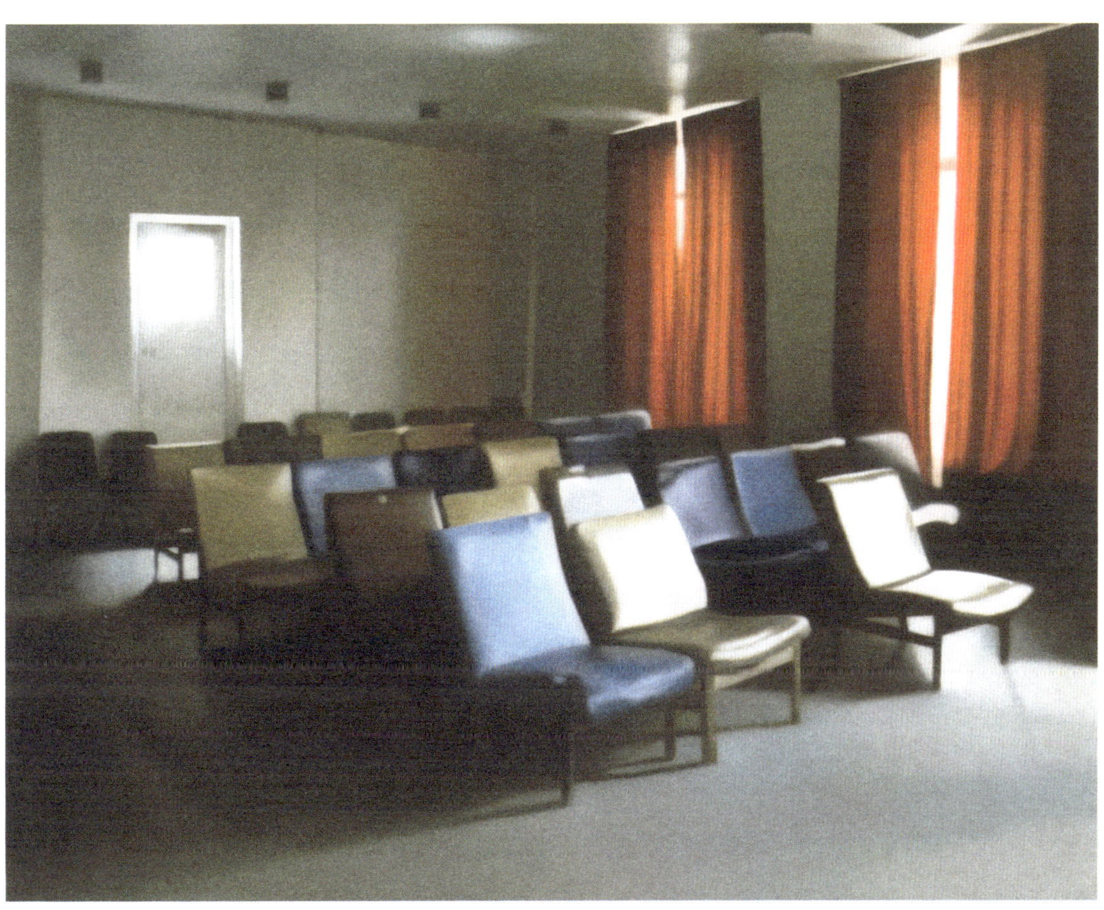

Fig. 17 Paul Winstanley *Viewing Room* 1997 oil on linen

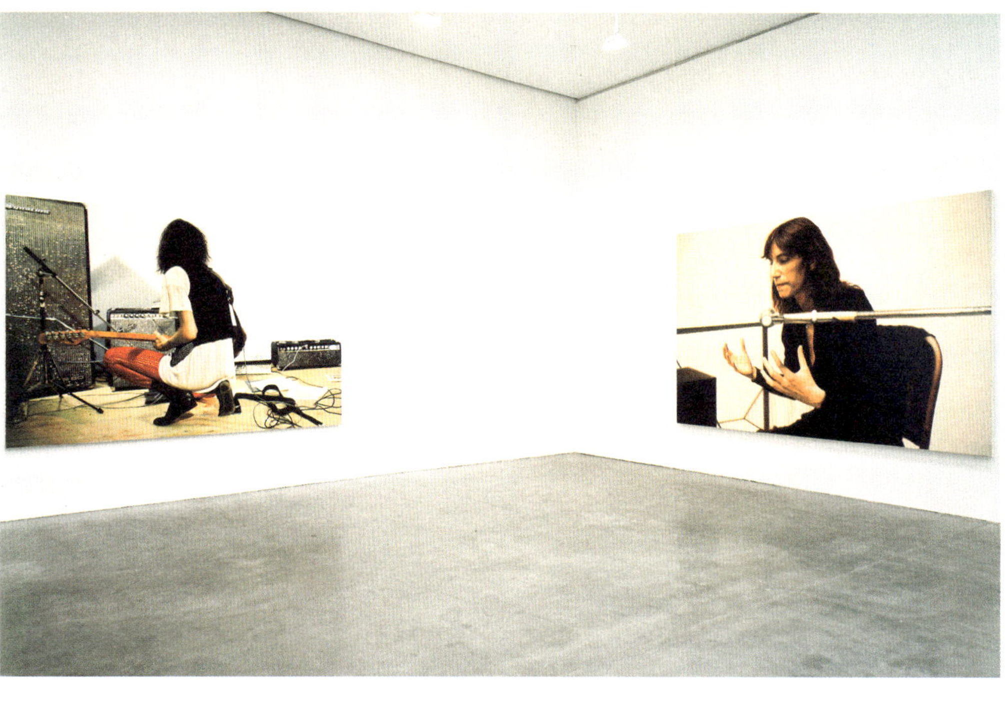

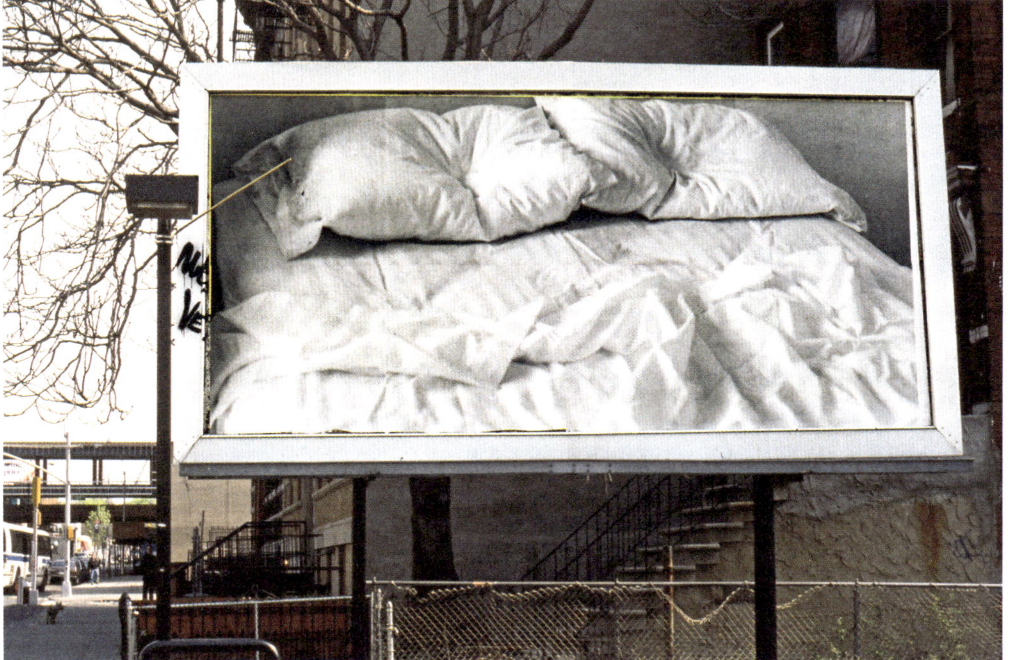

Fig. 18 Installation view of the exhibition *Franz Gertsch* at Gagosian Gallery, New York, 2005

Fig. 19 Felix Gonzalez Torres *"Untitled"* 1991 Installation at Third Avenue and East 137th Street, the Bronx, for *Projects 34: Felix Gonzalez-Torres*, Museum of Modern Art, 1992

working within a nearly hyperrealist mode, Celmins suggests a sense of infinite depth within the modest canvas. “I’ve always been interested in very impossible things,” she remarked in an interview with Gober in 2002. “Things blowing up, things disappearing in a breath. Things like the sky, which doesn’t even exist. There is no thing like the sky...and then trying to invent it on another surface.”(35)

Tauba Auerbach’s practice also explores surface qualities, as seen through contemporary modes of image production, from print to digital. She delves into the optical qualities of each, often rendering their literalness. Her *(Untitled) Fold* paintings (2011; plate 51), are made on canvas that the artist creases, rolls, and otherwise manipulates prior to painting. When laid flat, the canvas retains a topographic impression left by the folds, which forms the template for the work. Like the Photorealists before her, Auerbach uses a sprayer through which she releases thin layers of acrylic onto the canvas, creating an illusionistic ghosting of the formerly three-dimensional surface. At once a trompe l’oeil image and an abstract composition, the work is reminiscent of James Welling’s photographs of crumpled aluminum foil, while its palette recalls the intense patterning of op art.

Thomas Demand’s photographic tableaux, made as constructed environments, likewise dwell on surface. Often made from paper or cardboard, the “sites” he documents are sometimes real, sometimes imagined, and frequently based on other existing photographs. *Barn* (1997; plate 36) depicts a detail of Jackson Pollock’s celebrated Long Island studio reduced to an abstract and eerily artificial formation of slats and light. The film *Rain/Regen* (2008; plate 41) is a multisensory environment of moving image and sound that envelops the viewer in what appears to be a cloudburst. We stand before the darkened projection, lulled by the droplets hitting the pavement, transported to a more universal space or unspecified time. If the artifice eludes us, however, it is because this clever illusion has been created as a stop-motion animation, with candy wrappers forming the “splashing” raindrops and frying eggs providing the convincing soundscape of the rain shower.

Isaac Layman’s hyperreal photographic tableaux are made with a large-format 4 x 5-inch camera with a scanning back, with which he documents ordinary nooks and crannies in his Seattle home. Seemingly straightforward, his large-scale images, such as *Oven* (2010; plate 39), are actually deftly constructed collages that often weave together high-resolution pictures made from the same vantage point but with varying depths of focus. In a dreamlike way, this layering of day-to-day subjects into a singular image creates perceptual confusion, a heightened sense of the real, and a compelling jumping-off point into abstraction.

What connects these artists, whether inspired by photographs or life, whether representing surface or constructing an image, is that they are engaged in the intimate observation of things often overlooked. For many, recording these unremarkable spaces between events, or within scenes passed through when one moves from room to room or place to place can lead to a cerebral kind of abstraction. These works are, above all, documents of the instant of noticing.

For artists seeking to pictorialize these liminal moments in

(35) Celmins in conversation with Robert Gober in Lane Relyea, Robert Gober, and Briony Fer, *Vija Celmins* (New York: Phaidon, 2004), 25.

painting, the use of the "uncomposed," casual photograph remains as relevant now as it did to artists such as Bechtle in the 1960s. Dike Blair has made small-scale gouaches based on his own snapshots of ordinary landscapes and interiors as part of his larger practice since the 1980s. These intimate works on paper, which can take several months to execute, are a means of exploring his abiding interest, as he says, in presenting "transitional spaces and situations"([36])—the corner of a tiled bathroom or an empty parking lot illuminated by headlights (2010 and 2008; plates 44 and 46). When viewed together, these enigmatic fragments form a narrative about being conscious of life's mundane details and their fleeting moments of potential beauty.

Richter's *Lake Shore Drive, Chicago* (1992; plate 37), an oddly arranged picture plane of architectural angles and landscape, captures this essence, as do the paintings of Paul Winstanley, who has systematically focused his painted subjects on generic spaces, from waiting rooms and office lobbies to parking lots and conference tables (the *New Yorker* once called him "the Vermeer of corporate interiors").([37]) Winstanley's pictures possess a kind of agitated serenity—their lack of human presence (often signaled by arrangements of empty chairs) suggests an impending event, or perhaps something just missed (fig. 17). In more recent works, such as *Utopia 1* (2005; plate 52), the polished floors, plate glass, and steel mullions painted with absorbing attention to surface and light create a Dan Graham-like abstract grid of cool planes that gird the image against its depiction of nothingness, and quell any suspense we may harbor for more information. Far beyond the doors, past the manicured grounds, lies the faintest hint of the natural world, a murky tangle of trees refusing to conform to the sterile order within. Like Blair, Winstanley here merges the Photorealist interest in reflective, architectural planes with a whiff of the romantic embedded in lonely places.

Rudolf Stingel has also worked from photographs to create a sense of frozen cinema in his painting. Known for works he has characterized as "taking on the subject of painting,"([38]) he has covered the floor of Grand Central Station with patterned carpet, cloaked museum walls with silver material that accumulates etched graffiti of visitors, and revisited the processes of Photorealism. The latter works are often executed at billboard scale, as in a series of self-portraits of 2005-2006 (plate 50) based on intimate snapshots by his friend, artist Sam Samore. These images are reminiscent of the Photorealist canvases of Swiss artist Franz Gertsch (fig. 18), who in the 1960s began to paint monumental, strikingly realistic portraits and scenes of bohemian urban life, which Stingel says he found revelatory. "It was the way he painted it. When you get close to a Gertsch, it looks like an abstract painting by someone who doesn't know how to paint. But if you walk away it becomes sharp and fantastic. This kind of painting triggered my decision to become a 'contemporary artist,' and it always stayed in my mind."([39])

The black-and-white portraits Stingel makes are transposed from their photographic sources via a grid onto a grand scale. Unlike

(36) Dike Blair in conversation with the author, New York, May 11, 2011.

(37) "Art: Goings on About Town" *New Yorker*, May 19, 2008.

(38) Rudolf Stingel in conversation with Cay Sophie Rabinowitz, in "Portrait of the Artist as a Self-Portrait," *Parkett* 77 (2006): 104.

Close, however, whose earliest renditions of his own likeness (1967-1968; plate 4) were based on pictures selected for neutrality, or a "mugshot" quality, Stingel presents a more melancholic view, a figure resting on a rumpled bed. The painting recalls Felix Gonzalez-Torres' arresting AIDS-era billboard project (fig. 19) showing black-and-white photographic images of empty pillows imprinted by heads. Through the sheer scale of his works, however, and the fact that they are executed by hired assistants, Stingel adds a sense of remove more often associated with conceptual art than with realistic painting, bringing the "authenticity" in the picture back to the photograph itself. Here, we sense self-portraiture as a mechanical still, played out on the proportions of a movie screen. These works are, the artist says, "something more psychological...the only activity in these paintings is self-doubt."[40]

(39)
Rudolf Stingel, "1,000 Words: Rudolf Stingel Talks About His Latest Installation," *Artforum* (May 2005): 221.

(40)
"Portrait of the Artist as a Self-Portrait," *Parkett* 77 (2006): 107.

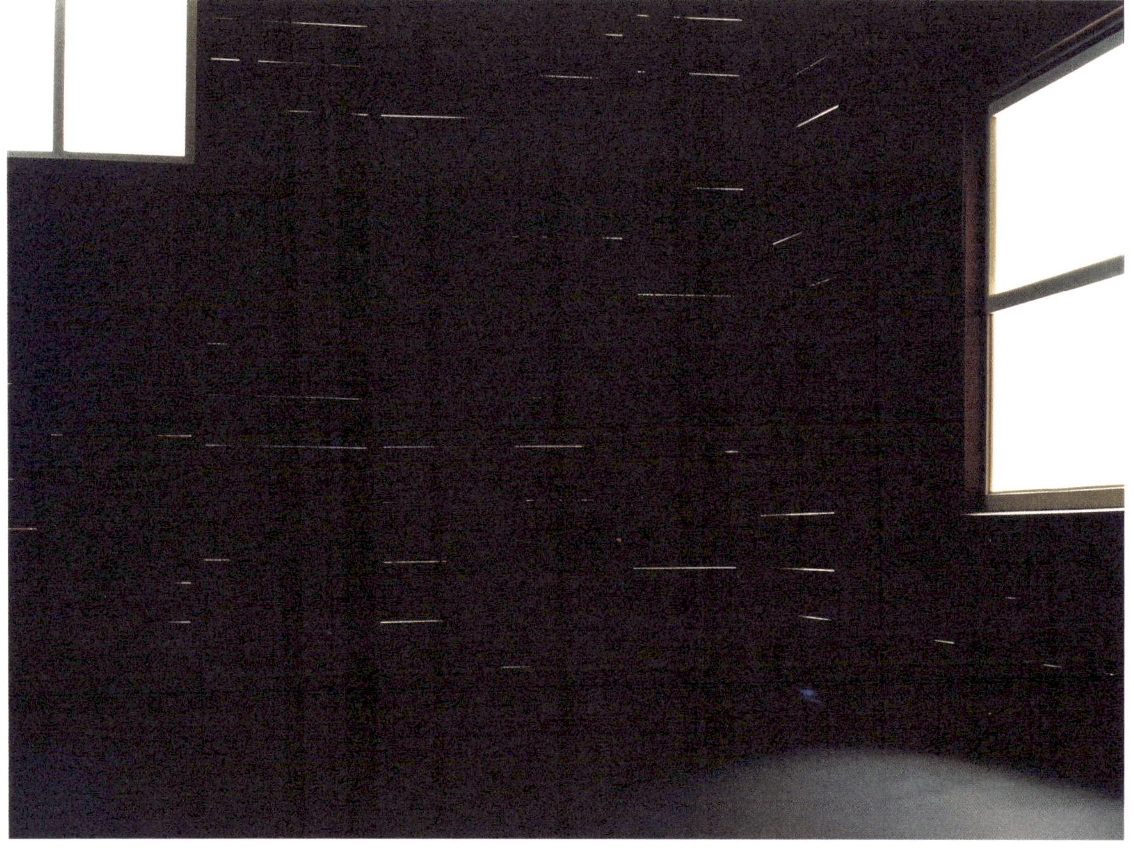

Plate 36. Thomas Demand *Barn* 1997 color chromogenic print

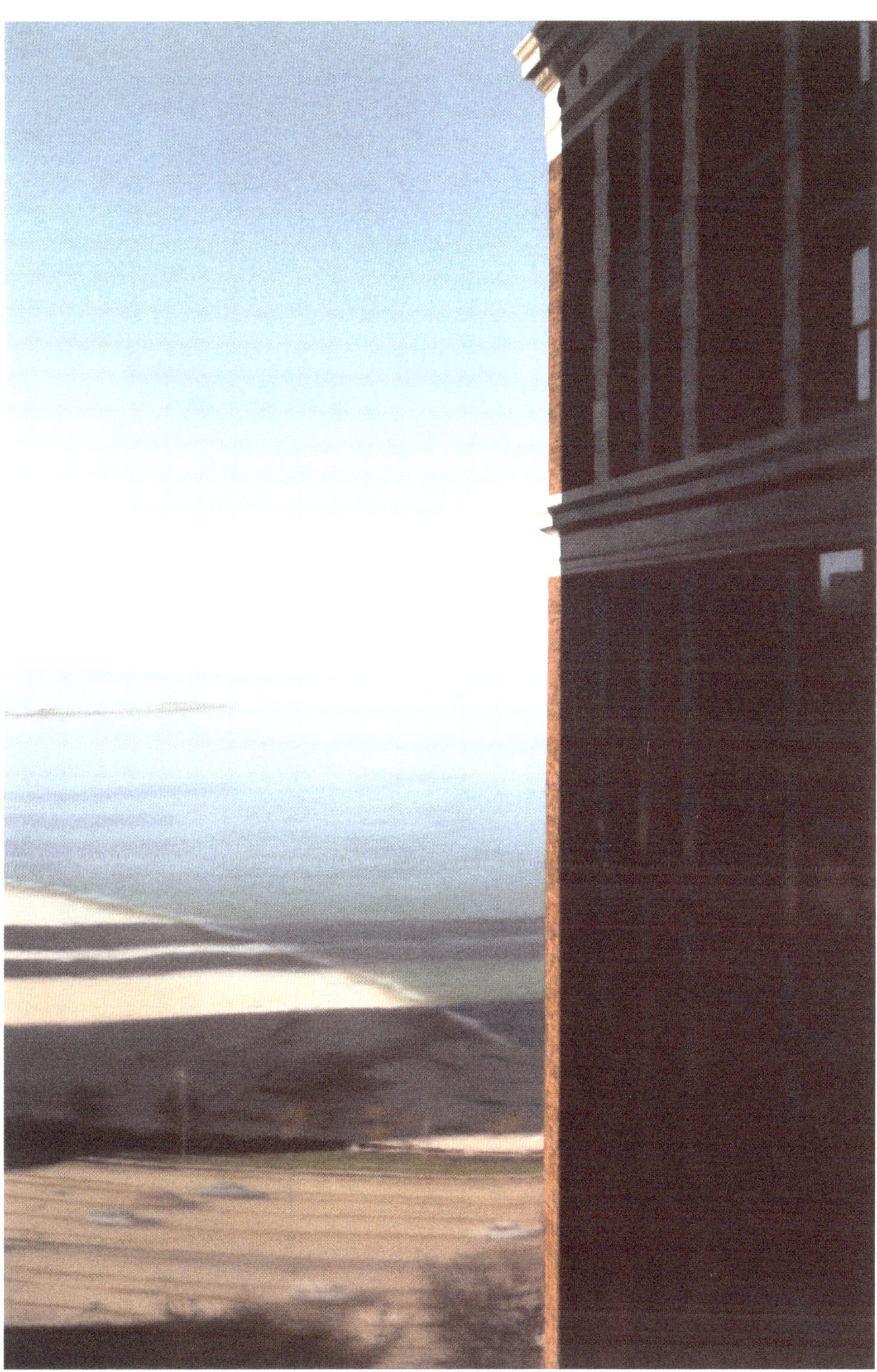

Plate 37. Gerhard Richter *Lake Shore Drive, Chicago* 1992 oil on canvas

Vija Celmins on the Night Sky Paintings

I ended up doing this extremely detailed work that I detest, but I have somehow worked myself into this space and I am hoping to work myself out. But I hate to abandon the work that I have cared for for so long.... I am leaving out the comet [from the source photograph] because I can't stand an event that exciting in there. I had the comet in there but now it is maybe millimeters under [the surface]. I have redone the image many times, on top of each other. I paint it and then I sand it off.... Each time I try to articulate it.... If I lose it, which I often do, then I paint it again, on top of itself. Somehow I think that the image then begins to have a sort of memory in it, even if you can't see it. It can build up a kind of dense feeling toward the end and then it makes me happy.... I am very suspicious of illusionism, so the space is flat and I like that.... What I'd like for it to do is give a little, so that it makes you want to go in a little bit.

Plate 38. Vija Celmins *Night Sky #6* 1993 oil on linen mounted on wood

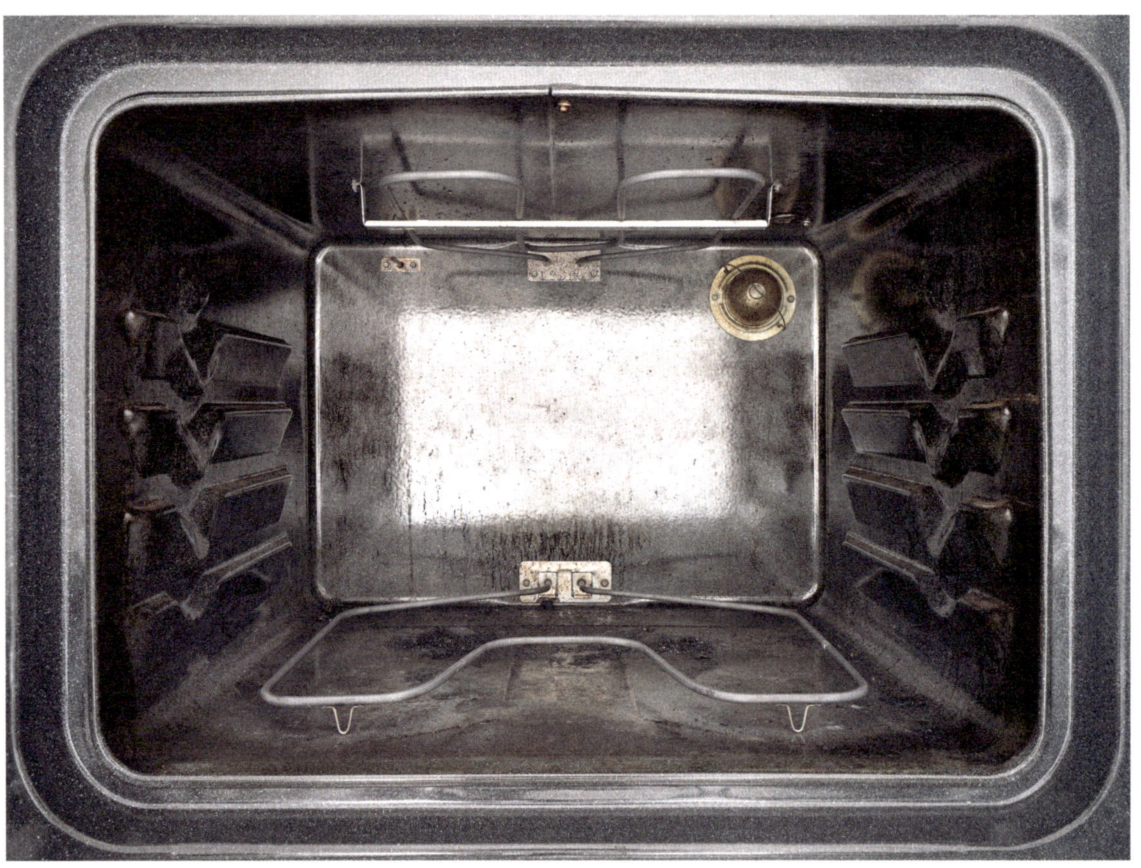

Plate 39. Isaac Layman *Oven* 2010 archival inkjet print

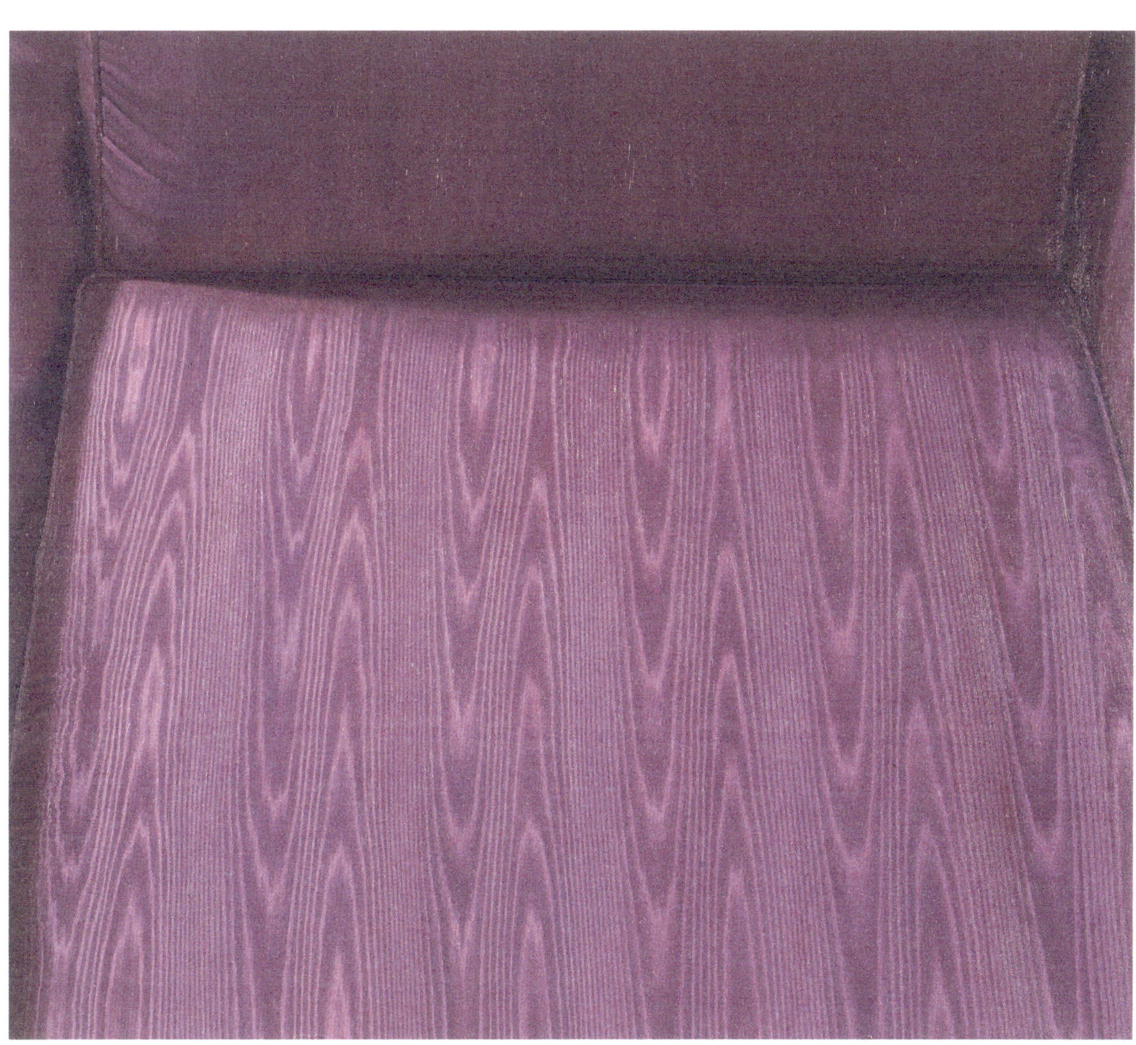

Plate 40. Catherine Murphy *Moiré Chair* 1991 oil on canvas

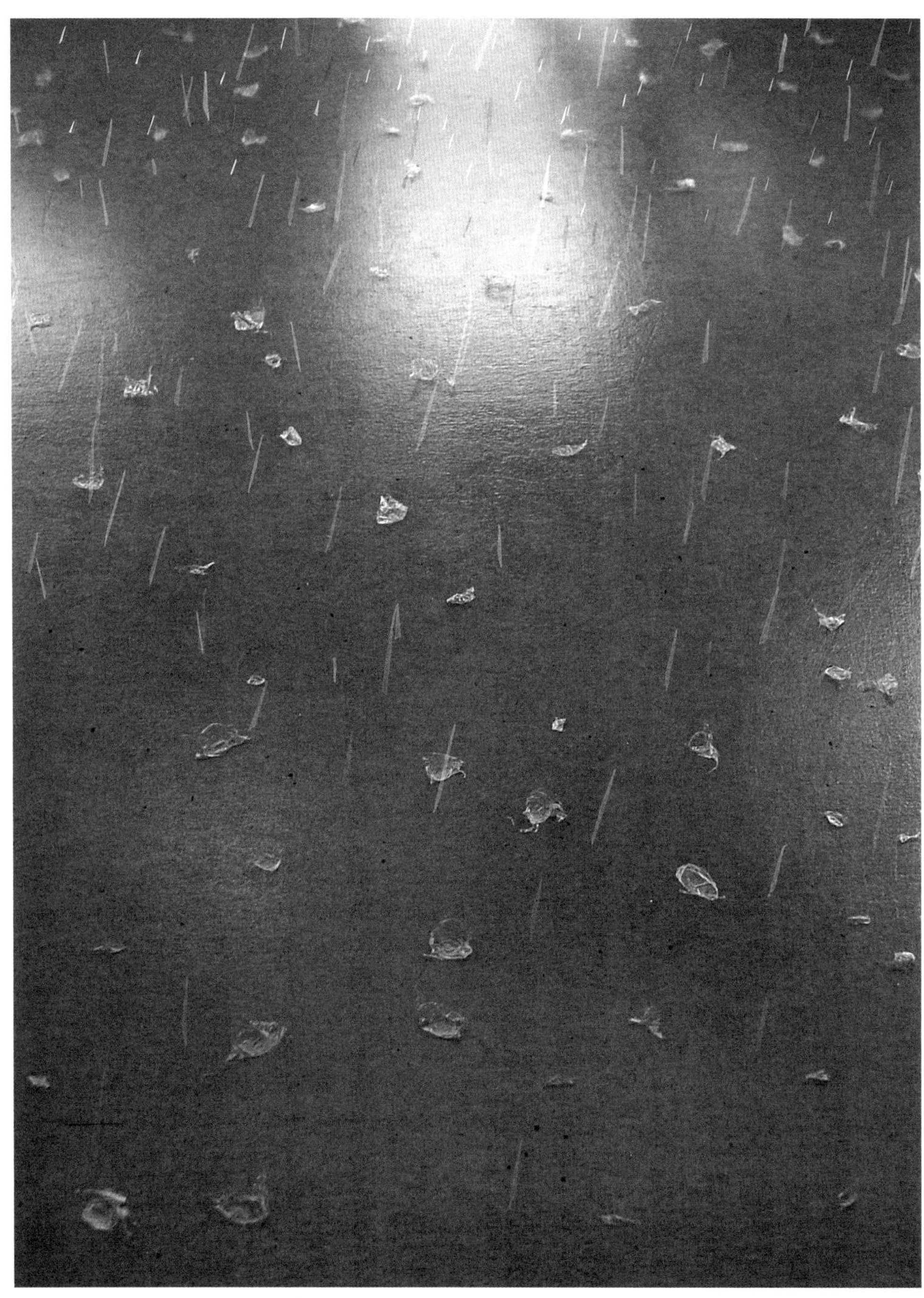

Plate 41. Thomas Demand *Rain/Regen* 2008 (still) 35mm film (color, sound) transferred to HD video

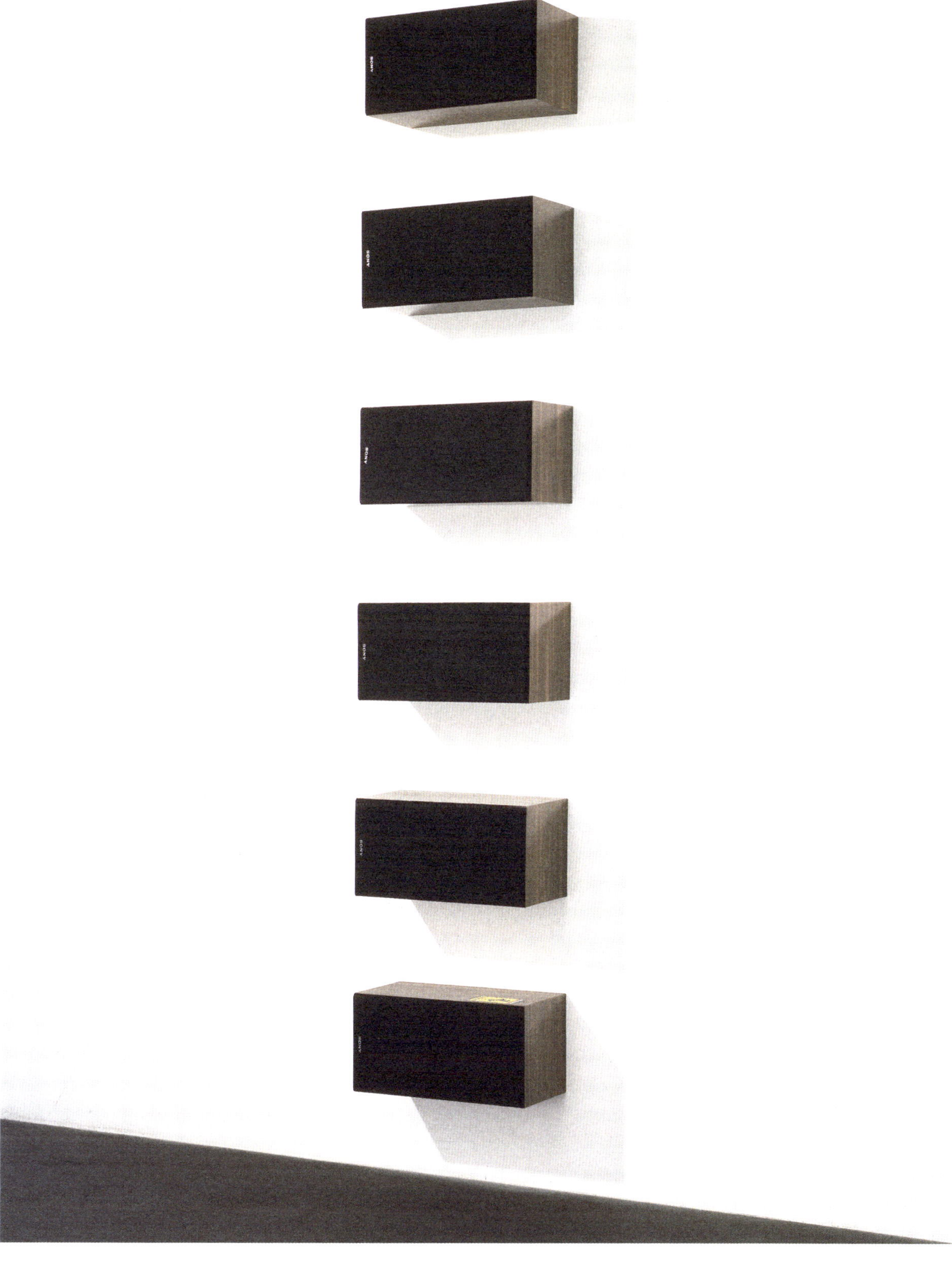

Plate 42. Kaz Oshiro *Sony Bookshelf Speakers* 2003–2004 acrylic, Bondo on stretched canvas

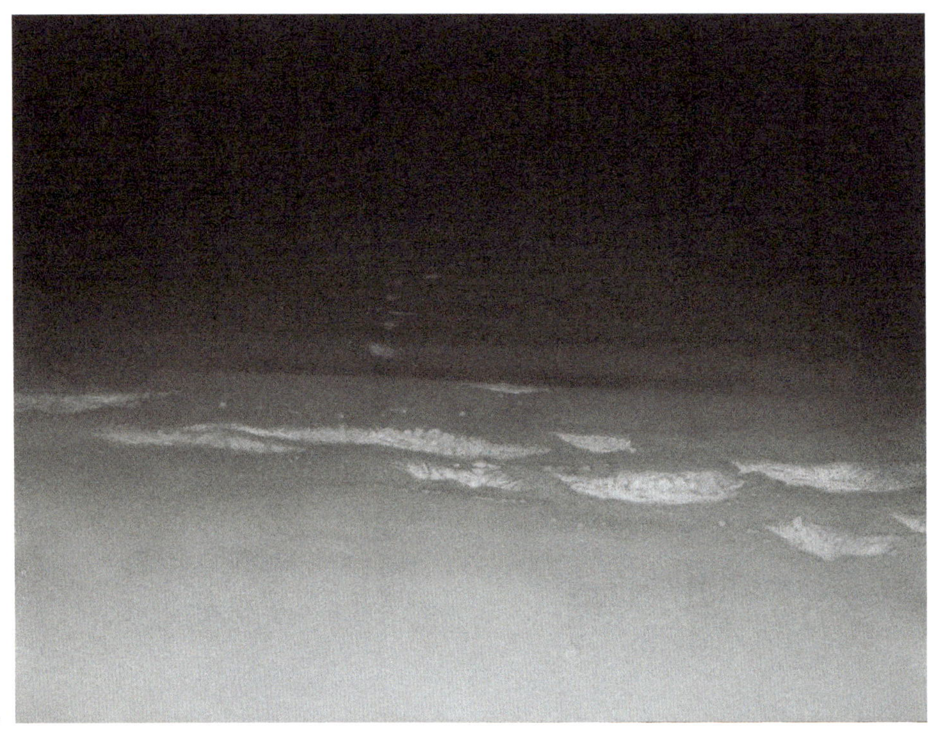

43.

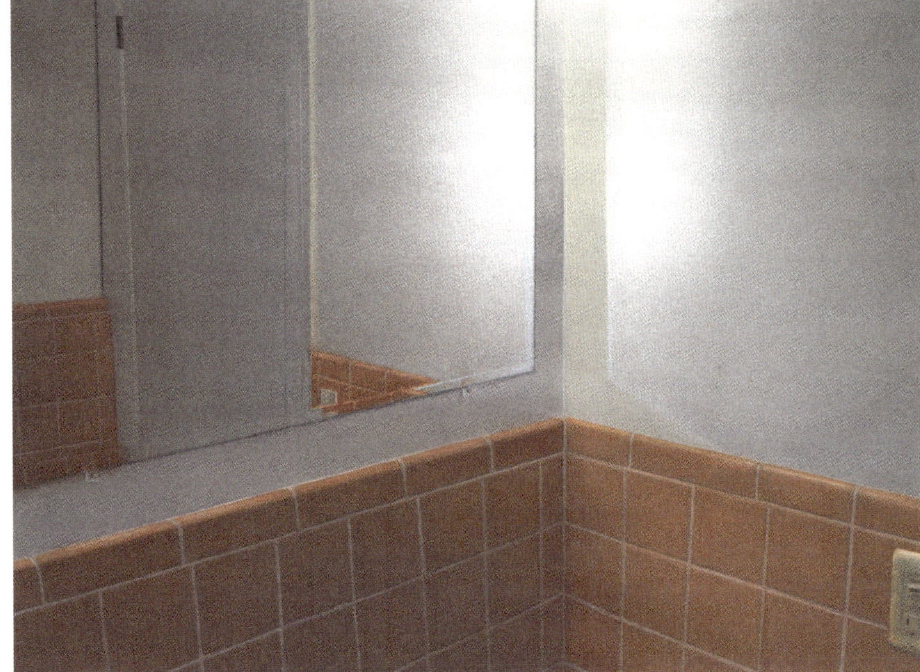

44.

Dike Blair

Plate 43. *Untitled* 2008
Plate 44. *Untitled* 2010
Plate 45. *Untitled* 2008
Plate 46. *Untitled* 2008

all gouache on paper

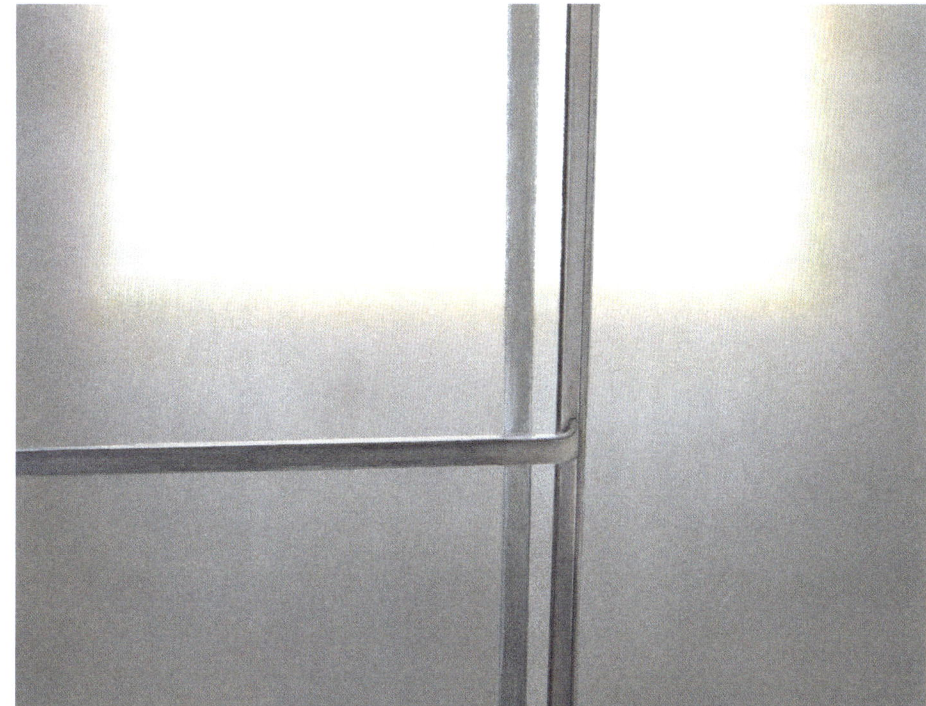

45.

46.

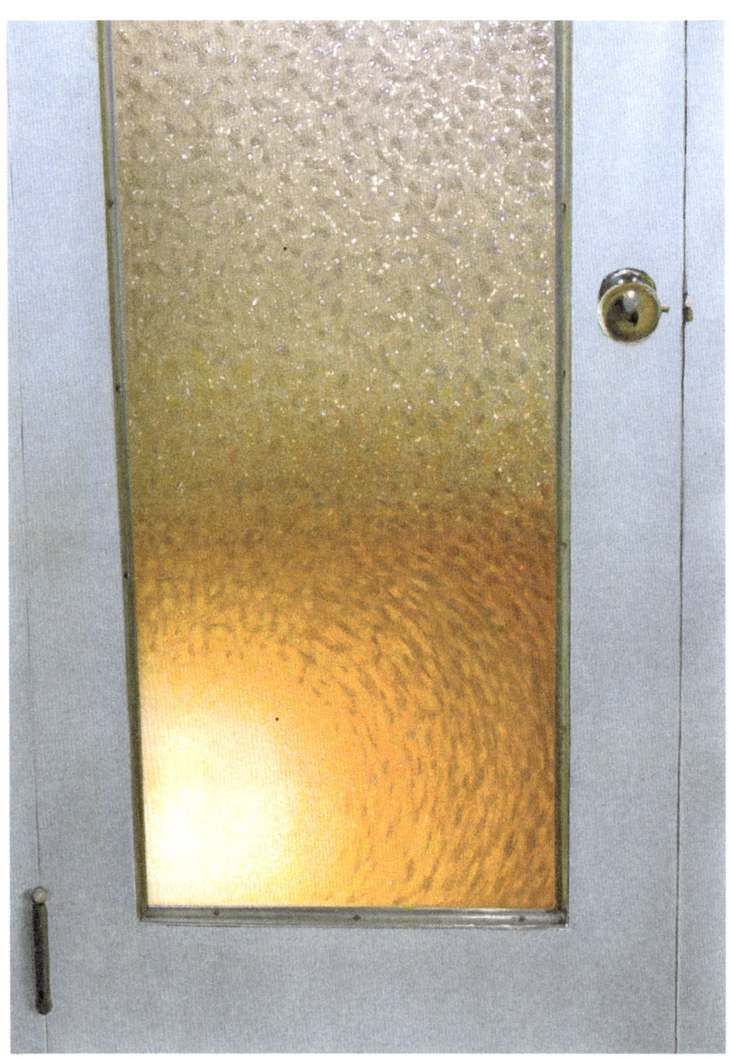

Plate 47. Dike Blair *Untitled* 2009 gouache on paper

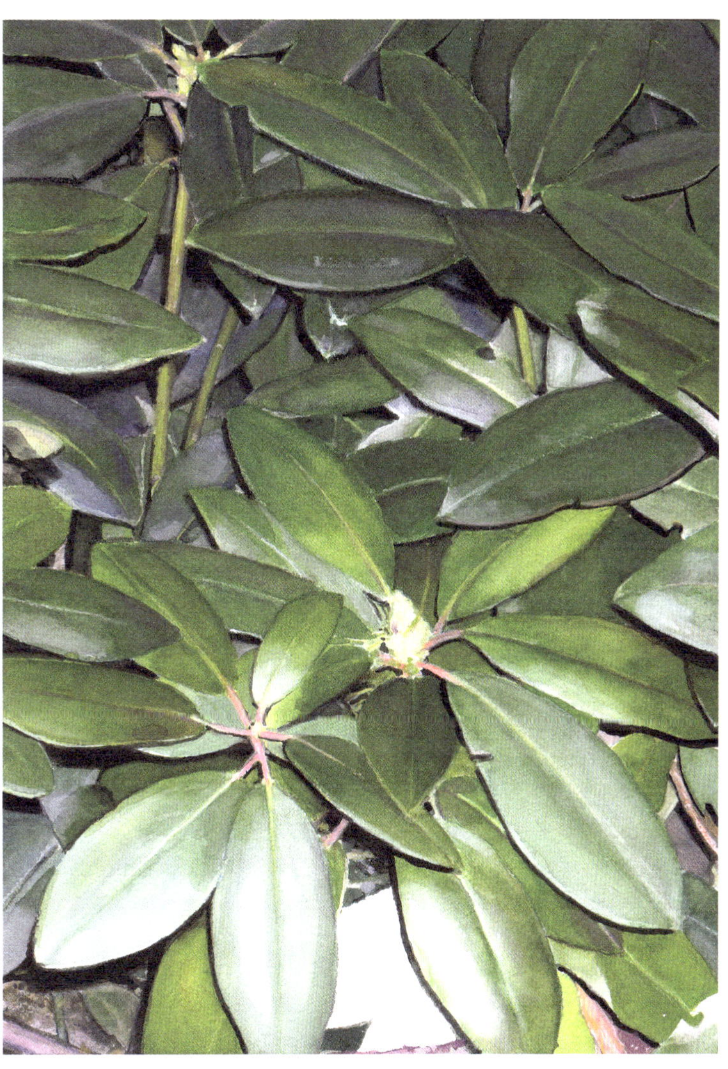

Plate 48. Dike Blair *Untitled* 2006 gouache on paper

Plate 49. Peter Rostovsky *Curtain* 2010 oil on linen

Peter Rostovsky on Curtain

What does it mean in Warholian fashion to "want to be a machine," to long for a kind of inhumanity that has to be constantly performed and repeated? Is this not a radical disavowal of an all too human vulnerability? Can we not read in the mechanical appeals of photorealism a kind of excessive sentimentality, a naïve expressionism that uses the camera and the photograph as a shield against trauma?

And likewise in expressionism's hyperbolic restatement of its humanity, is there not a silent concession to its opposite, a founding anxiety about inauthenticity, a mortal dread regarding the total triumph of simulation and technology?

However, it is important to stress that these are *unfulfilled* desires. No photorealist painting completely fools the viewer into the fact that it is machine-made; it entertains the fantasy, much like electronic music. And each autonomous artwork is only a temporary escape, a utopian space, "an orchid in the land of technology," to borrow a phrase that Walter Benjamin applied to the illusion of reality in film.

What these two positions in fact represent are two negative theologies that stand as sentinels, forever pointing to and away from a traumatically unresolved subject position—a position of the never sufficiently technological, and the never completely human. They are both Romantic positions and should be read as such: as positions of longing and disavowal, not of identity.

Why would this be important to emphasize? Because it answers the familiar question asked to every painter painting photographs. It's not about the ends, it's about the means. It's about the performance of painting that re-states the position, not the photolike product that it yields. In other words, it's about trying and failing to be a machine. Therein resides the futility and poetic nature of the practice. The failure marks the fragility and evanescence of the subject negatively, knowing that the alternative is to misname, to misrepresent, to conjure the opposite. This poetic is more latent, and seldom acknowledged in art that aspires toward indifference and inhumanity, but I hope that I have shown that every tin man has a heart, just like every photorealist hides an abstract painter.

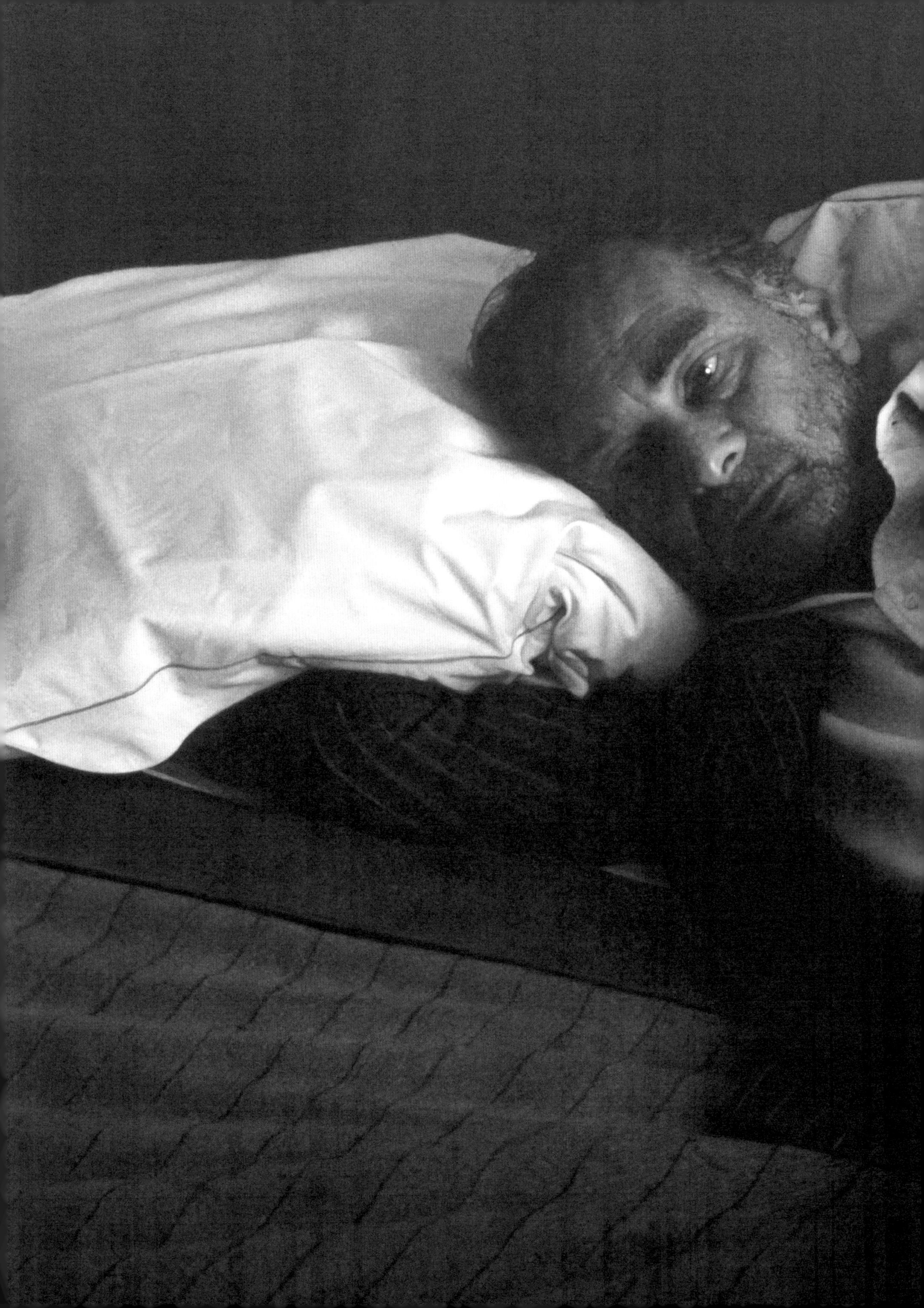

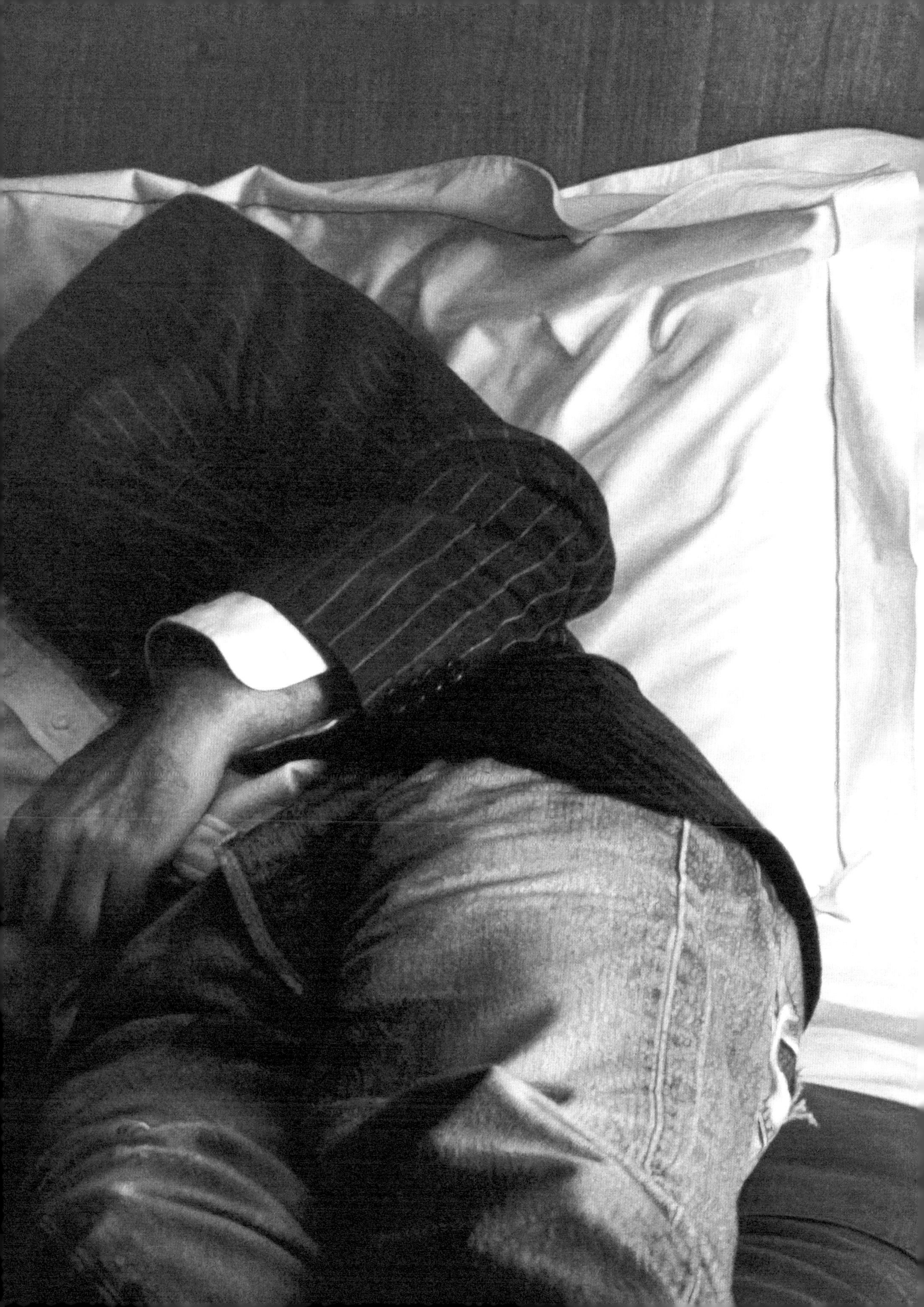

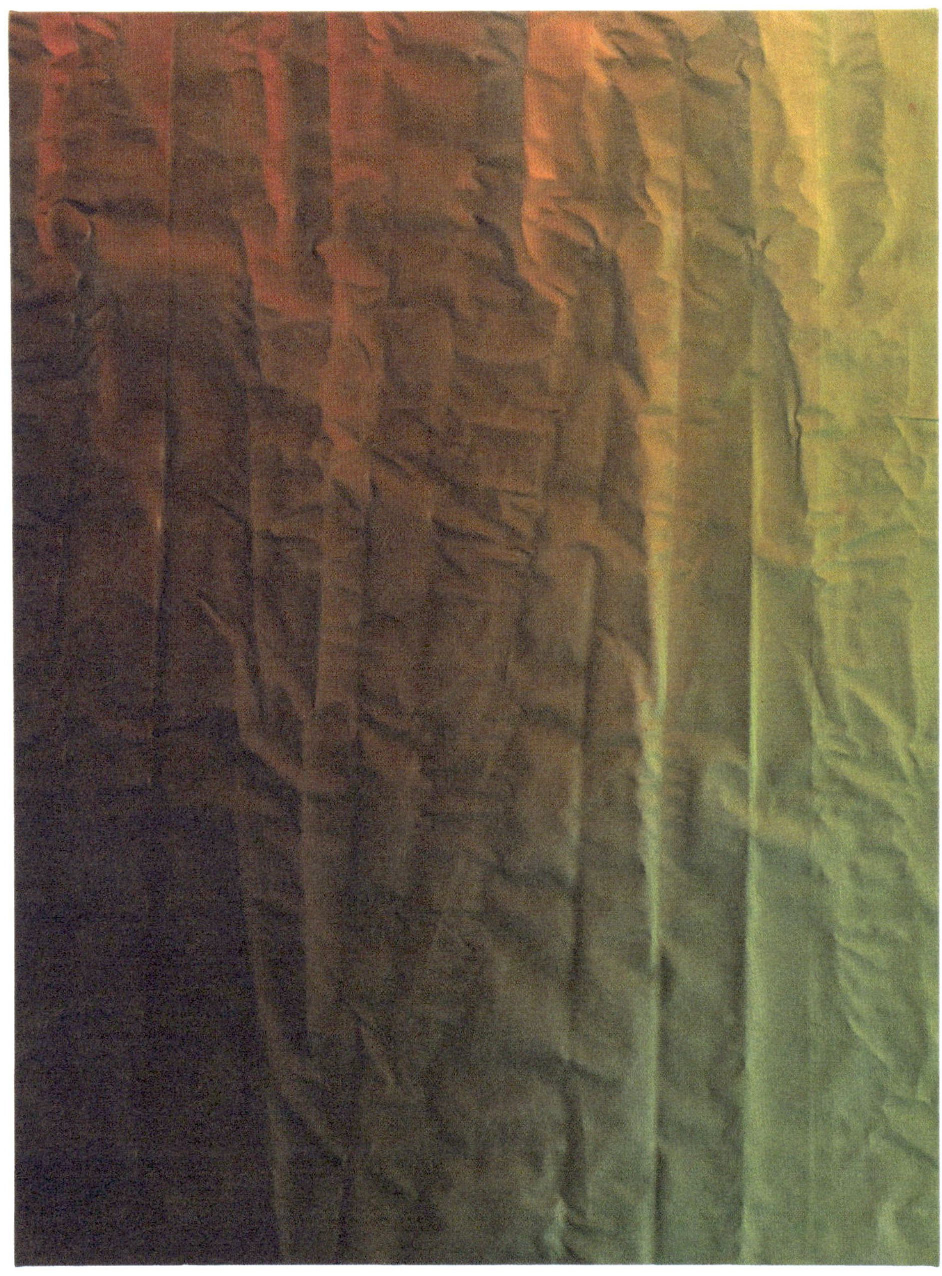

Plate 50. (previous page) Rudolf Stingel *Untitled (after Sam)* 2006 oil on canvas

Plate 51. Tauba Auerbach *Untitled (Fold)* 2011 acrylic on canvas

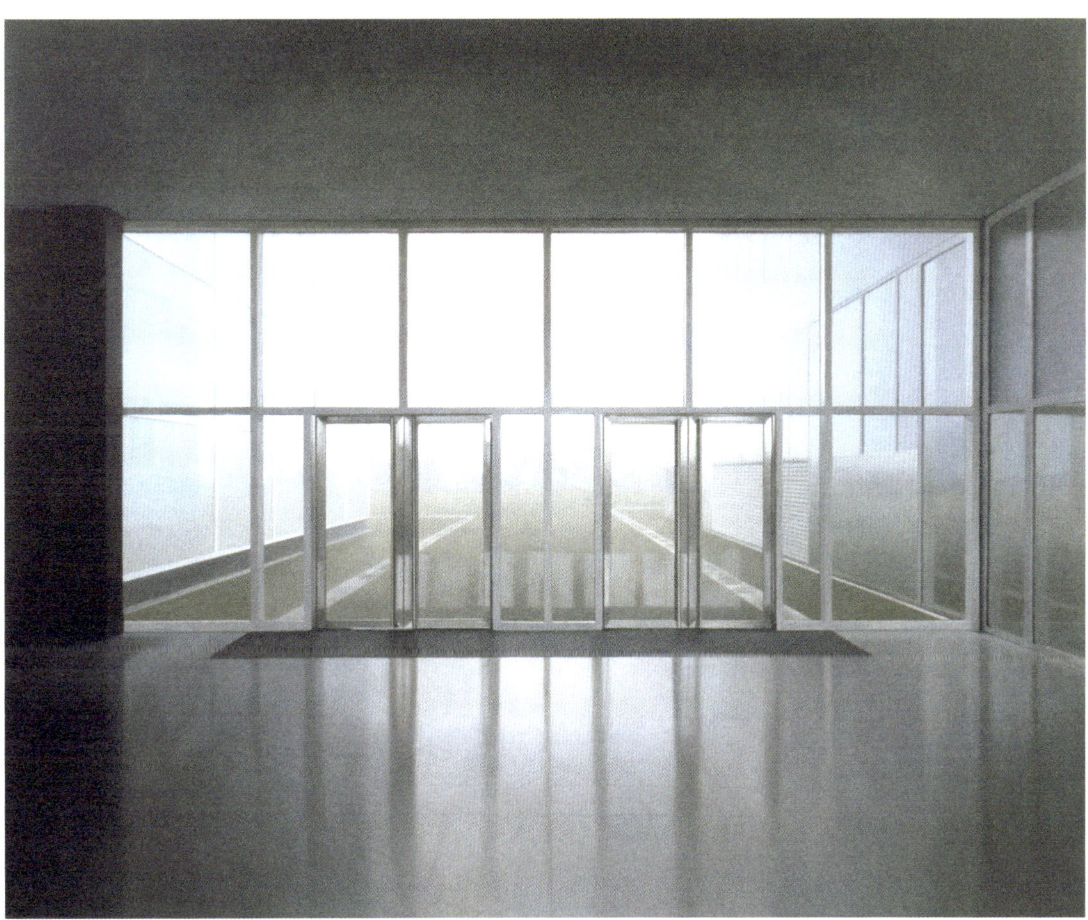

Plate 52. Paul Winstanley *Utopia 1* 2005 oil on linen

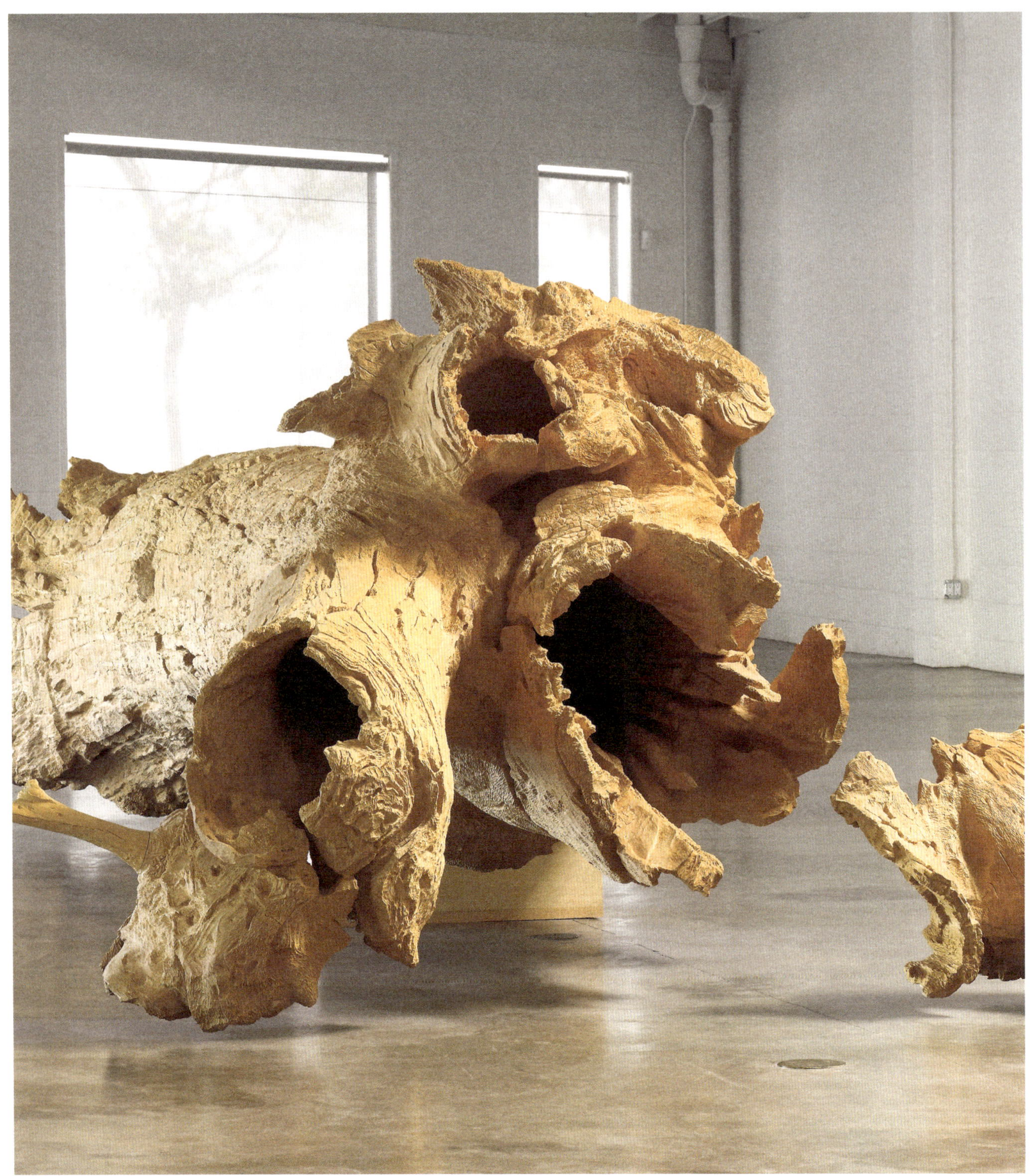

Fig. 20 Installation view of Charles Ray's *Hinoki* at Regen Projects, Los Angeles, 2007

H A N

SLEIGHT

E D

OF

Section 5
Handmade Sleight
of Hand

HAND

L I F E L I K E

D A M

"The homemade clothes [project] was going to be a public sculpture ... in a public theater. Called *Self Portrait with Homemade Clothes*, it was to be embedded as a two-minute trailer with the [regular] trailers. I was going to make my own glasses and shoes, and down in the studio I was cobbling my own shoes, and grinding my own lenses, but it became too much about that feat, and the craft." —Charles Ray[41]

Handmade Sleight of Hand

The work Charles Ray mentions here was conceived for Sculpture Projects Münster in 1997, but was ultimately never fully realized. Ray's abandonment of the effort points to the notion of the "feat" he describes, an artistic end that many artists discussed here achieve in one way or another, reconstructing three-dimensional objects with such detail that the sculptural renditions are indistinguishable from their real-life counterparts. Ray achieved this a decade later, with his sculpture *Hinoki* (2007; fig. 20), a tour-de-force merging of the real and the fabricated. The piece is based on an actual rotting tree Ray found in California, which he made into a carefully sectioned mold, then sent to Osaka, Japan, where it was recrafted by master carvers in a years-long process. Reincarnated in cypress (a different wood from the original tree), the sculpture now lives in a quiet, softly lit gallery at the Art Institute of Chicago. *Hinoki* is abstract—a ghost version of its live (dead) model, yet startlingly real, with precisely chiseled angles, crevices, and gnarled limbs.

Sunflower Seeds, a work of similar magnitude, was made by Ai Weiwei in 2009 as a commission for London's Tate Modern for its massive Turbine Hall, an atrium-like space that lends itself to spectacular, interactive works. The piece consisted of more than 100 million "seeds" made from cast porcelain hand-painted with slip (a form of liquid clay), then fired. Over several years, the seeds were painted by a team of more than 1,600 citizens from a village renowned for its porcelain (it had once supplied the imperial court). Spread across the great hall in a 4-inch-thick carpet, the piece was astounding in its sheer labor, its minimalist beauty, and its resonance as an emblem of Chinese cultural and political history. Until the ceramic dust proved dangerous for visitors to breathe,[42] the piece could be waded through, rolled in, and experienced by the handful.

By reimagining mass-produced goods or subjects from the natural world as sculpture, a number of artists in recent years have embraced an approach to their art that is above all about a rigorous, systematic way of working. This detached, more conceptual attitude toward the "handmade" can extend to the execution of the work, which is often, as in the case of Ray or Ai, produced by hired artisans or studio assistants. Given room to breathe as art, and rendered nonperishable through new materials, these objects call into question notions of permanence and ephemerality. Why were they chosen? What gives them license to exist, suspended in time, in this pristine space?

(41) Charles Ray interviewed by Doug Harvey in "The Charles Ray Experience at MOCA and Beyond," *LA Weekly*, December 2, 1998.

(42) See Roberta Smith, "At Tate Modern, Seeds of Discontent by the Ton," *New York Times*, October 18, 2010.

Like many works of conceptual art, viewer participation is often necessary for full appreciation and meaning. Duchamp's readymades achieved their impact because they were removed from their expected context and inserted into the exhibition arena, as Walter Benjamin characterized it, placing "the copy of the original into situations which would be out of reach for the original itself."(43) Many artists who make hyperreal sculpture use the space of the gallery as a means of giving it newfound meaning. As Danto has noted, context is key: "It is safe to say that the greater the degree of realism intended, the greater the need for external indicators that it is art and not reality."(44) Many artists working in this vein subtly, even subversively, install their sculpture in unexpected places—ceilings, cracks in the floor, unlit corners—with the intention that we may mistake them for something so commonplace that we overlook their careful fabrication. Like Hanson's figures sharing our personal space, these objects startle us into paying attention.

In 2009, Ugo Rondinone presented an exhibition at Sadie Coles HQ gallery in London that consisted entirely of what appeared to be unassuming found objects: pieces of "cardboard" propped against the wall (plate 59), precise rows of potatoes and walnuts, and denuded wooden branches. Arrayed throughout the spare gallery a là Richard Serra or Carl Andre, the works—at first seeming quite modest—gradually announced themselves as sculpture, with their perfect imperfections revealing that they were in fact cast in bronze, then hand-painted to match the originals.

This transmutation of materials, often from something disposable to something precious, can throw a subject's ordinariness into high relief. Jud Nelson's *Hefty 2-Ply* (1979; plate 54) is a facsimile of an ordinary kitchen trash bag made from Carrera marble, carved as classically as the drapery on a Bernini figure. Yoshihiro Suda's subject matter often comes from the natural world—flowers, dried leaves and twigs, or other humble plant matter, which he hand-carves from magnolia wood and paints with intricate detail. Works such as *Weeds* (2009; plate 62) are intended to be installed in cracks in the gallery floor or wall (the artist considers the space surrounding the piece to be part of the work). Likewise, Ruben Nusz's ashtray sculptures (2008; plate 73), formed from wax and installed in everyday situations as sly interventions, contain hand-modeled and painted cigarette butts scattered amidst cremation ashes—a highly personal portrait in an unlikely guise.

Some artists play off these strategies to respond to architecture. David Lefkowitz's miniature paintings of outlet covers (1991-2011; plate 55) are executed with deft brushstrokes in full trompe l'oeil. Installed near baseboards or floors where one would expect to find electrical access, the works, like Suda's, would be easily missed, were it not for the understated glimmer of color and the softness of the real canvas that catches the eye and separates these from their plastic hardware-store counterparts.

Susan Collis' sculptures are often meditations on the art gallery itself, and its life as a space once the objects it houses are gone. Her works appear to be things waiting to be swept into the trash bin, as in *Forever Young* (2009; plate 57),

(43) Walter Benjamin, "The Work of Art in the Age of Mechanical Reproduction," in *Illuminations*, trans. Harry Zohn (New York: Schocken Books, 1969), 220. First published 1936.

(44) Arthur Danto, "Works of Art and Mere Real Things," in *The Transfiguration of the Commonplace: A Philosophy of Art* (Cambridge, MA: Harvard University Press, 1981), 24.

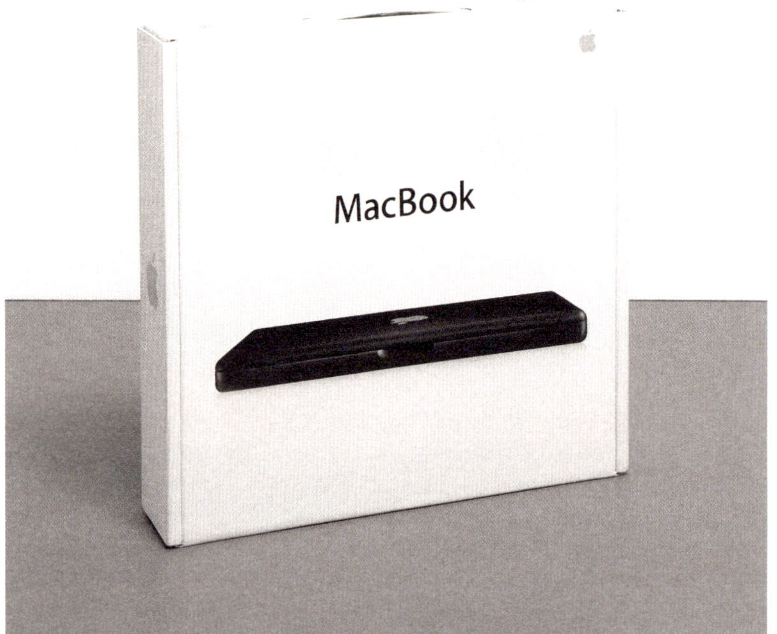

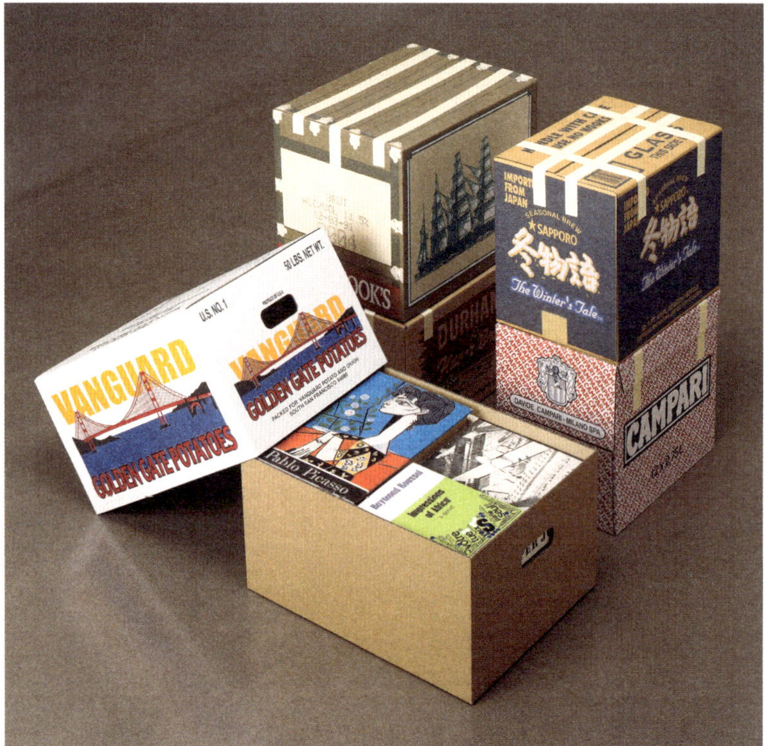

Fig. 21 Daniel Douke *MacBook* 2008 oil and acrylic on canvas and Bondo

Fig. 22 Steve Wolfe *Untitled (Vanguard/Cook's/Sapporo/Durham's/Campari Cartons)* 2001–2003
cartons: oil and screenprint on archival cardboard with wooden armatures
books: oil, screenprint, lithography, modeling paste, canvasboard, paper, wood

which resembles debris left from gallery construction such as bits of drywall and lumber piled on the floor. But these are fashioned from exotic hardwood veneers, mother of pearl, and silver, using the precision techniques of metal-smithing and marquetry. In similar works, Collis has embroidered spatters of "paint" onto canvas drop cloths and made screws (fig. 2) and wall anchors from solid gold and turquoise, respectively. Her sculpture *Refugee* (2007; fig. 16; plate 61), which clones the ubiquitous woven shopping bags used worldwide to transport domestic goods and laundry, is in fact a series of carefully joined drawings in pencil and ballpoint pen executed by a team of volunteers.

Daniel Douke has been making paintings portraying the particulars of found surfaces, such as Cor-Ten steel and cardboard, since the 1970s, when he chose to distance himself from the Photorealists by working in three dimensions, making painted constructions from custom-built canvases. His works that emulate cardboard do so quite physically: gesso is sanded into corrugated ribs, while each scuff, abrasion, dent, and tear is replicated with fidelity; he uses an airbrush to eliminate brushstrokes, and to achieve an effect that is "non-idealized and absolute."([45]) The antithesis of Warhol's towers of bright Brillo boxes, Douke's hyperreal cartons are lone specimens—from generic brown shipping boxes (1979; plate 20) to recent renditions of the seductive packaging for Apple computers and iPhones (fig. 21)([46]). Steve Wolfe has made trompe l'oeil boxes, too (fig. 22), but also the objects they contain—items we have enjoyed, used, and perhaps no longer need but can't part with, such as worn books and vinyl LP records—scrupulously hand-painted with what one critic called a "monkish devotion that turns feats of technique into icons of a deeply personal religion."([47]) *Untitled (Are You Experienced?)* (1993; plate 60), a handmade copy of this iconic Jimi Hendrix album, is enshrined in a gold-leaf frame as a relic of a moment in culture as well as the artist's own biography (all of the objects he crafts are based on his own belongings). It is also emblematic of a moment in time, an artifact of past technology, the LPs' physicality and worn grooves today supplanted by invisible digital files.

Like Douke and Wolfe, Kaz Oshiro is interested in the skins of objects—the pure surface reality presented to him through intense observation of an item that has lived in the world. His painted canvas panels are constructed as three-dimensional objects, and rest directly on floors or are mounted or propped against walls, his attempt to "make a painting without making a painting."([48]) His "models" are items that evidence use: worn appliances, stereo equipment plastered in rock band decals, or the rusted tailgates of pickup trucks, many of them geometric forms that he selects for their visual resonance with major postwar movements. *Sony Bookshelf Speakers*, (2003-2004; plate 42) is a modular progression of rectangular stereo equipment that references the rigors of Minimalism in its

(45)

Julie Joyce, "Endless Instant," in *Daniel Douke: Endless Instant*, exh. cat. (Los Angeles: Harriet and Charles Luckman Fine Arts Complex, California State University, Los Angeles, 2006), 17.

(46)

Since Rauschenberg and Douke's examples, more contemporary incarnations of re-created "cardboard" (often cast in bronze) have appeared in the work of Gavin Turk, Ugo Rondinone, Tony Matelli, and others.

(47)

Ken Johnson, "Books Read and Unread Are Turned into Totems, with Every Scuff Intact," *New York Times*, October 19, 2009.

(48)

Oshiro in conversation with the author, Los Angeles, May 14, 2011.

resemblance to the work of Donald Judd, though its meticulously painted details are far from Judd's pristine industrial surfaces. The splatters, stains, and graffiti on *Dumpster (Flesh with Turquoise Swoosh)* (2011; plate 66) recall the gestural bravado of Abstract Expressionism. Like the works of Douke, who was Oshiro's teacher, these "sculptures" are akin to stage props, meant to be encountered from a particular vantage point; if one views Oshiro's works from behind, for example, stretchers are revealed and the illusion dissolves into the material reality of the work (fig. 23).

Roxy Paine often constructs his hyperreal objects with a "cabinet of curiosities" approach. Carefully researched, and sculpted in the manner of a specimen in a natural history museum, his accumulations of mushroom species seem playful at first, but the poisonous colors command caution, as in "never pick a red mushroom" (2002; plate 75). Sigmar Polke has played with this theme, as has Carsten Höller, whose mushroom installations allude to psychotropic hallucinations and Alice's dream world. Like Suda's plants sprouting from the gallery floor, Paine's replicas rely on their new context for the reactions they invoke. He has said, "I really love this idea that something is foreign to its environment, but seems quite natural and quite at home. It's kind of a metaphor for sculpture in general."[49]

On one hand, these works evidence what might be seen as a kind of hypercraft—a fastidious attention to detail that spares no labor in its making. If looking at the work of Ray, Collis, Suda, Oshiro, and others noted here within the frame of conceptual art, however, these are works above all about process, and about the calculated procedures for executing them seamlessly. If one runs these objects through the paces outlined by LeWitt in his seminal article "Paragraphs on Conceptual Art" of 1967, many of these works derive their muscle as they conflate this complexity with simplicity. Tom Friedman's work, for example, can be read against LeWitt's pronouncement that "most ideas that are successful are ludicrously simple."[50] Friedman's humble materials—toothpicks, toilet paper, Play-Doh, chewing gum, human hair, masking tape—are most often refashioned into a representation of another ordinary thing, as in *Untitled* (2007; plate 56). While inherently playful and perhaps even irreverent in appearance, his work is undergirded by a strict framework not unlike that of the process artists of the 1970s who adhered to rigid parameters in the making of their work. Friedman recounts, "I identified for myself four basic elements: the material I would choose, the process of altering the material, the form that it would take, and its presentation."[51] This straightforward application of a methodical, procedural approach is key to the work of many of the artists discussed here. Despite the calculated nature of their construction, however, Friedman has referred to the viewing of his sculptures as ephemeral experiences: "Ideas have this kind of elusive nature to them in mind space....You have a solidity inherent in the materials.... But they are also like apparitions; they just appear, but they are not real."[52]

(49) Roxy Paine, interviewed by Tod Williams, *BOMB* 107 (Spring 2009), archived at http://bombsite.com/issues/107/articles/3278.

(50) Sol LeWitt, "Paragraphs on Conceptual Art," *Artforum* 5, no. 10 (June 1967): 80.

(51) Tom Friedman, "Dennis Cooper in Conversation with Tom Friedman," in Bruce Hainley et al., *Tom Friedman* (London and New York: Phaidon Press), 12.

(52) Ibid, 29.

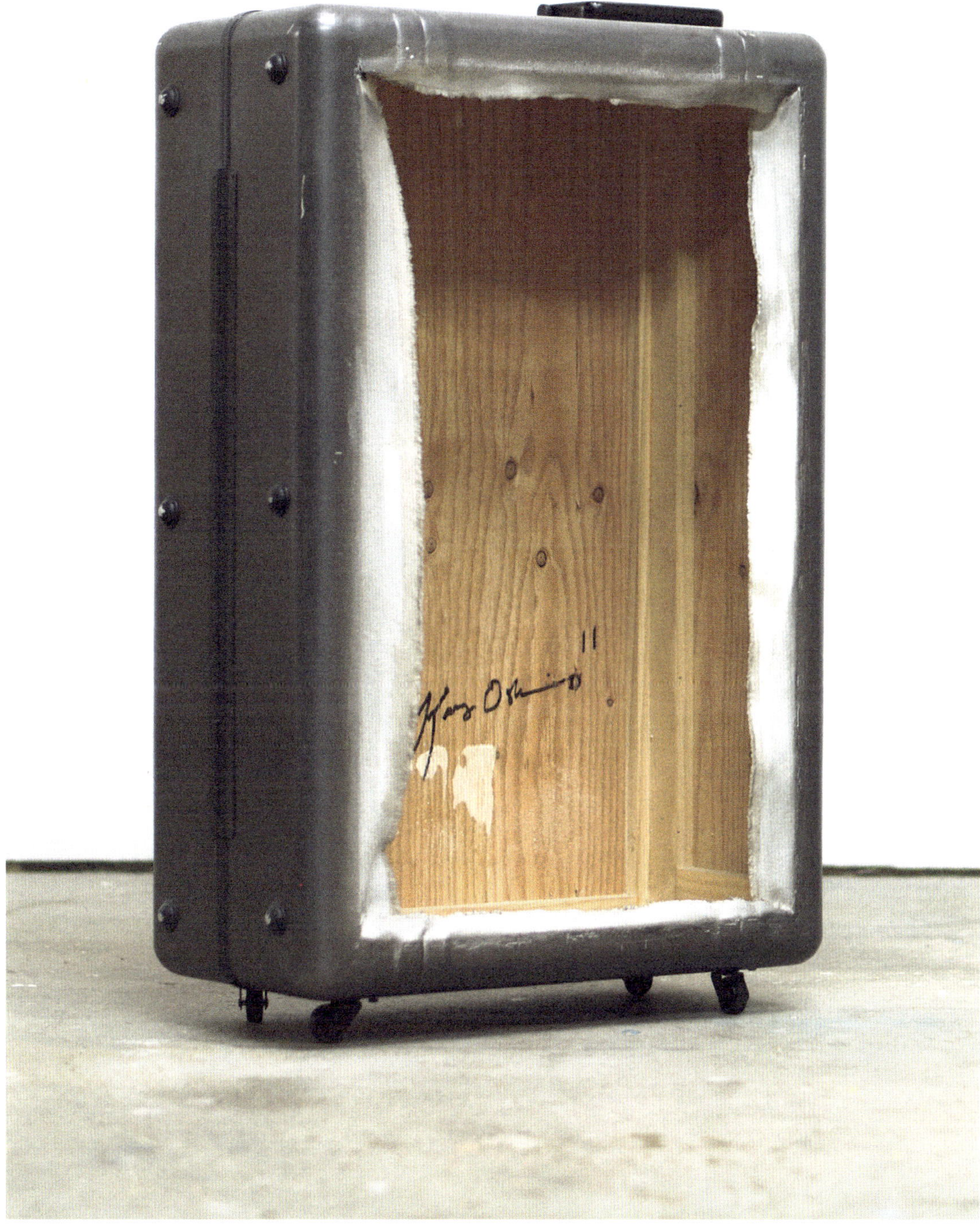

Fig. 23 Kaz Oshiro *Zero Case Spinner (gun metal—torn FRAGILE stickers)* 2011 acrylic, Bondo on stretched canvas, caster wheels

Mungo Thomson's work shares this notion of viewer experience, often balancing, as he has said, "intellectual inquiry with a desire to be entertained." This often transpires through the discovery of his works as incidental events or minimal gestures. His 2001 piece *Between Projects* (plate 53) is composed of twelve "pencils" (painted sculptures fabricated in actual size) found scattered across the ceiling (fig. 24), as if launched there by a frustrated writer. Thomson's work often focuses on banal objects or situations that somehow take on lives of their own, exhibit some kind of contradiction, or are conceived by "going after 'bad ideas,'"(53) then investigating ways they might be repurposed as art through viewer participation. To this end, he has hand-drawn his own graph paper, which he has distributed for other artists to use; fabricated human-scale, six-foot rulers from scratch; and made beer bottles from blown crystal. The projected video installation *New York, New York, New York, New York* (2004; plate 33) presents four scenes of Manhattan street life, which, after a series of visual cues ranging from golf carts to palm trees, are revealed to instead be views of Hollywood sets depicting the view of "New York" at Fox, Paramount, Universal, and Culver Studios. Thomson has successfully used the mise en scène of the studio setups as readymades, borrowing four prefabricated illusions in the service of a fifth.

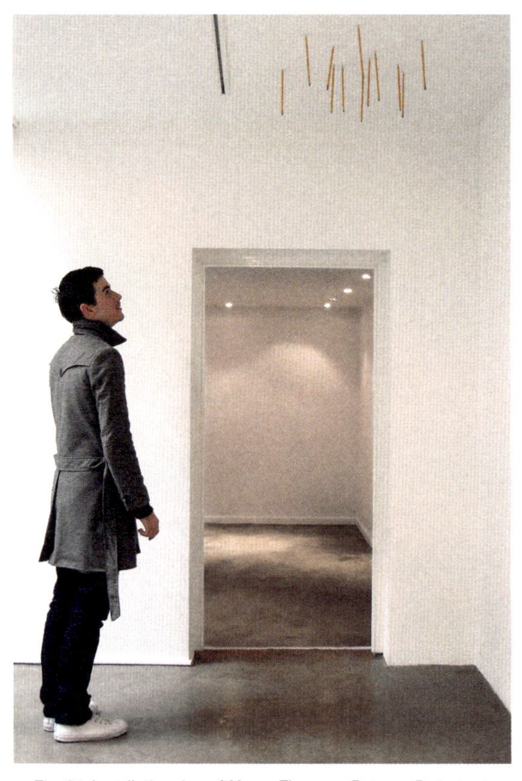

Fig. 24 Installation view of *Mungo Thomson: Between Projects* at Kadist Art Foundation, Paris, 2007

While artists such as Thomson have emphasized viewer encounters as performative actions, there are others for whom the performance is in the labor itself. The making of this sort of work is often durational, which allows it to be tracked, documented, and recorded. For Keith Edmier, the process of making his installation *Bremen Towne*, a sculptural re-creation of the kit home in suburban Chicago where he spent his formative years, was as important to the piece as the finished product. While he initially considered casting every element as sculpture, he soon became more engaged with the quest for sources and materials. His approach was forensic: months were spent combing through vintage catalogues, then on the online resale juggernaut eBay, searching for items lurking in the backgrounds of his family snapshots. Like an obsessed Hollywood set designer (he once worked in the film industry and as an assistant for artist Matthew Barney), Edmier strove not just for the general "look" of the space, but for historical accuracy whenever possible with materials and finishes. If something wasn't available, he pursued an alternate method of

(53) Adam Carr, "Between Projects: An Interview with Mungo Thomson," *UOVO* 12 (November 2006), 114.

manufacture. In the house's kitchen (2006-2007; plate 65), a single linoleum tile from the original house was scanned, then laser-etched into composite tile to complete the floor; a vintage dinette set couldn't be located, so was sculpted instead; wallpapers were hand-drawn from photographs, then re-silkscreened (see insert between plate 65 and page 136); and museum posters that had hung in the rooms of the original house were laboriously remade as actual paintings rather than the photographic reproductions they once were. In contrast to Gober, who in 1979 made a model of a home he remembered from his childhood and then set it on fire,[54] Edmier reclaims his past with his dogged pursuit of authenticity. Room by room, his *Bremen Towne* project becomes his own revisionist self-portrait.

While many artists have made a realistic, physical record of something through sculpture, others have investigated this idea through drawing, which has historically been a medium by which to indulge in scrupulous detail. Its intimacy can allow prolonged engagement with a subject, resulting in works that are, perhaps more than any other technique, a record of the labor of the hand. A number of contemporary artists in the past decade have used drawing as a vehicle through which to simulate other images or surfaces, many of them employing the photograph as a point of departure. While this is sometimes done to make a handmade replica of the photographic image—an original copy as an end in itself—this type of image-making largely descends from a postmodern view of appropriation, of reframing and reclaiming the found image, and perhaps taking a critical stance in relationship to it. For many artists working in this way, execution of image can involve a high degree of process-oriented discipline. Hearkening back to Close, LeWitt, and other artists who emerged in the 1960s and took a systematic approach to creating images or structures in units, many artists working with drawing continue to use the grid as a means of transcription. But unlike Close, a number of them are interested in the object quality of the photograph itself as much as the image contained within it. Rather, many have followed the path laid forth by Celmins' drawings circa 1968, which showed her found clippings and personal letters and snapshots as still lifes, hovering on their own illusionistically rendered grounds as if pinned to a bulletin board.

This practice of embracing the paper fragment as an object of three-dimensional interest in itself can be seen in recent work by Dan Fischer, who bases his drawings on found images of well-known artists or works of art. His drawings, reminiscent of artist portraits by French painter Jean-Olivier Hucleux, who was sometimes shown alongside the Photorealists in the 1970s, have a surface quality that is true to their source—in this case a photocopy or Xerox as opposed to an actual photograph (plates 67-72). Likewise, Paul Sietsema's self-portrait (2009; plate 64) seems to flicker strangely before us—it isn't quite "photographic." Its particular source is not a physical photograph but a picture the artist discovered of himself on the Internet, then remade as a drawing from the image as he experienced it on the screen, reclaimed in ink on paper as each pixel was replicated by hand.

(54) Gober has noted that the house, reconstructed in 1980 as a dollhouse-scaled rendition, was "loosely based on my paternal grandmother's house." Robert Gober in *Robert Gober: Sculptures and Installations 1979-2007*, ed. Theodora Vischer, exh. cat. (Basel, Switzerland: Laurenz Foundation, Schaulager Basel; and Gottingen, Germany: Steidl, 2007).

Object Lesson 4

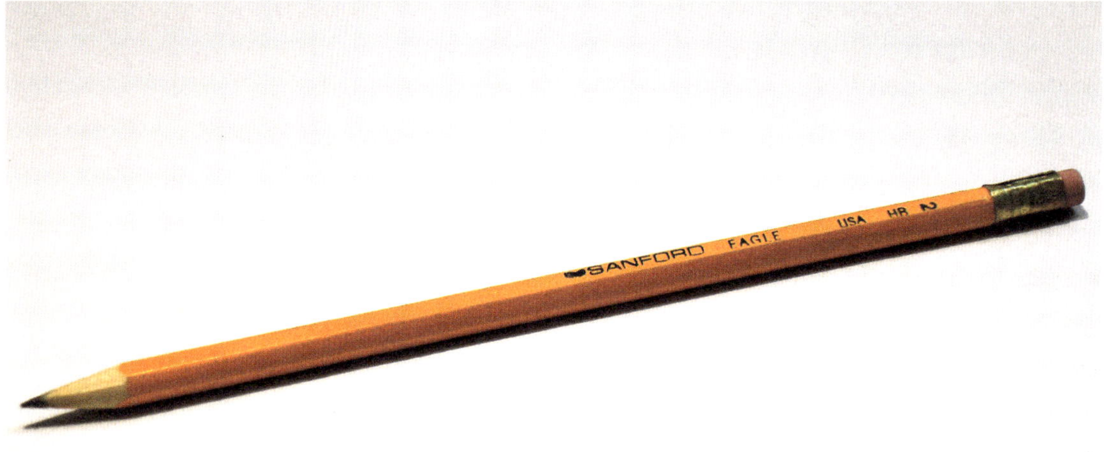

Plate 53. Mungo Thomson *Between Projects* 2001 (detail) handmade pencils

Mungo Thomson on Between Projects

I think pencils in factories are made with a lead core and two pieces of wood stuck together around it, then paint, eraser, etc. I did a version that was more in line with what I was capable of in my studio at the time, since the piece was so much about art being my "job" now (after getting my MFA and having my first commercial gallery show) and reporting to the studio as if it was an office (not to mention the studio-as-office turn in conceptual art) and hanging around there waiting for inspiration to strike, and making the waiting the inspiration. Hence the title. So I took wooden dowels, sanded them into hexagonal shafts, drilled holes down their centers and dropped fitted leads in with wood glue. Spray-painted the exterior, had a custom stamp made based on pencils I had in the studio ("Sanford Eagle") and stamped them with black enamel. Hand-fashioned tin fittings for rubber erasers. Then sharpened them and stuck them in the ceiling. There was a high failure rate with all those stages and it took a couple of months.

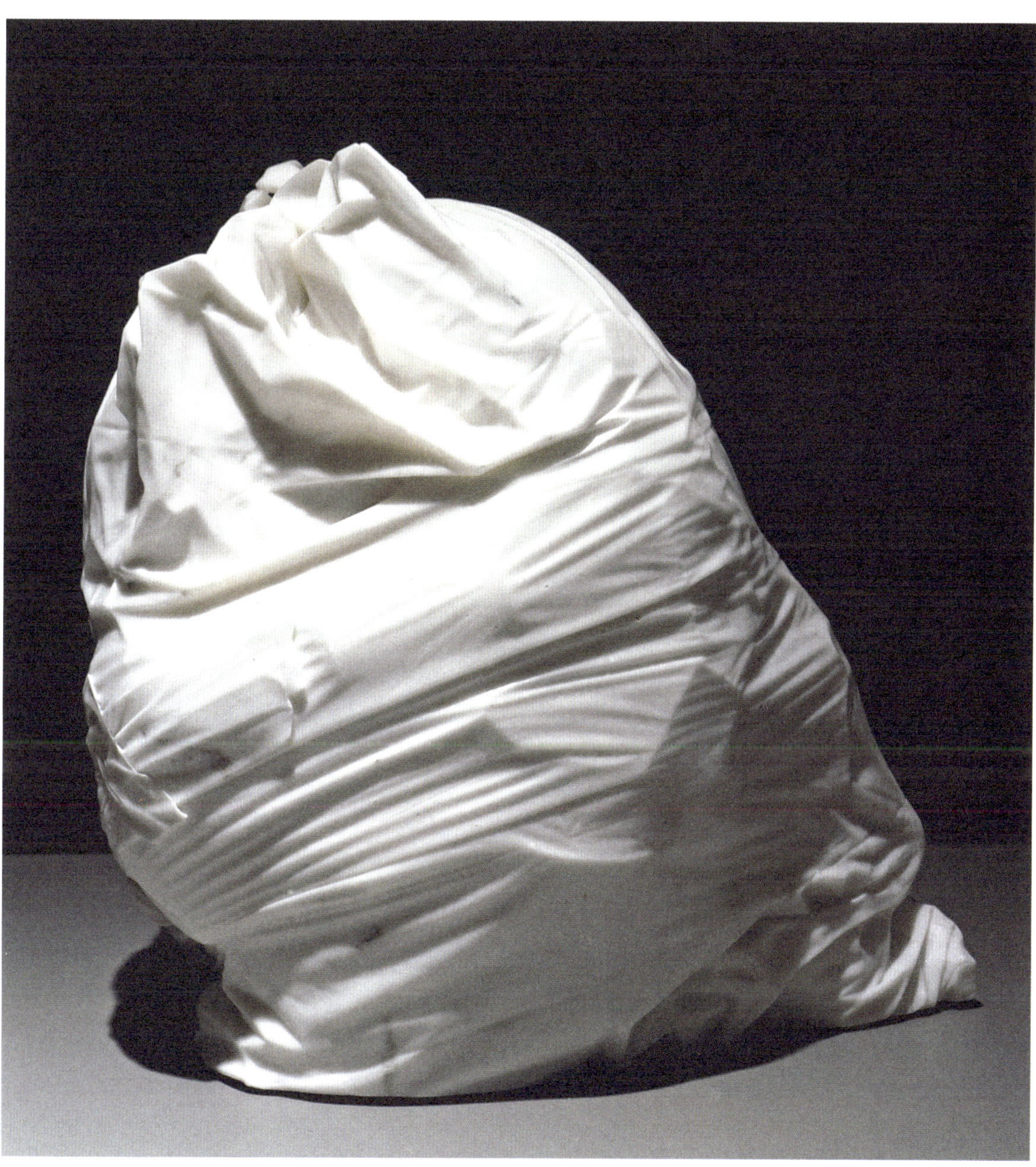

Plate 54. Jud Nelson *Hefty 2-Ply* 1979–1981 marble

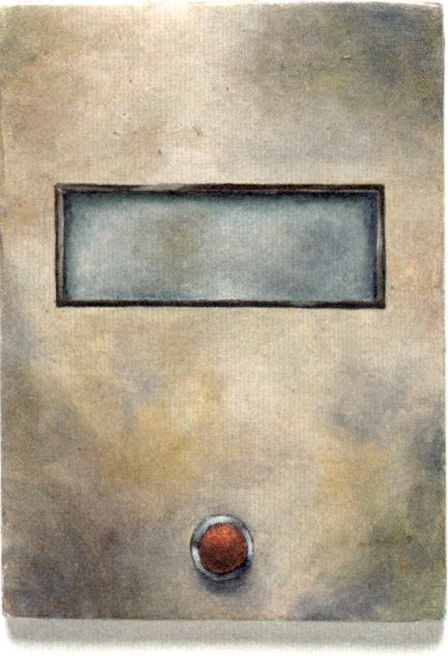

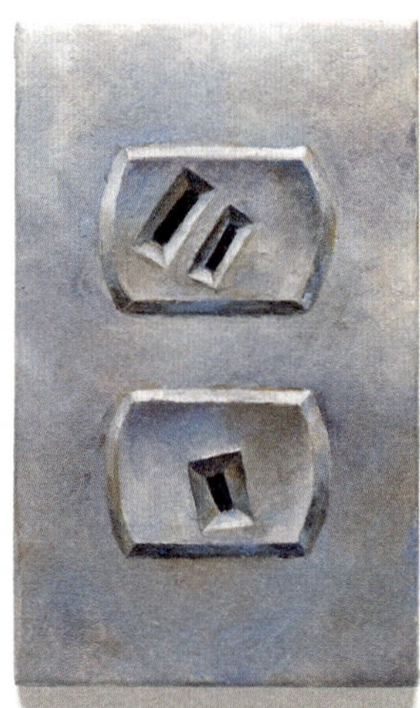

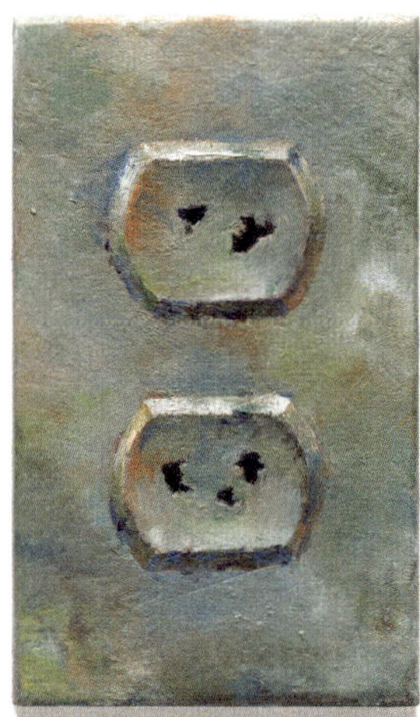

Plate 55. David Lefkowitz Selections from *Fixtures* 1991–2011 oil on wood panel

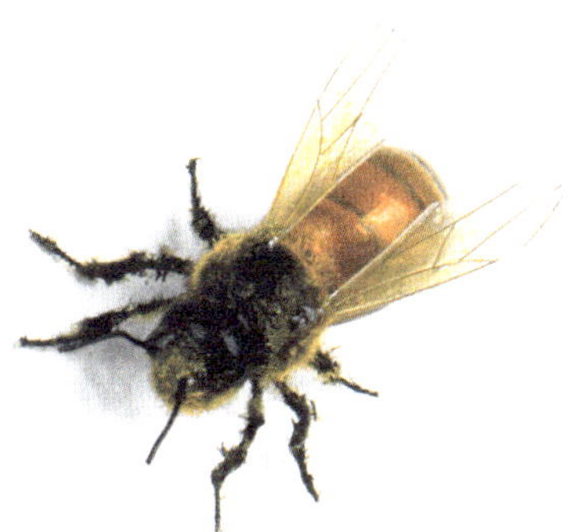

Plate 56. Tom Friedman *Untitled* 2001 clay, wire, fuzz, hair, plastic, paint

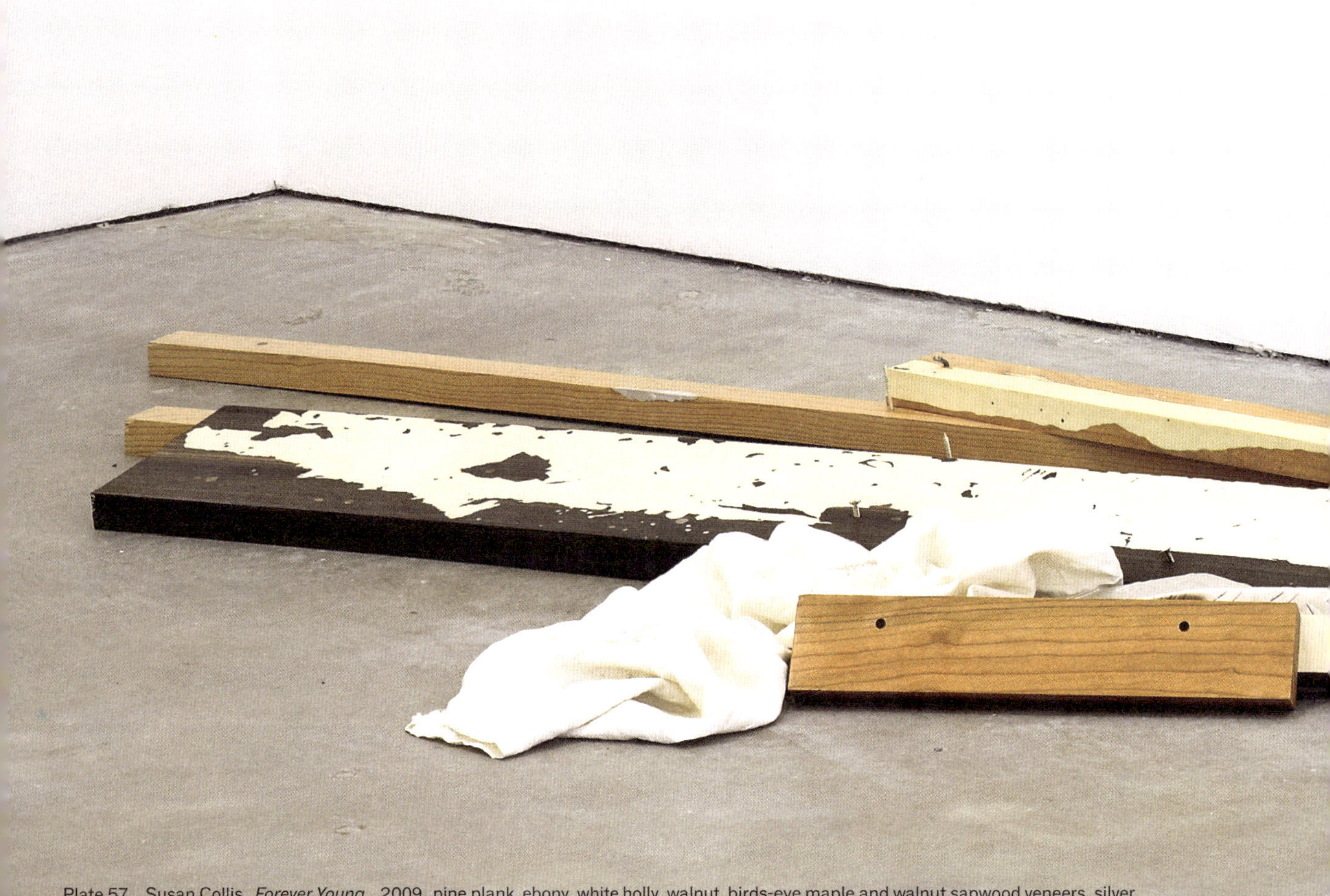

Plate 57. Susan Collis *Forever Young* 2009 pine plank, ebony, white holly, walnut, birds-eye maple and walnut sapwood veneers, silver, platinum, laminated chipboard, garnets, cedar of Lebanon wood, smoky quartz, black diamonds, oxidized silver, mother of pearl, white gold, smoky topaz, amber, mahogany, tulipwood, embroidery linen, thread

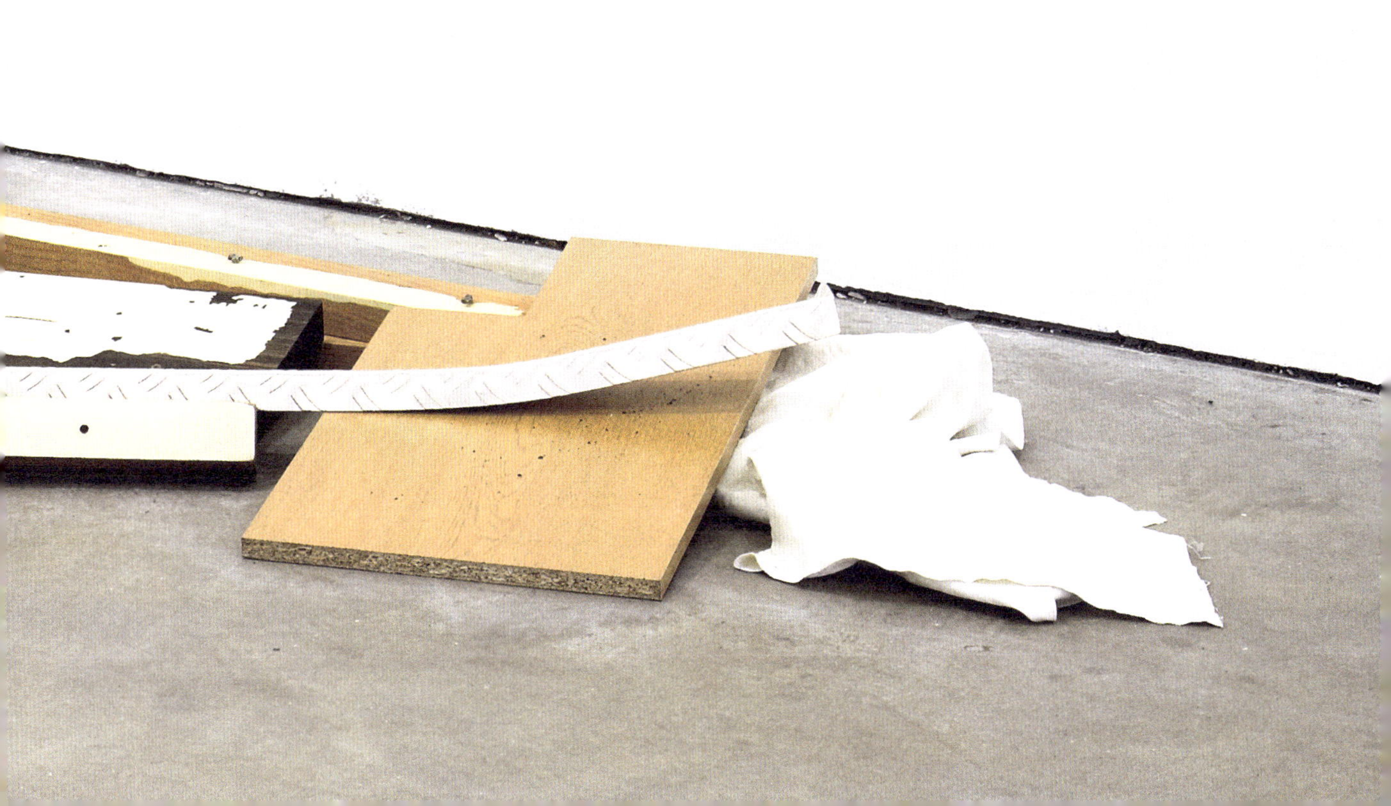

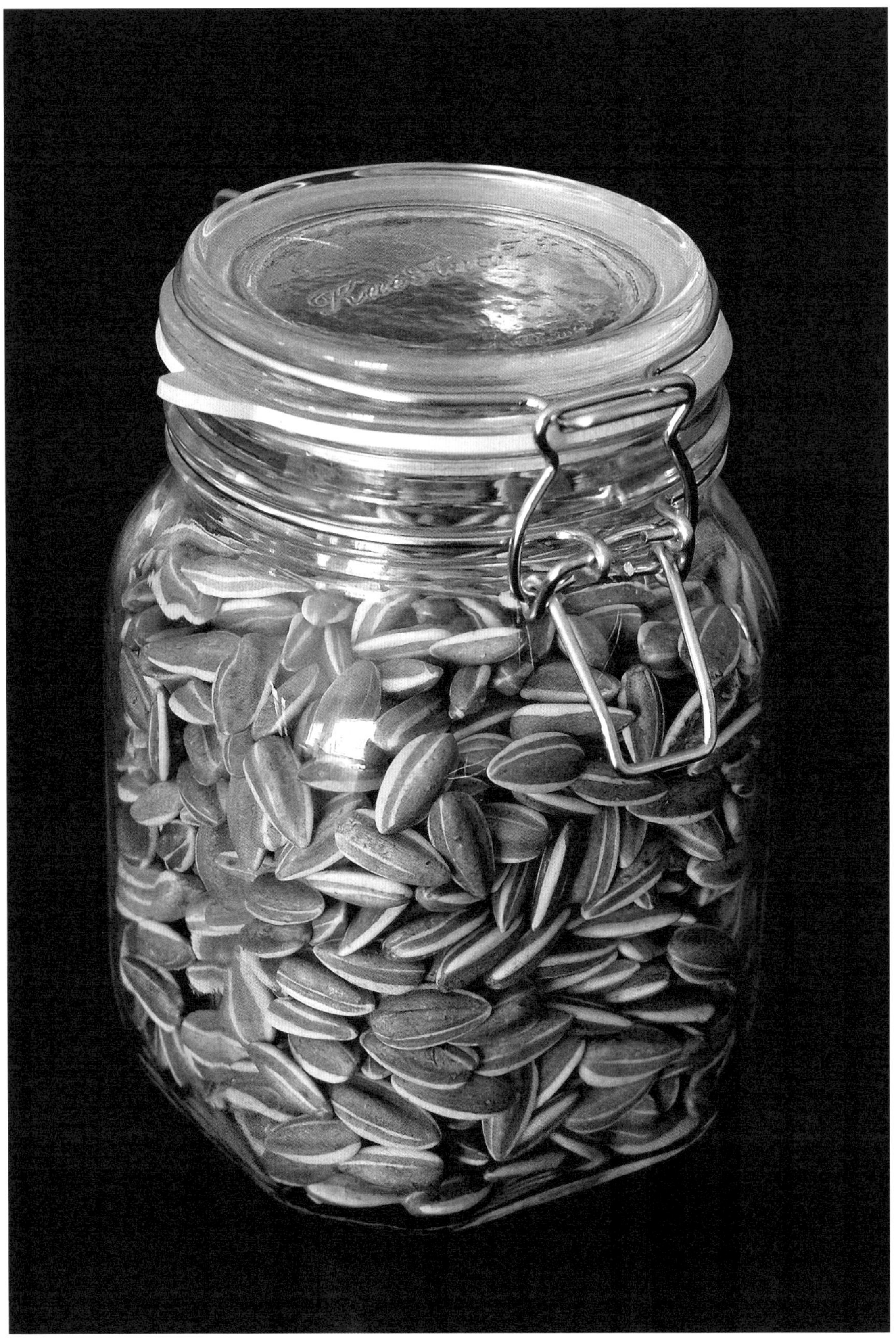

Plate 58 Ai Weiwei *Kui Hua Zi (Sunflower Seeds)* 2009 1,000 porcelain sunflower seeds, sculpted and painted by hand, manufactured in Jingdezhen, China, in glass jar inscribed with title and artist's name

I think people will have the impression that they are real sunflower seeds, but they are fake seeds. It takes them a while to adjust their minds. They would always say, "Is that possible?" Then they would pick up a few. Some would even want to put them in their mouth to try.

I always think art is a tool to set up new questions. [Creating] a basic structure [that] can be open to possibilities is the most interesting part of my work. I want people who don't understand art to understand what I am doing.

Normally porcelain production requires around 30 stages. You cannot really escape from it. The sunflower seeds are made in a town called Jingdezhen; it is about 1,000 kilometers from Beijing. In the old times, the whole town made porcelains for the emperor's court. For generations people refined the shape of a bowl or a vase; it was a very fixed language.

We have been working here [in Jingdezhen] for five or six years, to try and find out the possibilities of applying the old technique to modern contemporary language. Because of the quantity—it takes 1,600 people and more are involved in the project in this town—that means almost everyone knows someone who is making "sunflower seeds." Even the taxi drivers talk about it, but nobody understands it. If you tell them it is for an exhibition, nobody understands why you have to accept this.

The actual production is very much like the old times. You have a group of people working together—different people take different positions. When it comes to painting, it needs the most people because on every seed, each side takes three to four strokes. The most skillful ones take three strokes; for some it takes four or five.

In the political arena, the paintings always had sunflower seeds. Whenever Chairman Mao comes out there are sunflowers around him. That means Chairman Mao is the sun and all the ordinary people loyal to the party are the sunflowers. Sunflowers supported the whole revolution, spiritually and in material ways.

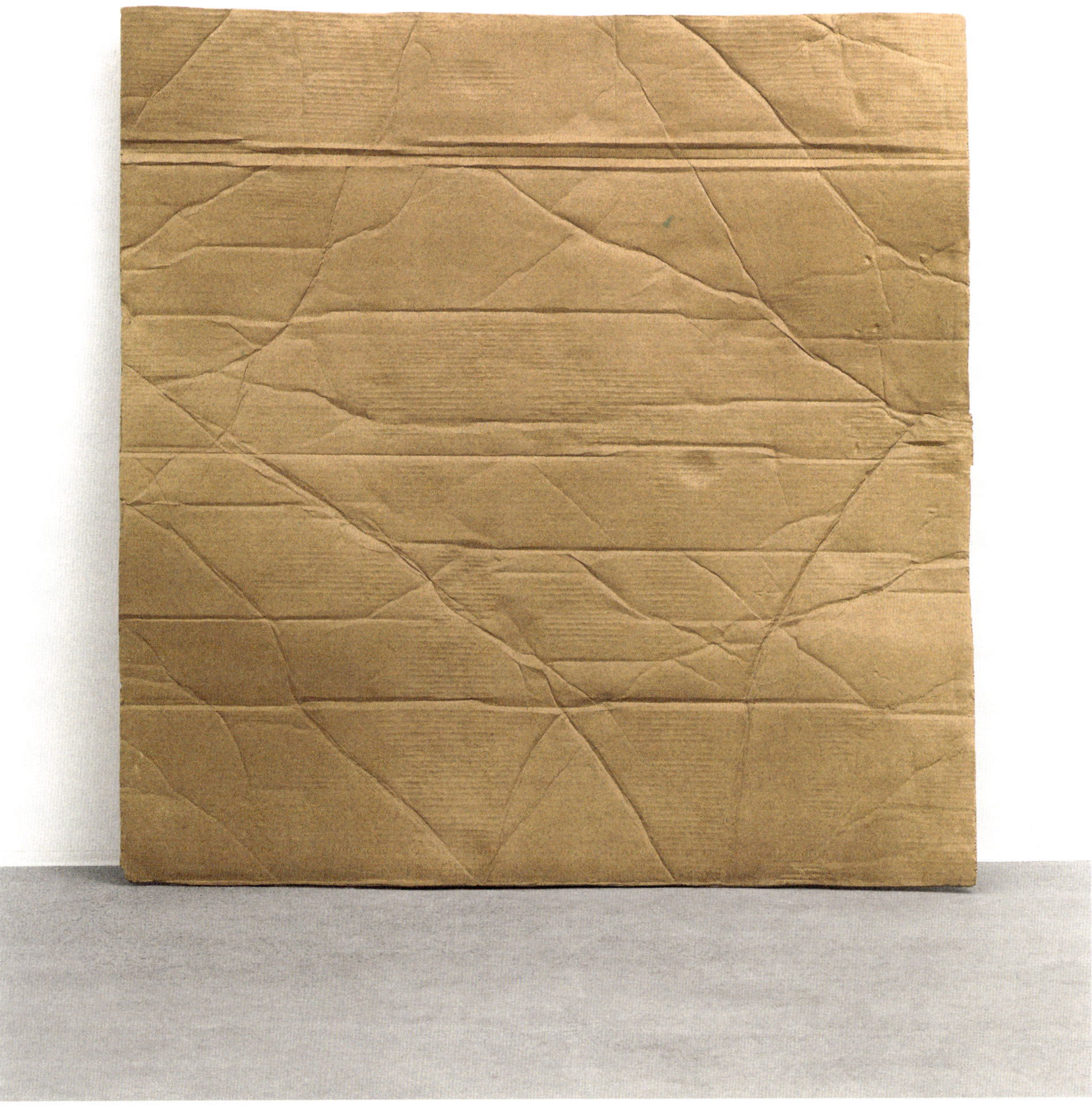

Plate 59. Ugo Rondinone *still.life. (cardboard leaning on the wall)* 2009 bronze cast, lead, paint

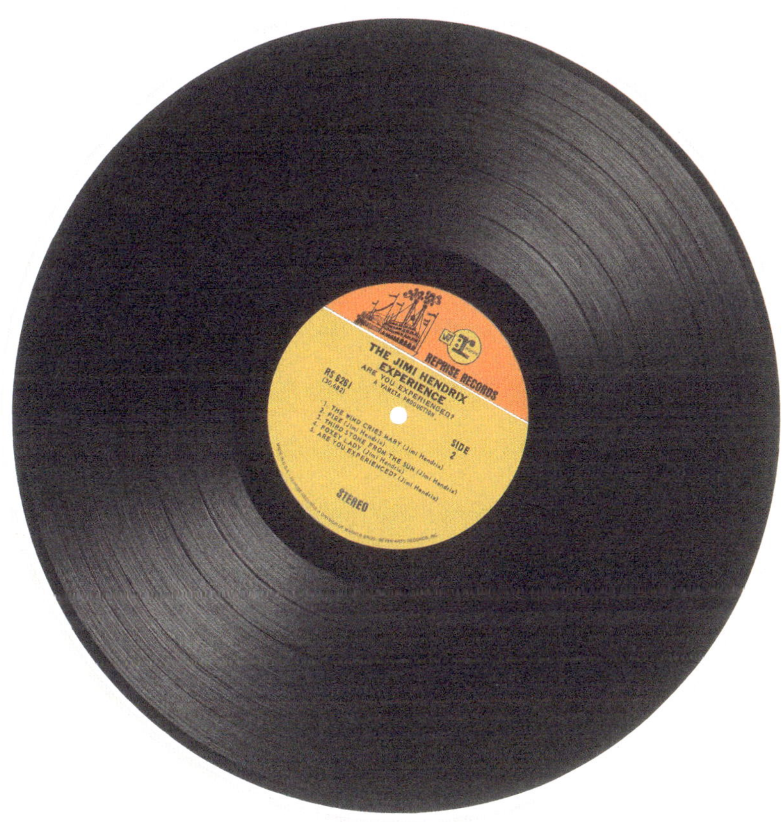

Plate 60. Steve Wolfe *Untitled (Are You Experienced?)* 1993 oil, enamel, lithography, modeling paste on board

Susan Collis on Refugee

The series of hand-drawn bags, begun in 2007, don't rely on any type of precious material; it is almost the opposite, it is more to do with the labor and time expended.... With drawings in particular, there are certain things that feel so personal, like the way you put your pencil on the paper, if it is gestural at all, and so on. How can you give that to someone else to do? So maybe that is another thing about those bags, they are so absolutely ungestural, they are so much about drawing out a grid and filling in the squares. When assistants would come to the studio I used to spend half an hour apologizing to them, saying, "This is what you are going to be doing today, I am so sorry that I thought this up and that you're going to have to do it!" It feels like bringing somebody into your madness, but they absolutely loved doing them. It is a basic thing, filling in boxes, listening to Radio 4, and just chatting. I used to be there at the end of the day saying, "Right then, it is time to go now," but the volunteers would say, "I won't be long; I just want to finish this bit." There is something very addictive, although that is not quite the right word.

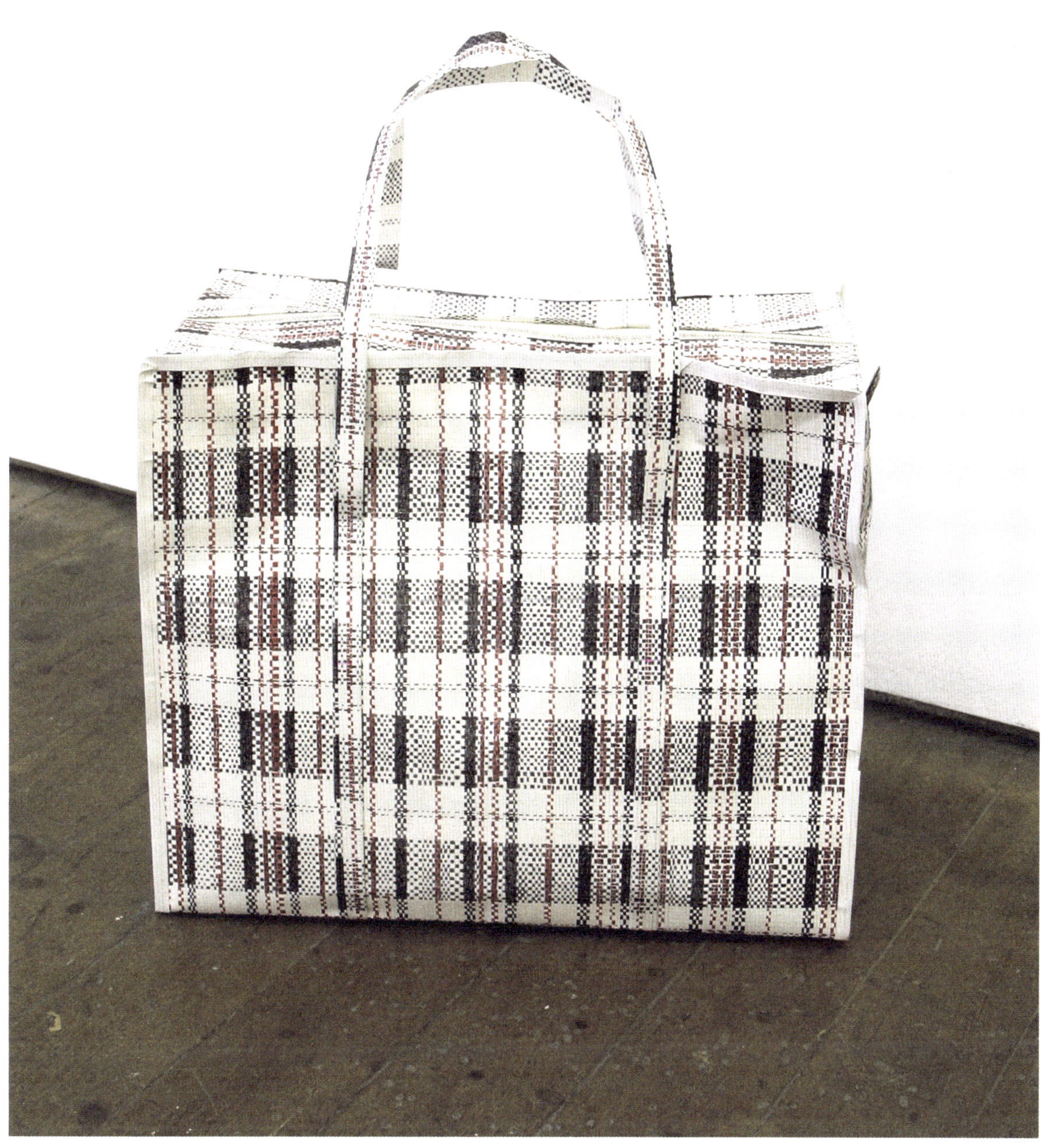

Plate 61. Susan Collis *Refugee* 2007 ballpoint pen, pencil and glue on paper

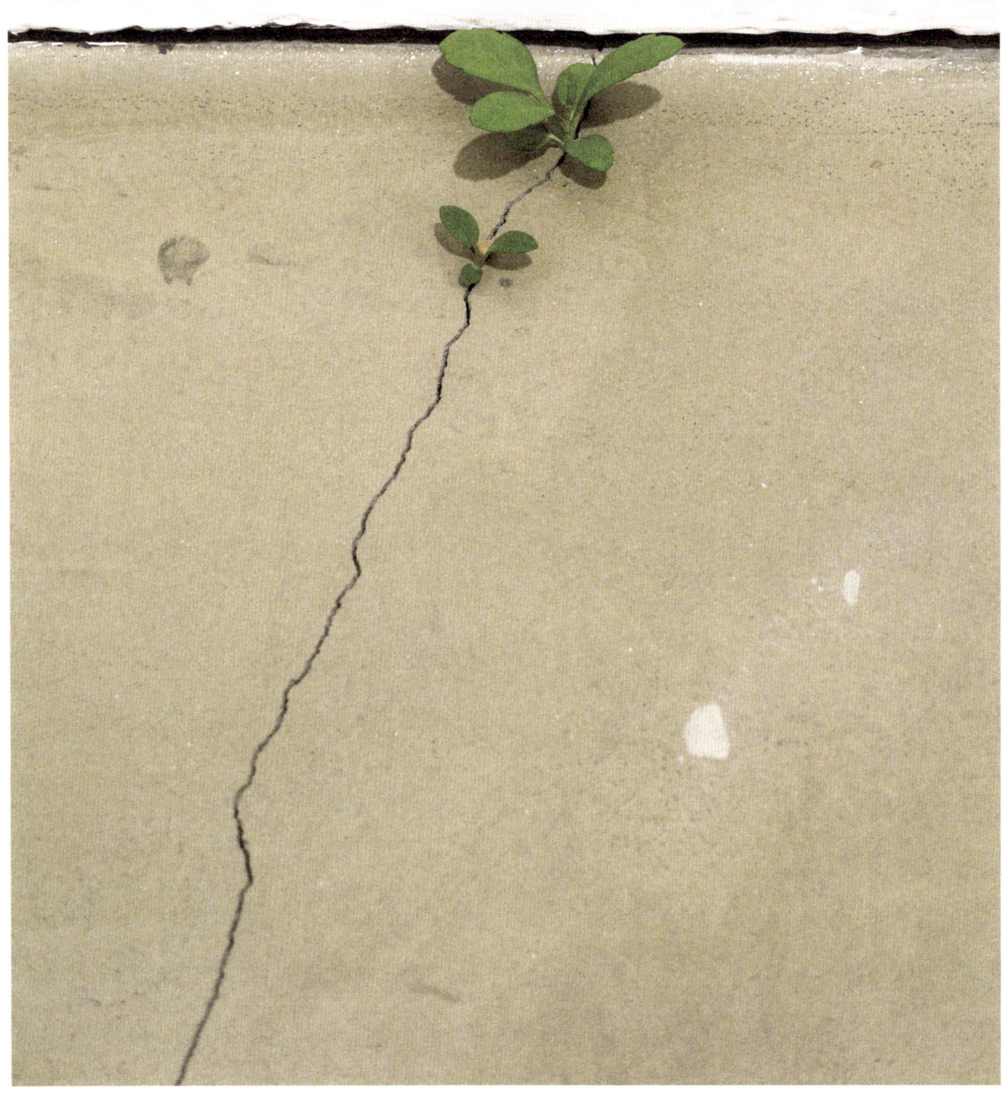

Plate 62. Yoshihiro Suda *Weeds* 2008 painted wood

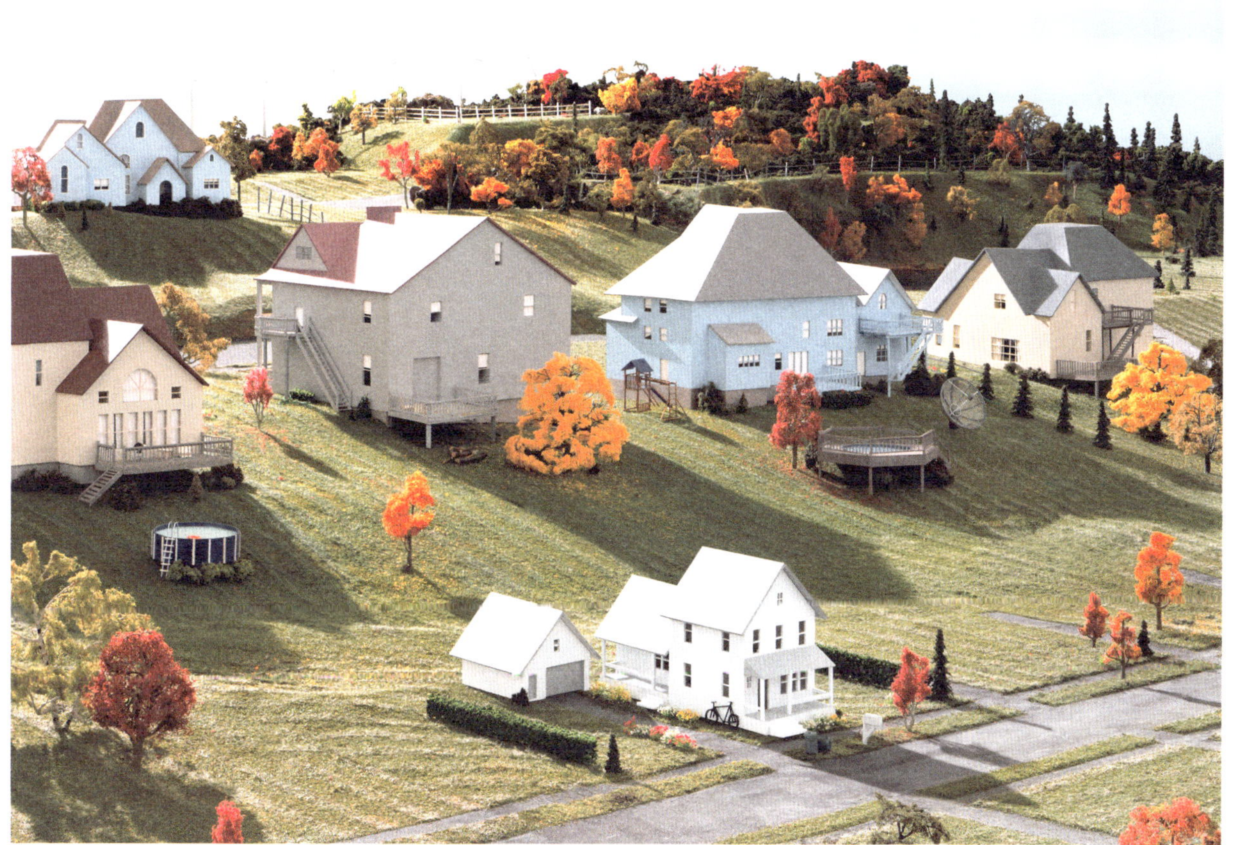

Plate 63. James Casebere *Landscape with Houses (Dutchess County, NY) #8* 2010 framed digital chromogenic print mounted to Dibond

Paul Sietsema on Untitled ink drawing

I agreed to have my picture taken by a photographer who was shooting Los Angeles artists.... I forgot about the image until I came across it while looking up another LA artist. My photo popped up next to theirs, and I dragged it to my desktop without thinking. I opened it at some later point and zoomed in as I usually do when looking at clipped images, as I'm always interested in the pixel/grain structures. I found the pixel formation to be compelling and almost immediately saw that the form could easily be building blocks for something that is handmade. I liked the idea of making a self-portrait that was actually an image taken by someone else, put into the slipstream of the Internet—a highly public and arguably impersonal place—and then appropriated back by me.... The drawing was built up, based on the structure of the pixels, and it was pieced together and not laboriously so, probably more meditatively.... For me, any form of rendering is simply about invisibility, about having 100% variability in where you place information in an image.

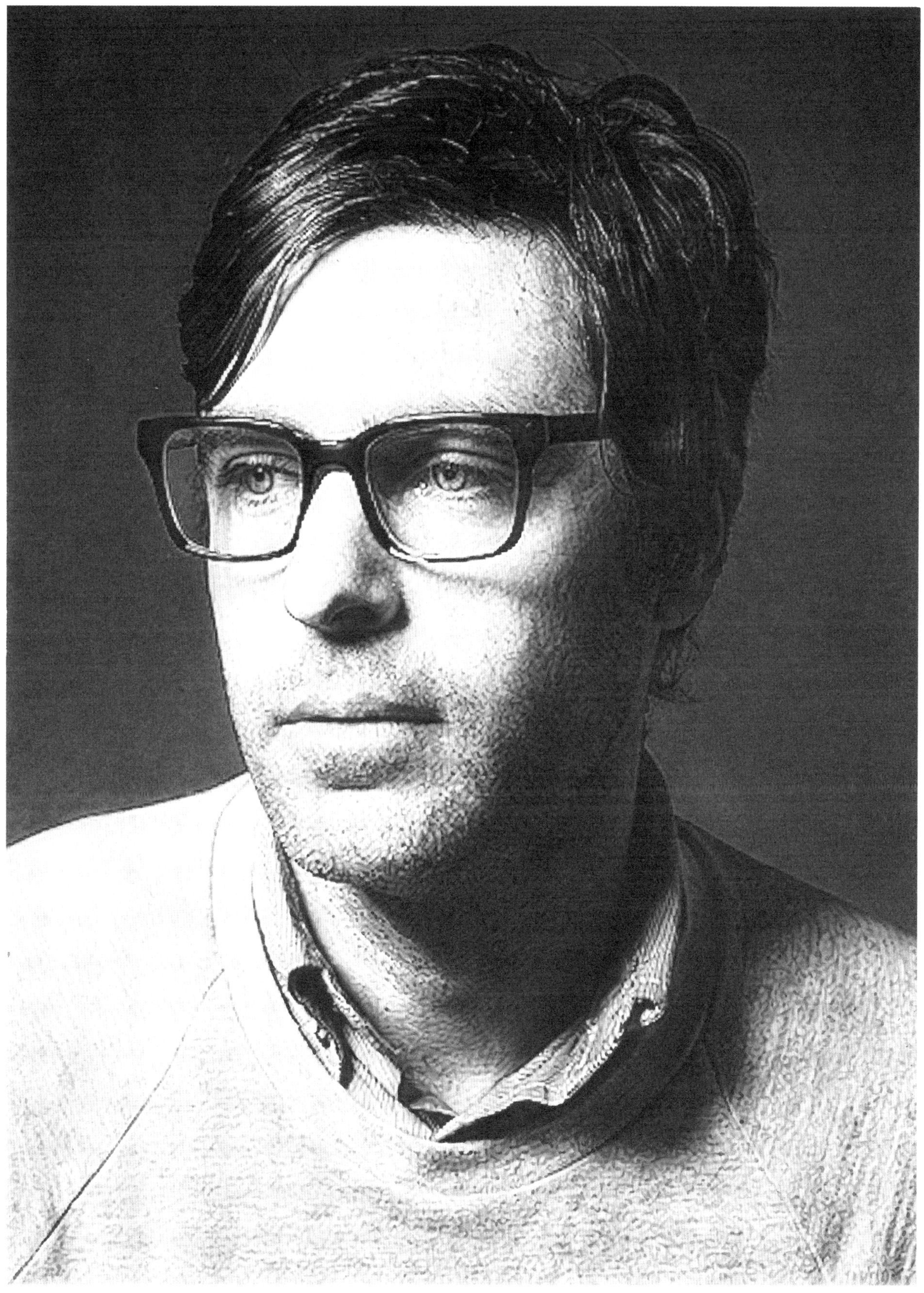

Plate 64. Paul Sietsema *Untitled ink drawing* 2009 ink on paper in artist's frame

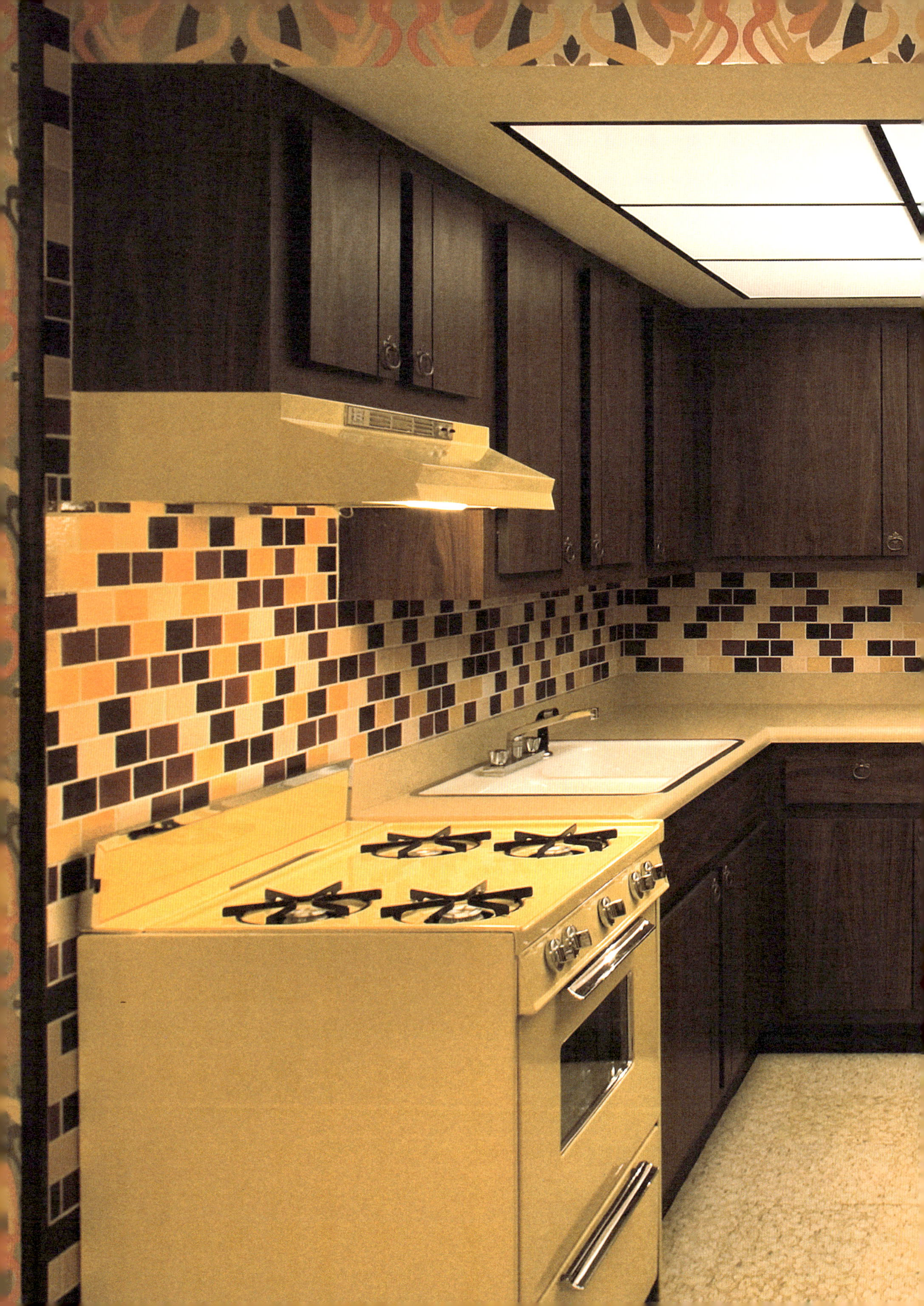

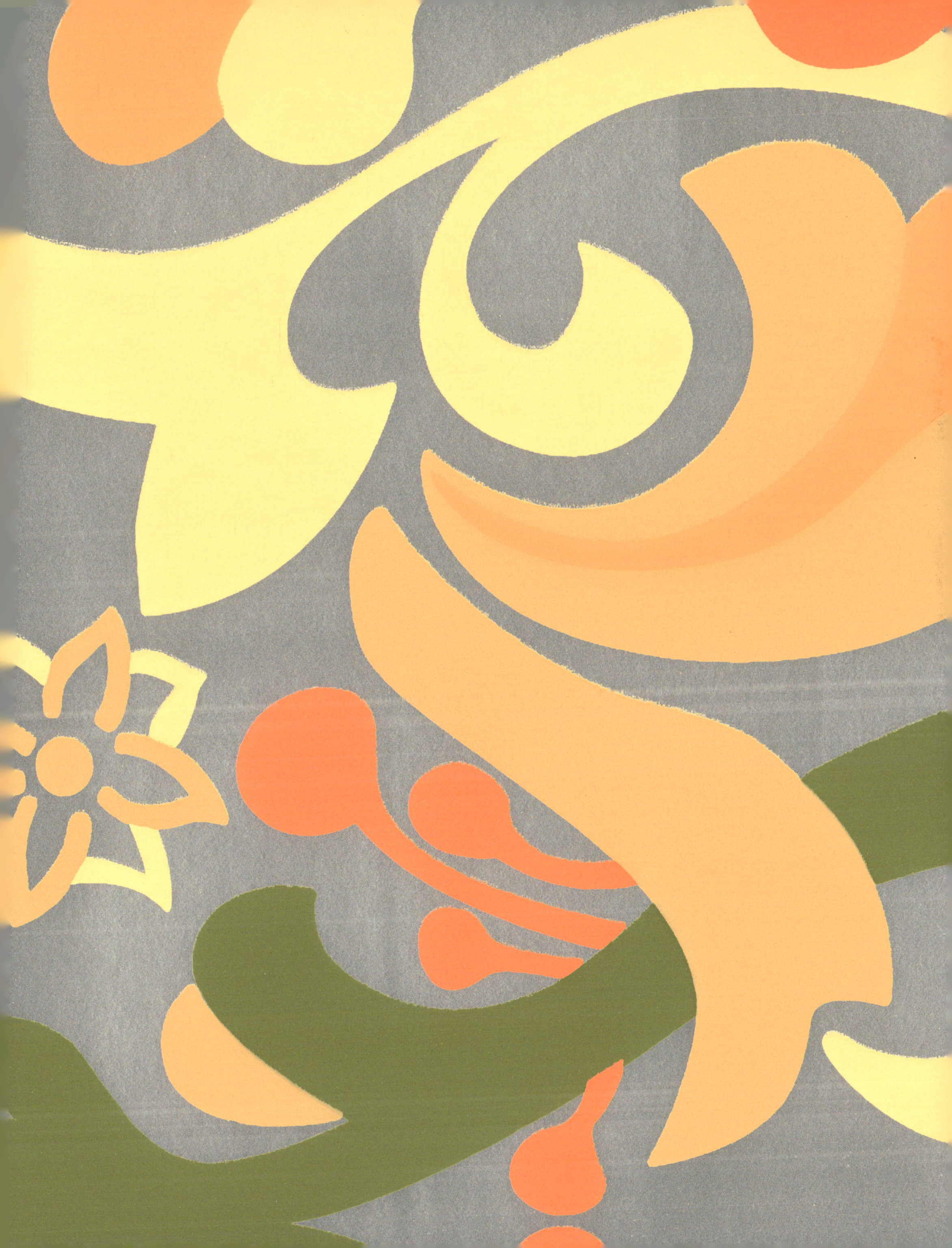

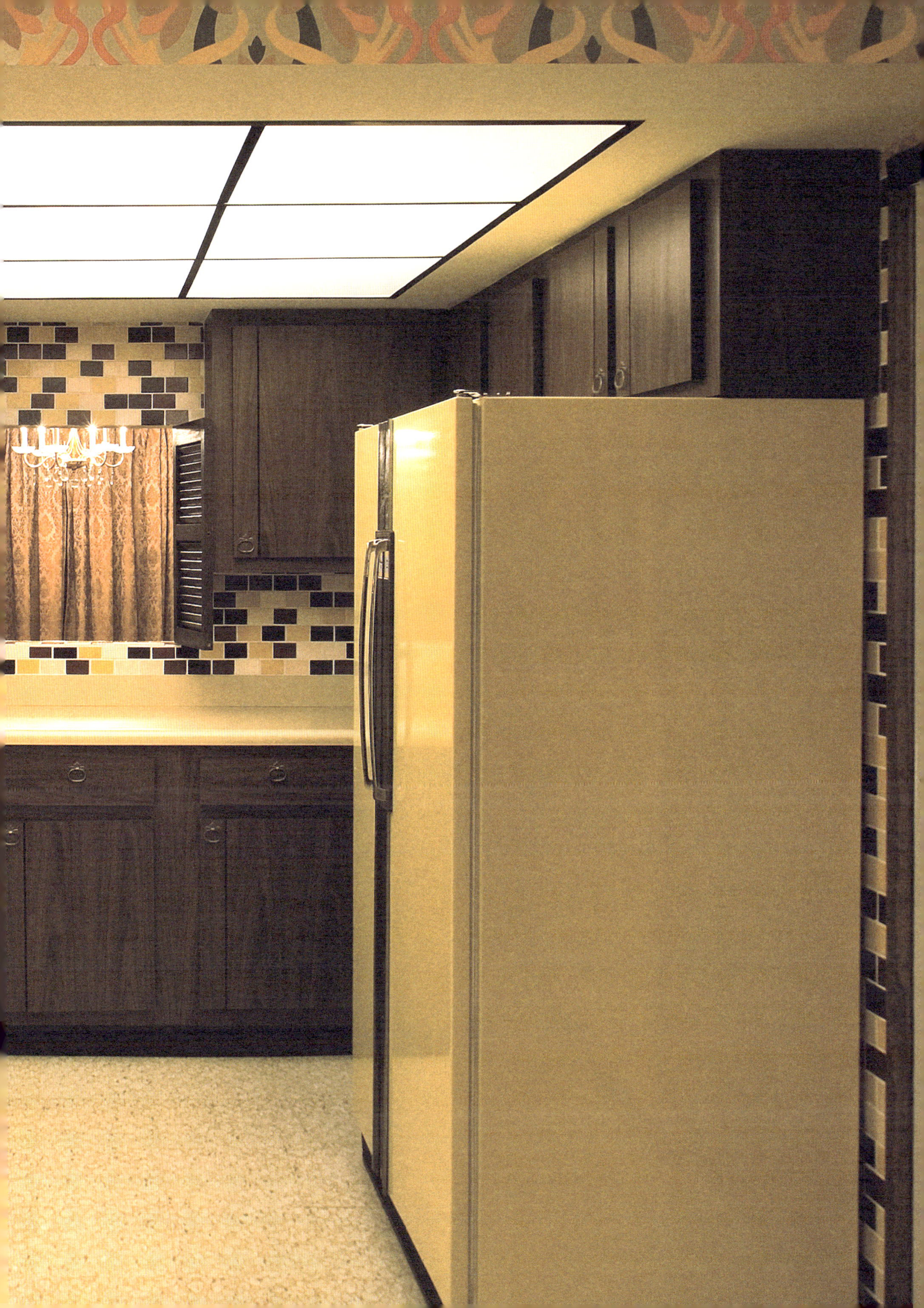

Object Lesson 8

Keith Edmier on Bremen Towne

Bremen Towne was an idea I'd been thinking about prior to [my 2008] show at Bard College. It had been floating in my head for a number of years based on the sales brochure of my parents' home I had obtained around 1999 off of eBay. It was just one of these things I had around.... I didn't really have the idea of constructing this house back then.... As it turned out, the interior dimensions of my parents' home from the original blueprints fit directly into one of the galleries at the museum. At that point I started considering it more as an art object, or as a sculpture more than an installation.... The main visual references were family photographs, mostly taken during critical events or holidays or birthday parties. My process involved going through the photo album—everything. They were all pictures of people posing, so I started looking at the spaces [in the background].... I ended up buying the whole decade of both Sears and JCPenney catalogues up until that time, the early '70s. Through that I was able to identify some products based on visual descriptions or in the family photographs.... I initially went to a place that has all kinds of wallpapers and floorings from other periods, used a lot for movies and things like that. I heard they had thousands of wallpapers. It turned out I couldn't find the exact wallpaper that was in the house. I guess at that point I started thinking it was more interesting for me to remake it, and to remake it more or less new. I wanted to represent the time element, the moment before the day of the family moving into the new house. It wasn't supposed to look lived in.

I think I was initially interested in doing that to have some kind of separation from taking a real object that was loaded with personal history or some sentimental thing. It was a way of moving from a subjective to an objective position.... [I was interested] in just thinking about the whole interior of the house itself as a cast, or this negative space. I thought about how the house is essentially the space that shapes us, that shapes oneself.... I think that my reason to make it, or to make almost anything, went beyond just the visual aspects of it, or the idea of re-creating an illusion of the thing. I've always been more interested in a certain level of representation or pictorial literalness.... I like words or descriptions like "actual" or "actual scale." I like the idea of "what is real?"

Plate 65. (previous page) Keith Edmier *Bremen Towne* 2006–2007 (detail) building materials, reproduction and vintage fabrics, furnishings, fixtures, finishes

Insert: Keith Edmier *Kitchen Psychedelia* 2012 foil paper hand-silkscreened with water-based inks

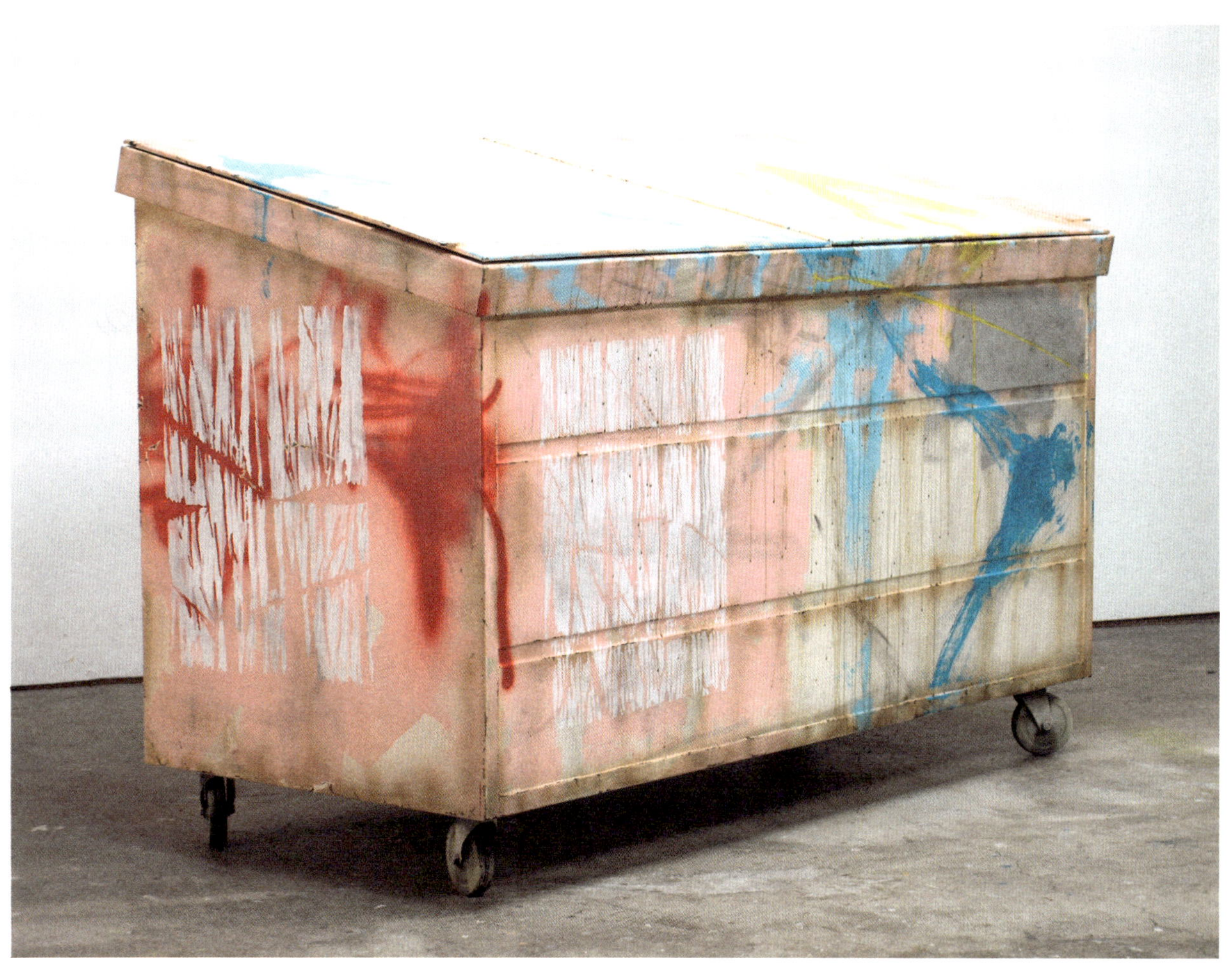

Plate 66. Kaz Oshiro *Dumpster (Flesh with Turquoise Swoosh)* 2011 acrylic on stretched canvas, caster wheels

Object Lesson 9

Kaz Oshiro on Dumpster (Flesh with Turquoise Swoosh)

This dumpster for *Lifelike* is the fifth that I have made.... I like the dumpster because I can experiment with the idea of abstract painting. I am always interested in the painter's issue.... I have been trying to find an area where representational painting and abstract painting coexist. With the dumpster, I can simulate or manipulate the idea of abstract painting directly on its surface. The work appears to be representational painting, but I am always thinking of it as abstract painting, with the details of paint drips, dust, and rust.... I see myself as a still life painter who's trying to be an abstract painter; I think the dumpster kind of shows this transition.

When I paint, I don't use photographs as a reference.... Everything that I want to paint is done from memory. Since the dumpster is a functional object, there are some important elements that I have to be aware of. I have to take measurements in order to know the physical volume. But sometimes I encounter problems when I try to replicate the shape exactly as an existing dumpster. So I try to combine the details and sometimes I find myself having to simplify the parts.... I don't know if it is noticeable, but usually dumpsters have metal channels that a forklift can insert into. I've omitted that detail from the piece because it was hard to make. For me, as long as the object I make has a physical volume that is close enough to the real object, then it serves its purpose.

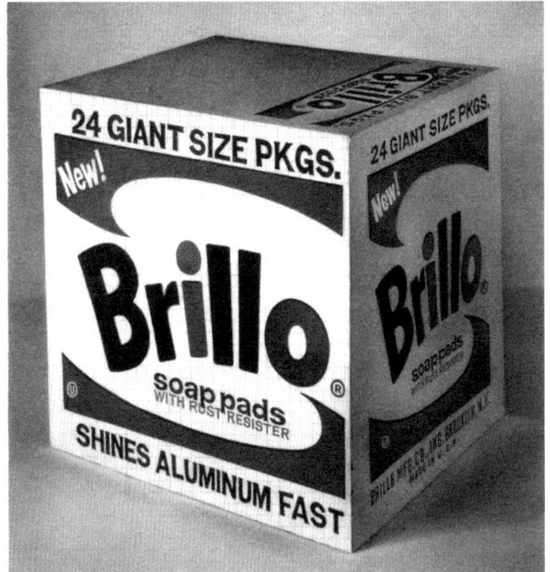

67.

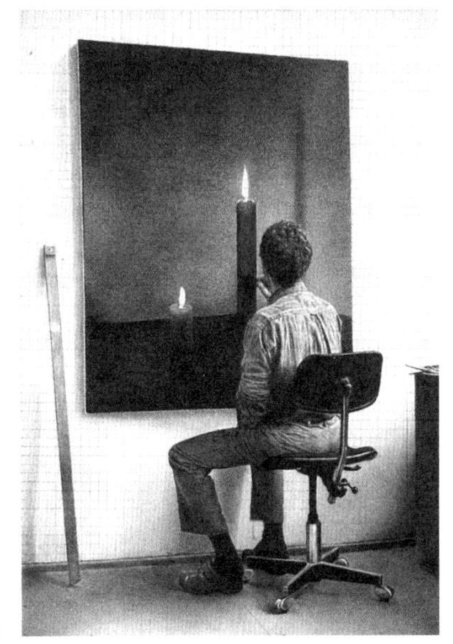

68.

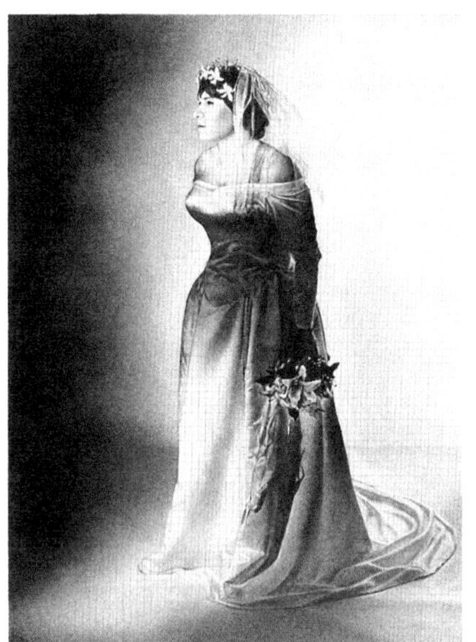

69.

Dan Fischer

Plate 67. *Warhol Brillo Box* 2009
Plate 68. *Gerhard Richter* 2002
Plate 69. *Robert Gober* 2003
Plate 70. *Tom Friedman* 2001
Plate 71. *Charles Ray* 2001
Plate 72. *Thomas Demand* 2005

all graphite on paper

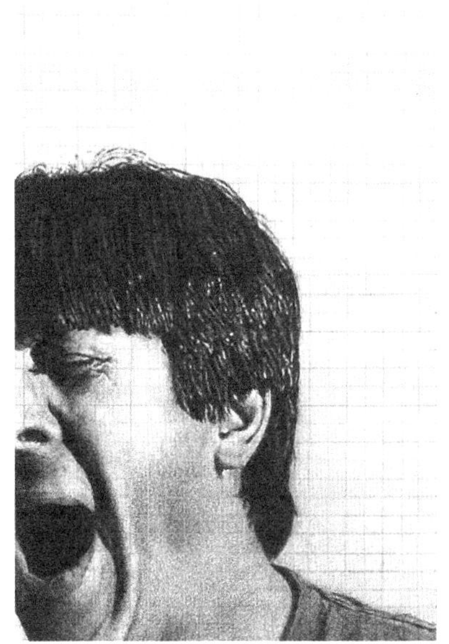

70.

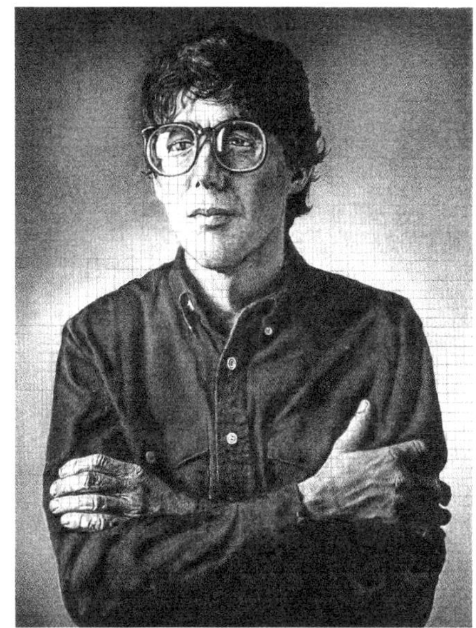

71.

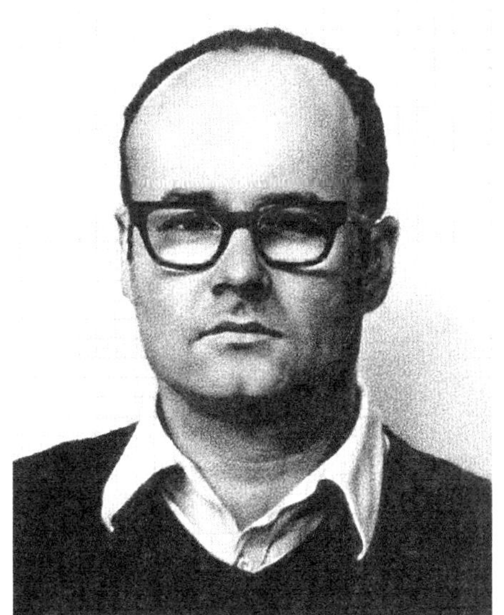

72.

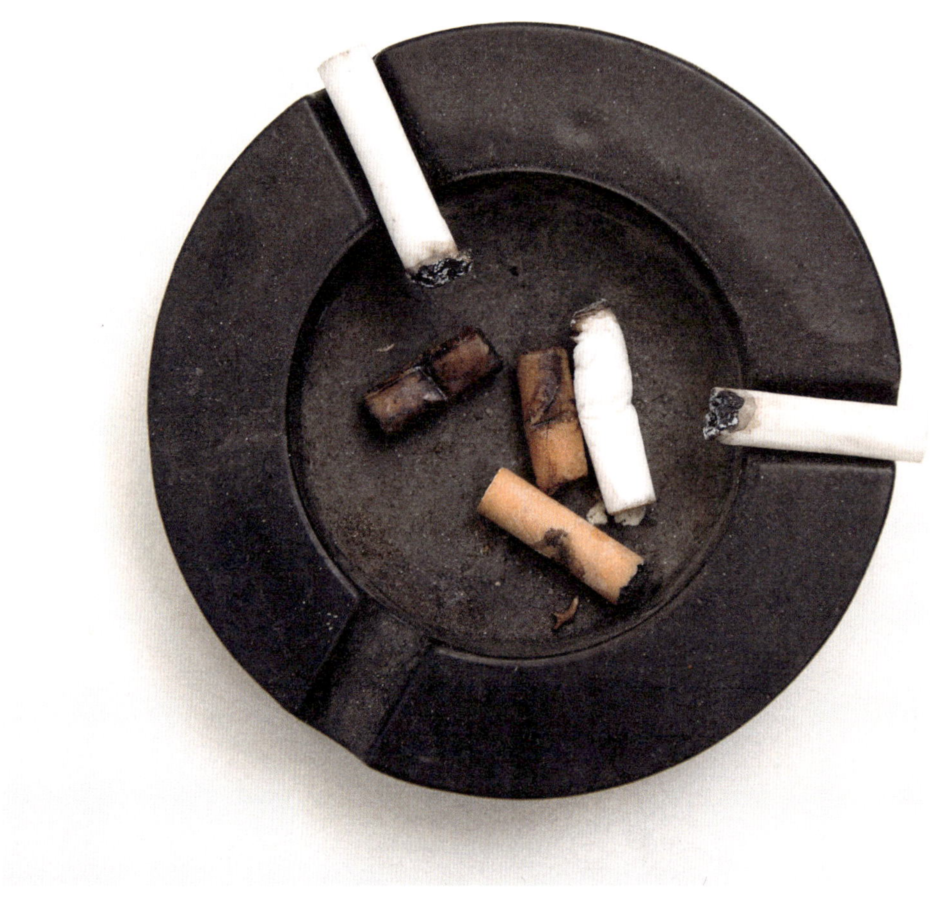

Plate 73. Ruben Nusz *Nothing good happens after midnight/everything good happens after midnight* 2008
acrylic, oil, tea, walnut ink on wax and resin with incense and cremation ashes

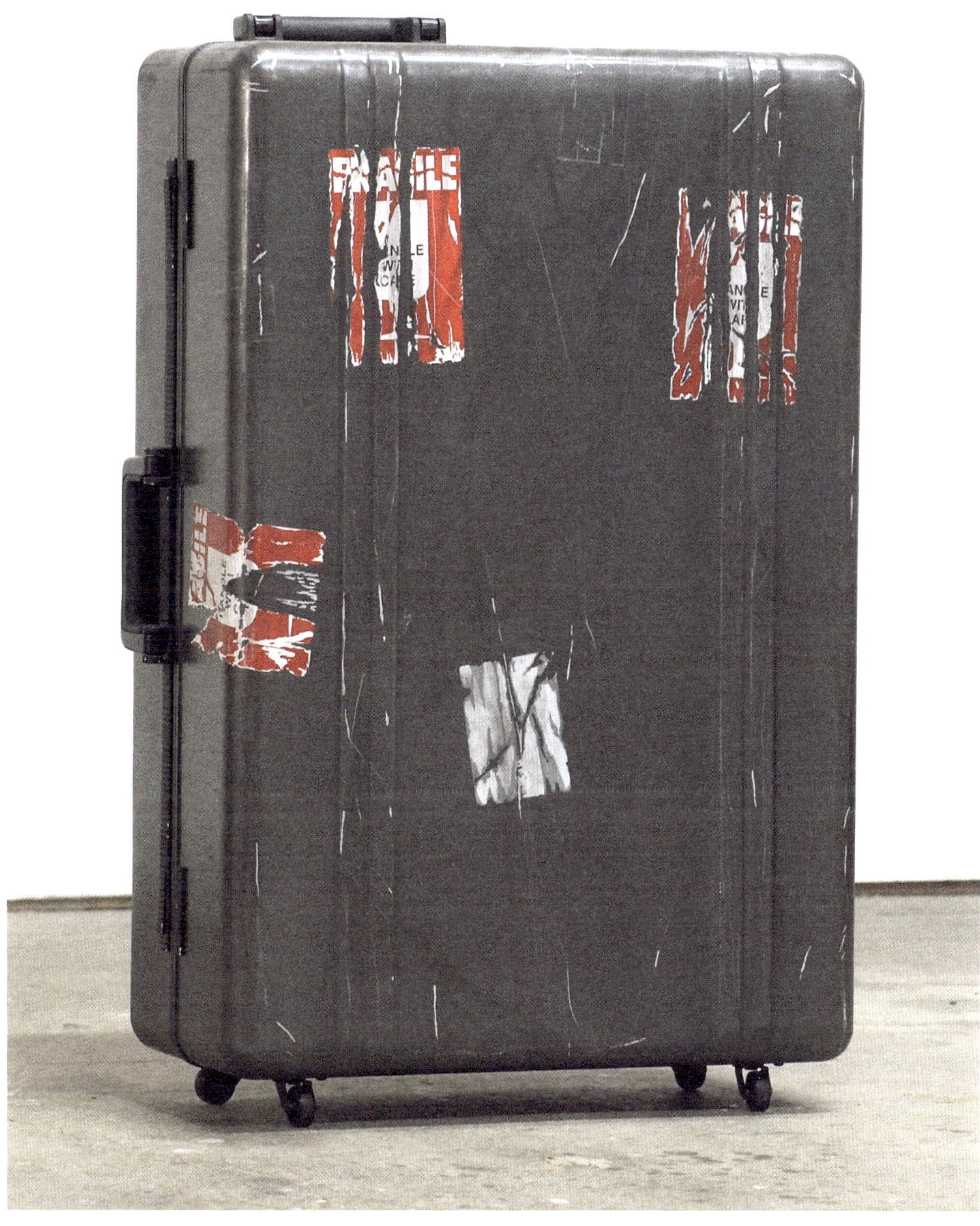

Plate 74. Kaz Oshiro *Zero Case Spinner (gun metal—torn FRAGILE stickers)* 2011 acrylic, Bondo on stretched canvas, caster wheels

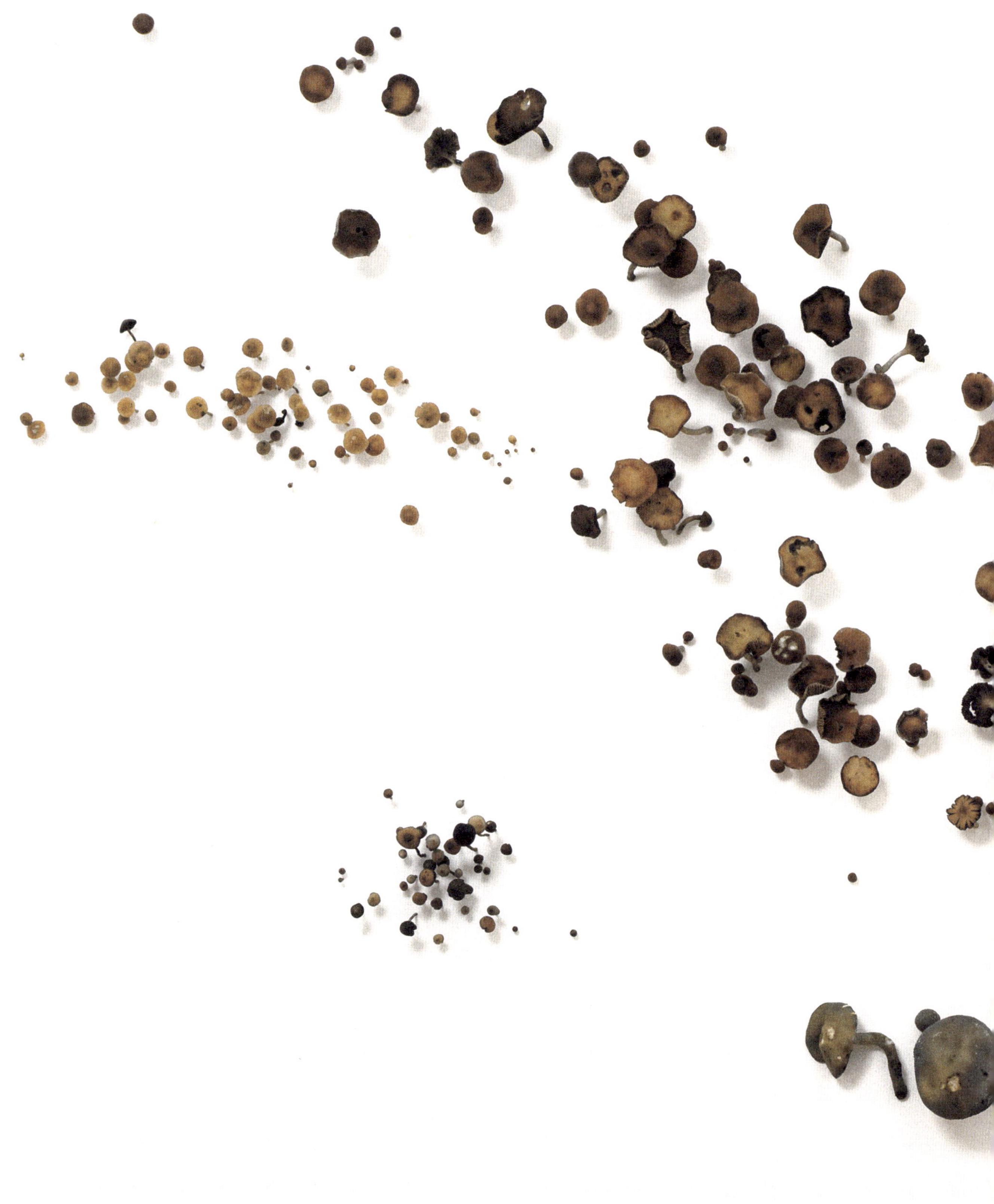

Plate 75. Roxy Paine *Untitled* 2002 polymer, lacquer, oil on wood frame

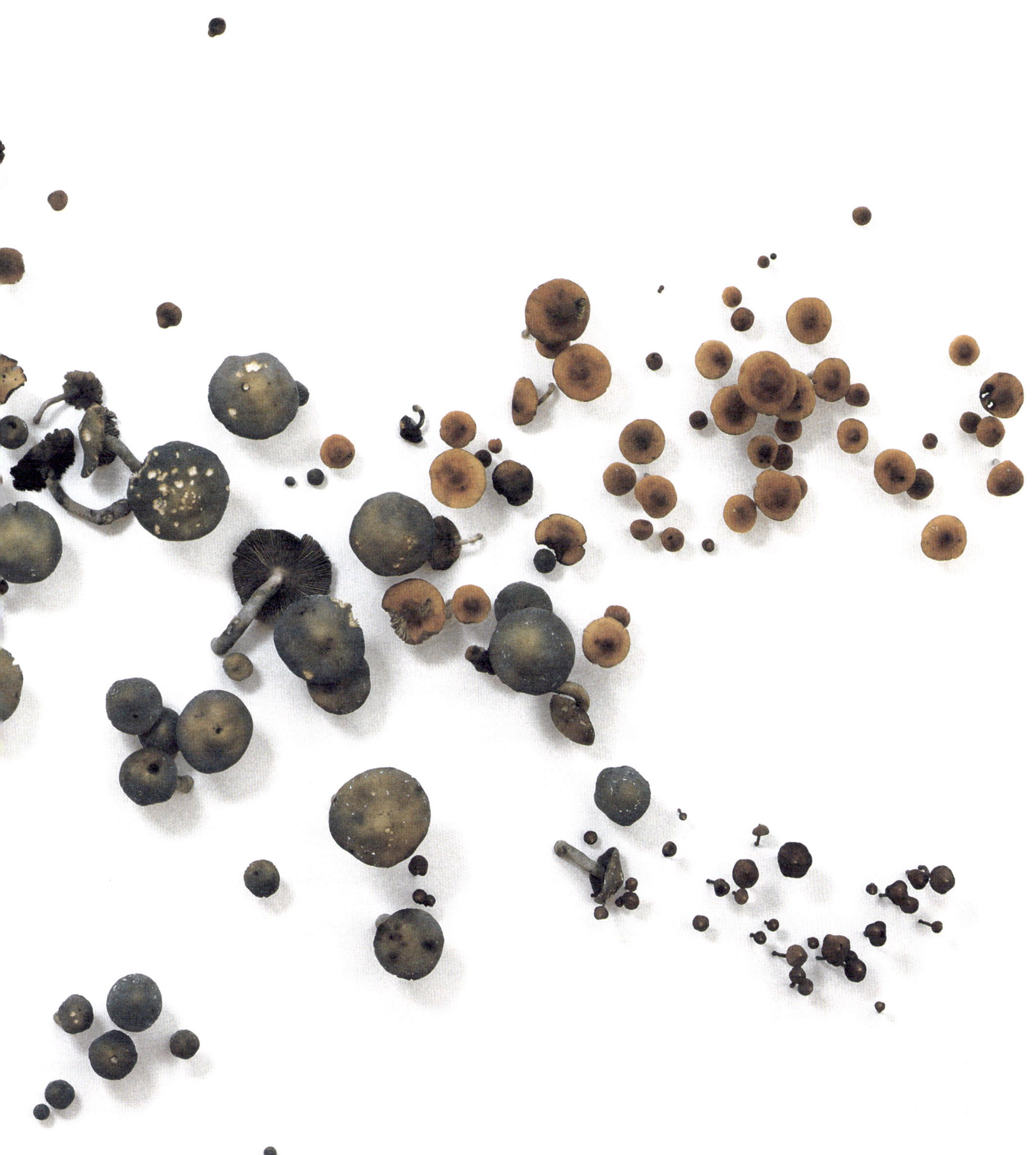

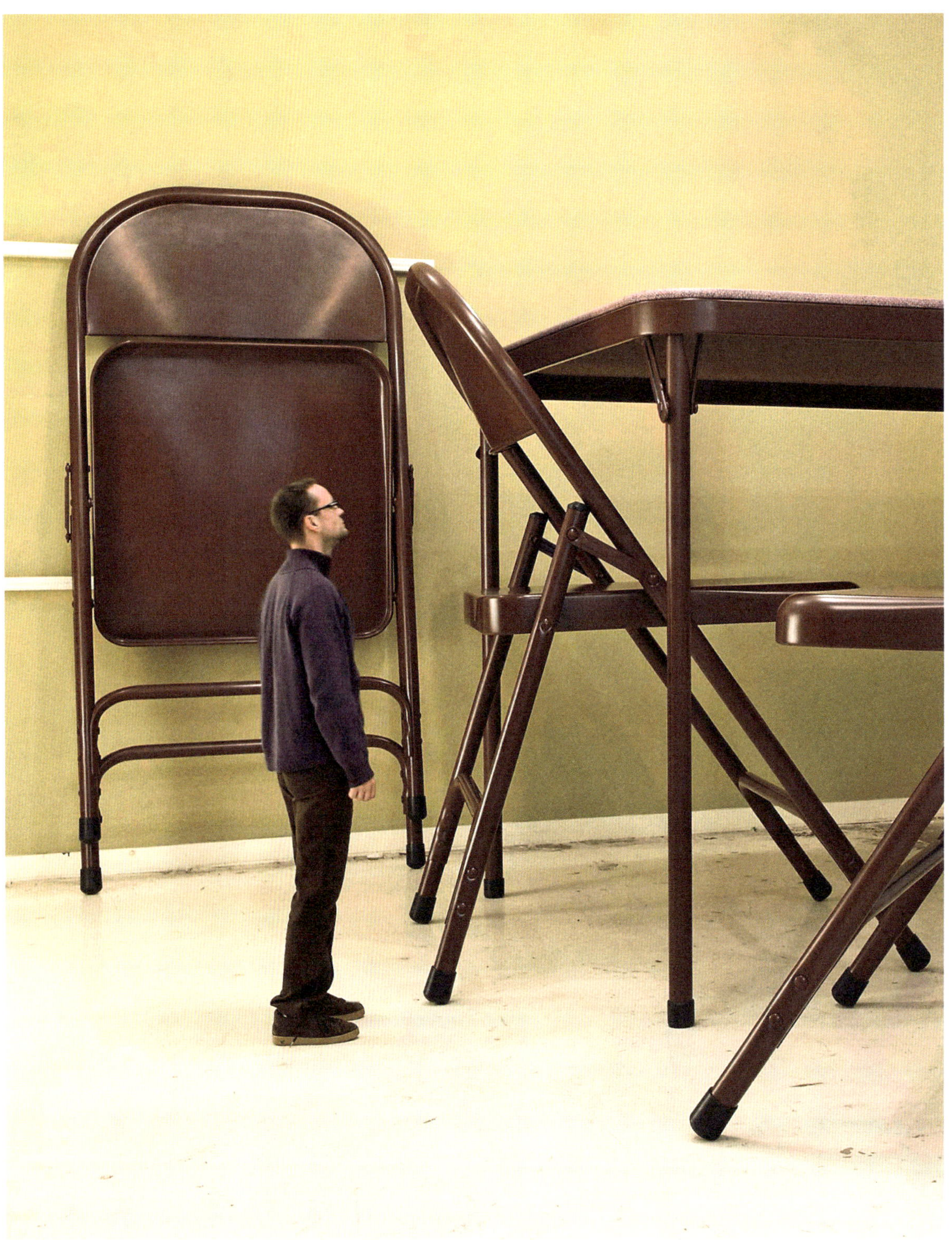

Fig. 25 Robert Therrien *No title (Folding table and chairs, brown)* 2006 (installation view) paint, metal, fabric

S P E

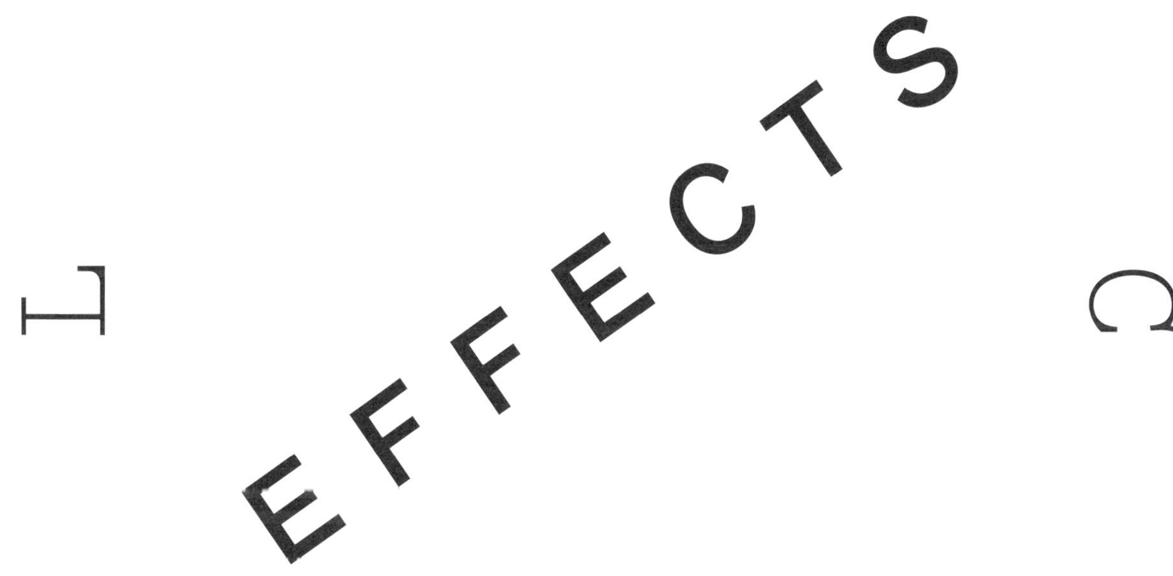

L C

L
I
F
E

L
I
K
E

Section 6
Special Effects: The Real as Spectacle

A I

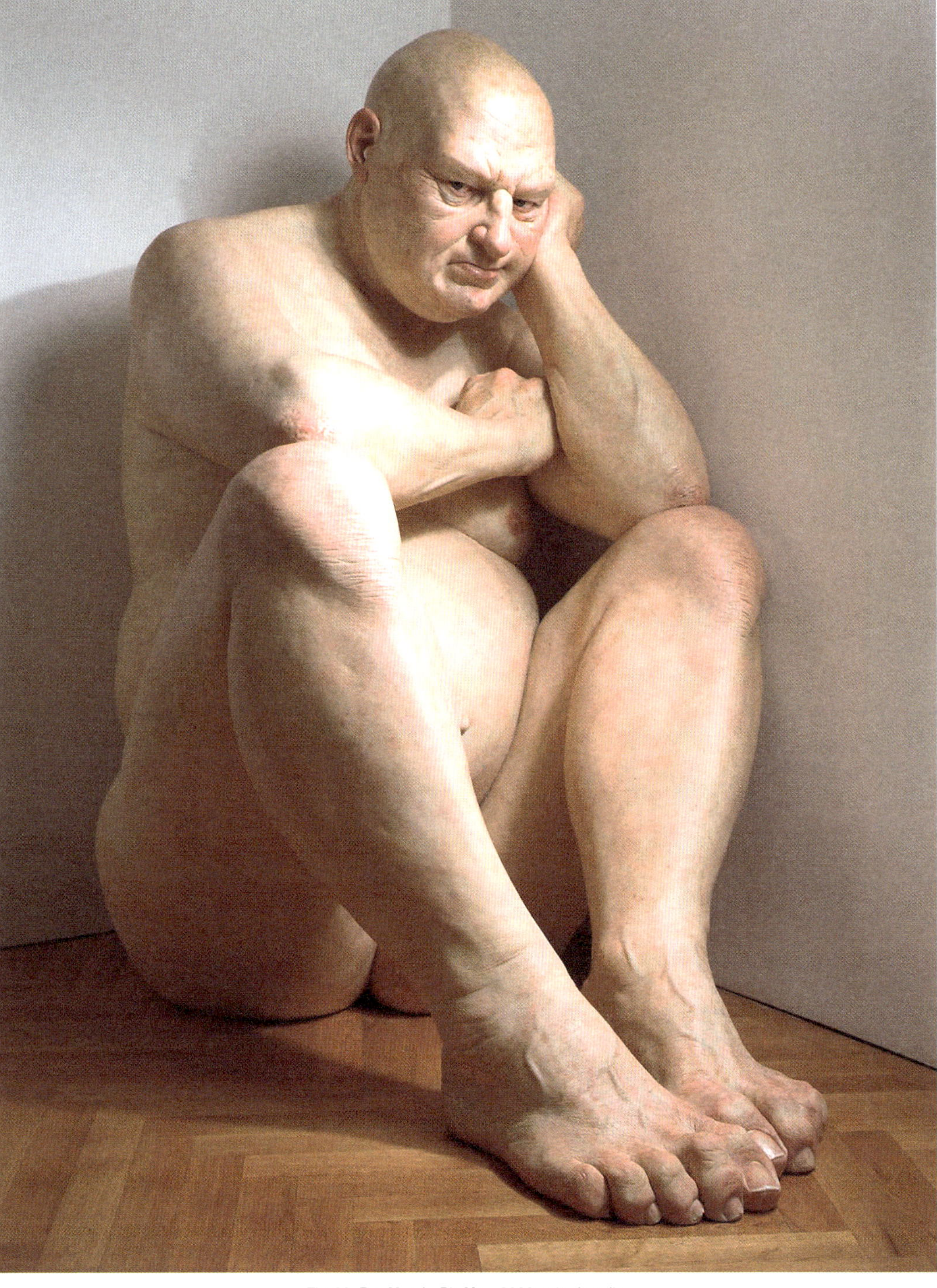

Fig. 26 Ron Mueck *Big Man* 2000 mixed media

Special Effects: The Real as Spectacle

While many artists since the 1960s have used hyperrealism to uncover the poetic, the uncanny, and the cerebral in ordinary things, others have employed fastidious craftsmanship in their work to shock, humor, surprise, or to invoke a *Through the Looking Glass* experience within the familiar. These works can alter one's perception through their surprising size, unusual installation, or sheer absurdity. These are artists who are intent on choreographing the experience of the audience, perhaps tapping into a childlike sense of wonder and amusement, while at the same time acting as magicians or tricksters, teasing out a sense of unease, disorientation, or even fear.

Maurizio Cattelan's use of trompe l'oeil realism veers beyond the surreal to the madcap. His sculptural tableaux often present objects or situations that play in the continuum from improbable to impossible: a lifelike horse embedded headfirst in a gallery wall; the Pope impaled by a meteorite; a kneeling child-size Hitler—all fabricated with exacting detail in a range of scales. The premise of *Untitled* (2001; plate 76)—a portal, in this case an elevator, that beckons with opening and closing doors and blinking lights, but which ultimately goes nowhere (even if one *were* six inches tall)—relates to the artist's project called *The Wrong Gallery* (fig. 28), which he conceived in 2002 with curators Massimiliano Gioni and Ali Subotnick. The "gallery," which was located prominently in New York's Chelsea gallery district, was marked by a steel and glass door, perfectly integrated with the neighborhood's slickly designed spaces embedded in former industrial and commercial architecture. However, the door could be peered into but not entered, an exercise in befuddlement, as is the case with many of Cattelan's pieces. His elevator, like most of his other works, was fabricated by outside sources, a strategy in keeping with the legacy of conceptual art, and with Cattelan's assertion that "I am not the best person to make it."[55]

It is not a coincidence that a handful of artists working in this vein have a background in special effects. Like Mueck, who has made dramatic, hyperrealistic renderings of the human form (fig. 26), often at a greatly exaggerated scale, Evan Penny's sculptural busts of ordinary individuals are enlarged several times their original size (2005; plate 77). Though we see these likenesses as fragments, and recognize them as sculptural reliefs on the gallery wall, they are nonetheless arresting. In addition to depicting facial features with a scrupulous level of detail (real hairs sprout from sculpturally formed follicles, etc.), Penny is well-versed in optical tricks such as anamorphism, where each angle of approach on the part of the viewer is carefully considered. His subjects are not reassuring sentries; they stare us down, confront us, make us feel uncomfortable.

Leandro Erlich's works confound as well by questioning how the body relates to the works being experienced. Often incorporating video, mirrors, architectural structures, or machines, Erlich's sculptural installations present the everyday urban experience as a funhouse of optical illusions. Like Edward Kienholz, whose tableaux placed the viewer in a kind of participatory three-dimensional film still, often complete with visual effects and sound, Erlich creates environments that transport the viewer—if only momentarily—into

(55) Alexi Worth, "A Fine Italian Hand," *New York Times T Magazine*, October 11, 2010: 70.

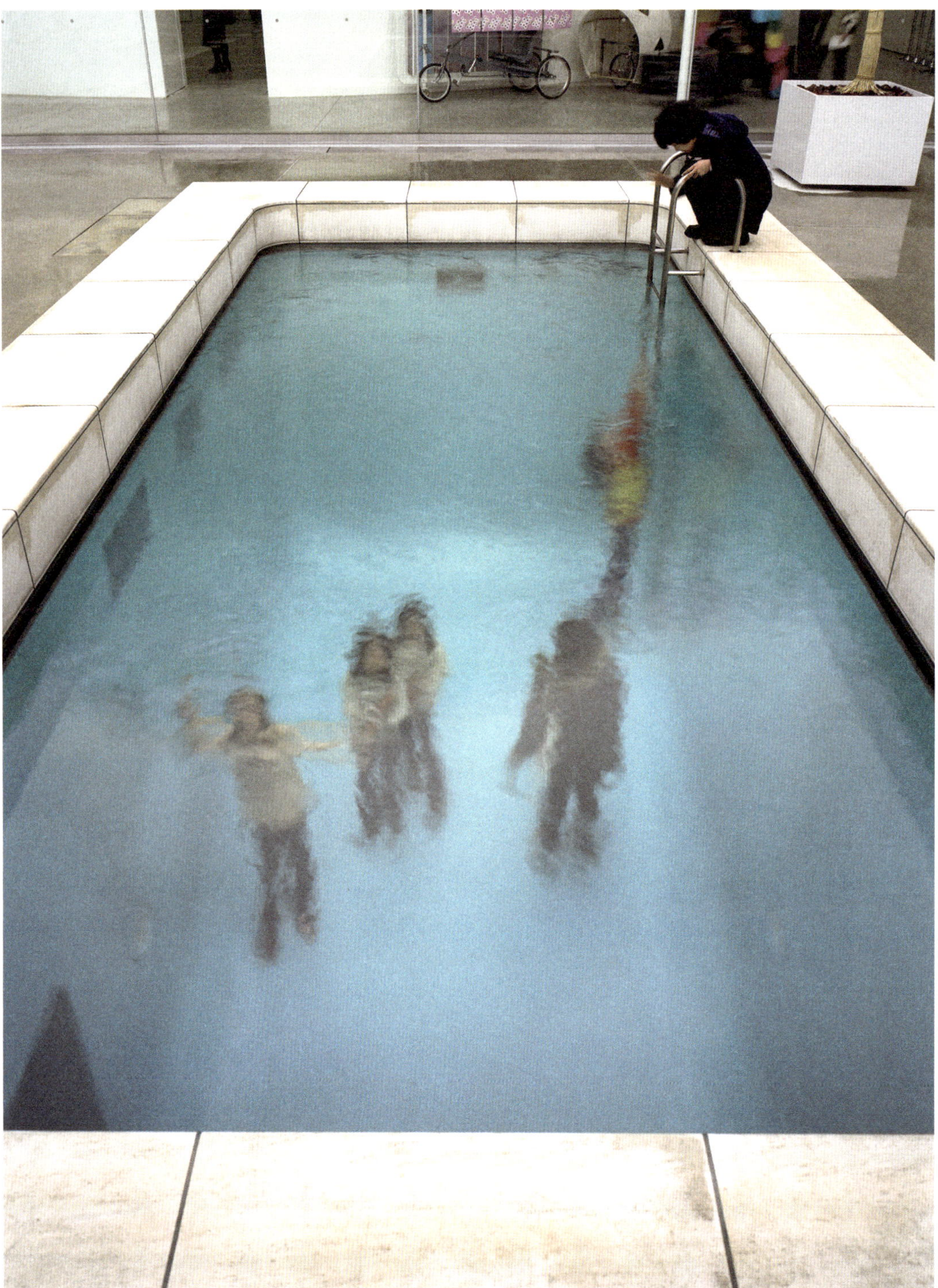

Fig. 27 Installation view of Leandro Erlich's *Swimming Pool* at the 21st Century Museum of Art of Kanazawa, Japan, 2008

another space. In the case of *Subway* (2010; plate 78), this is the Buenos Aires metro. Video here meshes seamlessly with sculpture as one stands before the subway door, gazing through the window at the passengers in the adjacent car. The moving image is disconcerting; not real, but convincing in a way that is magnetic and ultimately entertaining. In his larger sculptural environments such as *Swimming Pool* (1999; fig. 27), the interaction is all the more immersive, as Erlich builds veritable sets for our experience of his grand illusions.

Like artists working in sculpture who install works in unexpected locations, some whose practice engages with the moving image strive for subtlety. Jeon Joonho's video *The White House* (2005-2006; plate 79) presents a large-scale projection of ordinary US currency. It stands before us in all its glory, the White House as seen on the back side of the $20 bill, resolute, its engraving permanent and reassuring. Something, however, is amiss. Is it counterfeit? No, something is moving. Over the course of a half hour, an animated workman systematically begins painting out the windows of the building, "whitewashing" its facade.

When working in sculpture, a number of artists have continued to embrace scale shifts as a mechanism for viewer engagement. Like Oldenburg, whose Colossal Monuments (many made with his collaborative partner, the late Coosje van Bruggen), are extra-large exaggerations of everyday items—pool balls, banana peels, clothespins, shuttlecocks, and the like—intended for placement in the landscape, a number of artists today work with quotidian subject matter on a greatly exploded plane, elevating it to something grand and imposing. Robert Therrien's work has long investigated items of household use—plates, pots and pans, hardware—and distilled them into structures that toy with the language of minimalism as they flat-footedly present the everyday. His *No title (Folding table and chairs, dark brown)* (2008; fig. 25; plate 80) is a fully functional rendition of this ubiquitous institutional mainstay, painted in its various versions in utilitarian shades of brown, green, and gray. Under it, the viewer is Lilliputian, forced to experience the forest of steel legs like a child hiding among guests at a dinner party. Similarly, Jonathan Seliger's *Heartland*, a larger-than-life carton of milk (2010; plate 81) plays to this sense of wonder and amusement. Like Douke, Seliger is preoccupied with the sculptural rendering of containers—shopping bags, take-out cartons, everyday grocery items—which he often makes on a grand scale using techniques of auto-body fabrication, from the metal structures to their bright, imperviously painted surfaces. The works have a decidedly post-Pop flair, recalling Oldenburg's *Store*, for example, yet in their slickness and industrial fabrication aligning themselves, like Therrien's work or the objects of Katharina Fritsch, with a minimalist sensibility.

In various ways, the works noted here all cater to a sense of play, and the idea that perhaps what surrounds us is remarkable enough in its literalness for us to take notice from time to time. By allowing a fluency with the techniques of industrial fabrication to remain on equal footing with the handmade, borrowing from the language of the entertainment industry, and embracing experiential one-liners as a means of launching to more conceptual ends, artists who work with realistic content in this way create works that edge toward spectacle while the subject matter remains humble.

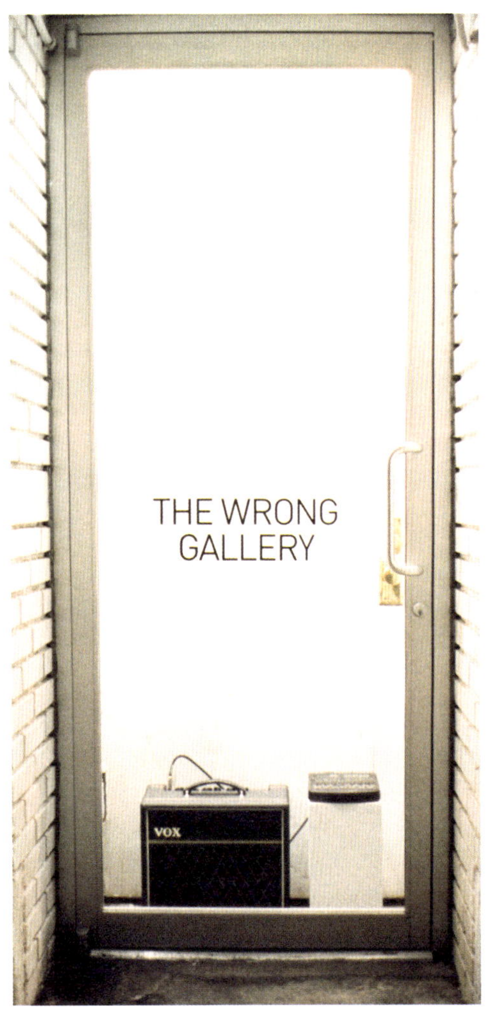

Fig. 28 Installation view of Martin Creed's *Work No. 122: All the sounds on a drum machine* (1995–2000) at the Wrong Gallery, New York, 2002

* * *

In a series of statements from 1985 entitled "Fifty Helpful Hints on the Art of the Everyday," artist Allen Ruppersberg wrote, "The act of copying something allows the use of things as they are, without altering their original nature. They can then be used with ideas about art on a fifty-fifty basis, and create something entirely new."(56) By employing mimetic realism as a vehicle by which to consider the experience of ordinary life, the artists gathered here have persistently investigated the processes of vision and perception, harnessing them as works of art. In an age where outlandishness is hard to achieve, and shock is relative, the experience of encountering the utterly mundane reimagined through an artist's careful hand or sly recontextualization can appear striking, even radical. Simplicity can be beautiful, but also startling. Ordinary things, when presented anew, have the capacity to disturb, bewilder, or delight. Subjects found by accident can have surprising resonance, as Richter once noted: "I consider many amateur photographs better than the best Cézanne."(57)

An artist's process of seeking out neutral subjects that can then become something on which to project other ideas is central to conceptualism as well as to the use of trompe l'oeil in contemporary art. We are currently in an era of post-readymade art, where the simple act of removing an object from the context of everyday life and denoting it as art calls into question a now-sustained legacy of such acts, and an acknowledgment of this rich history. Fusing this sensibility with an abiding interest in the average stuff of life has continued to provide potency for artists both conceptually and materially.

The artists in *Lifelike* have revisited the notion of what it means to become, in the words of LeWitt, "the machine that makes the art." Whether they strive in this endeavor for process over product or product by way of process, this preoccupation with "trying and failing to be a machine," as Rostovsky has mused, is often what produces futility, thus poetry. And Oshiro has said, "The work I'm doing doesn't look like I'm making decisions."(59) His uncomplicated statement is telling, as it underscores the adage of how appearances can deceive; yet more importantly, alludes to what is a key strategy deployed by each artist considered here, in which straightforward presentation of the simulated object or image masks what is an elaborate set of decisions and more often than not a rigorous studio practice and intense interest in labor and craftsmanship. Working within deceptively simple means, each of the artists in this exhibition has forged a carefully assembled set of criteria about the construction, presentation, and reception of their art.

To the latter point, how then should art of this nature be received? To be sure, the recognition of imitation has within it powers of both enchantment and disorientation, or, as Baudrillard called the sensation, "a slight vertigo—that of some previous life."(59) If an encounter with carefully fashioned reality in the context of art causes us to be thrown off balance, if we find ourselves startled by something simple where we expect to find complexity, if something unremarkable sustains our attention, we have been affected by the imitation. Art has always had at its edge an inherent unsteadiness, as artists push further into new, uncharted terrain. The persistence of the real in contemporary art is an often unexpected reminder of this possibility.

(56)
Allen Ruppersberg, "Fifty Helpful Hints on the Art of the Everyday," in *The Secret of Life and Death* (Los Angeles: Museum of Contemporary Art/Santa Barbara: Black Sparrow Press, 1985), 111-114. Reprinted in Stephen Johnstone, ed., *The Everyday: Documents of Contemporary Art* (London: Whitechapel Gallery, and Cambridge, MA: MIT Press, 2008), 56.

(57)
Gerhard Richter, "Text for exhibition catalogue, Galerie h Hanover, 1966," in Hans-Ulrich Obrist, ed., *Gerhard Richter: The Daily Practice of Painting: Writings and Interviews 1962-1993* (Cambridge, MA: MIT Press; London: Anthony d'Offay Gallery, 1995), 55.

(58)
Kaz Oshiro interviewed by Glen Helfand, in *Kaz Oshiro: Common Noise*, exh. cat. (Paris: Galerie Frank Elbaz, 2007), 26.

(59)
Jean Baudrillard, "The Trompe l'oeil," in *Calligram: Essays in New Art History from France*, ed. Norman Bryson (Cambridge, MA: Cambridge University Press, 1988), 56.

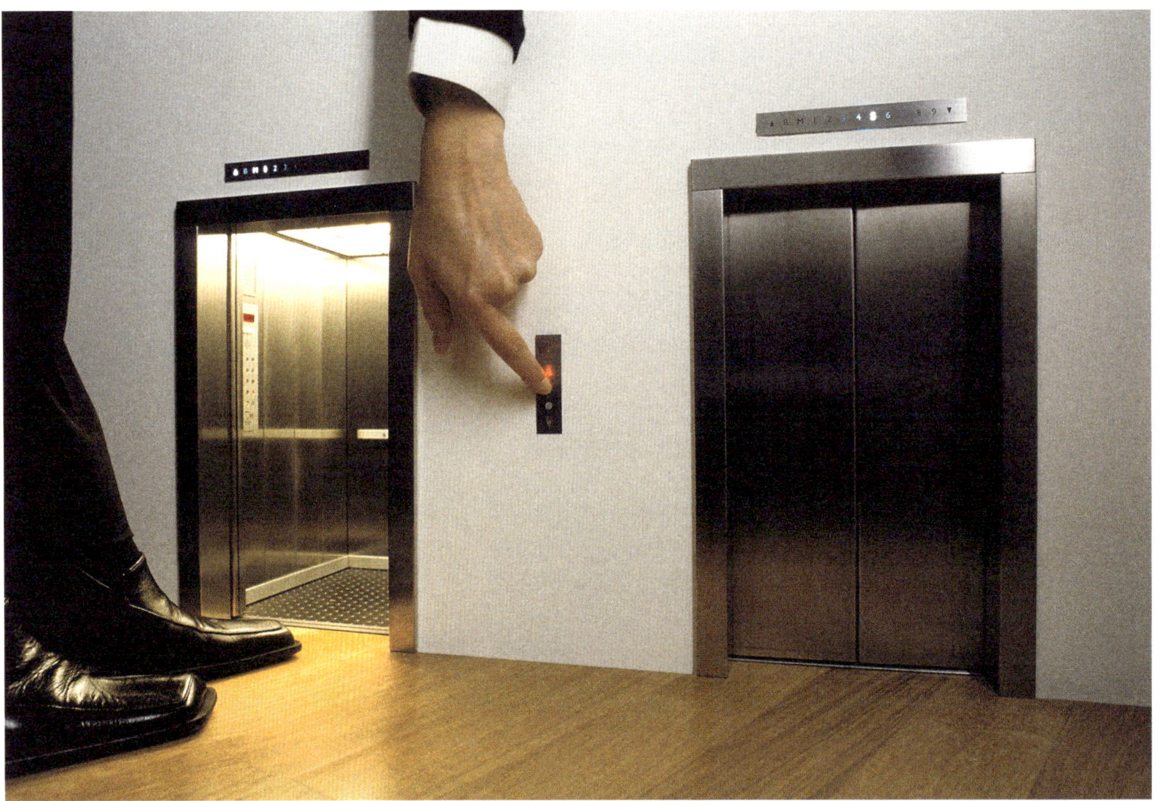

Plate 76. Maurizio Cattelan *Untitled* 2001 (installation view) mixed media/assemblage/collage; powered device, miniaturized elevator cabs with computer chips, working mechanical doors and lights

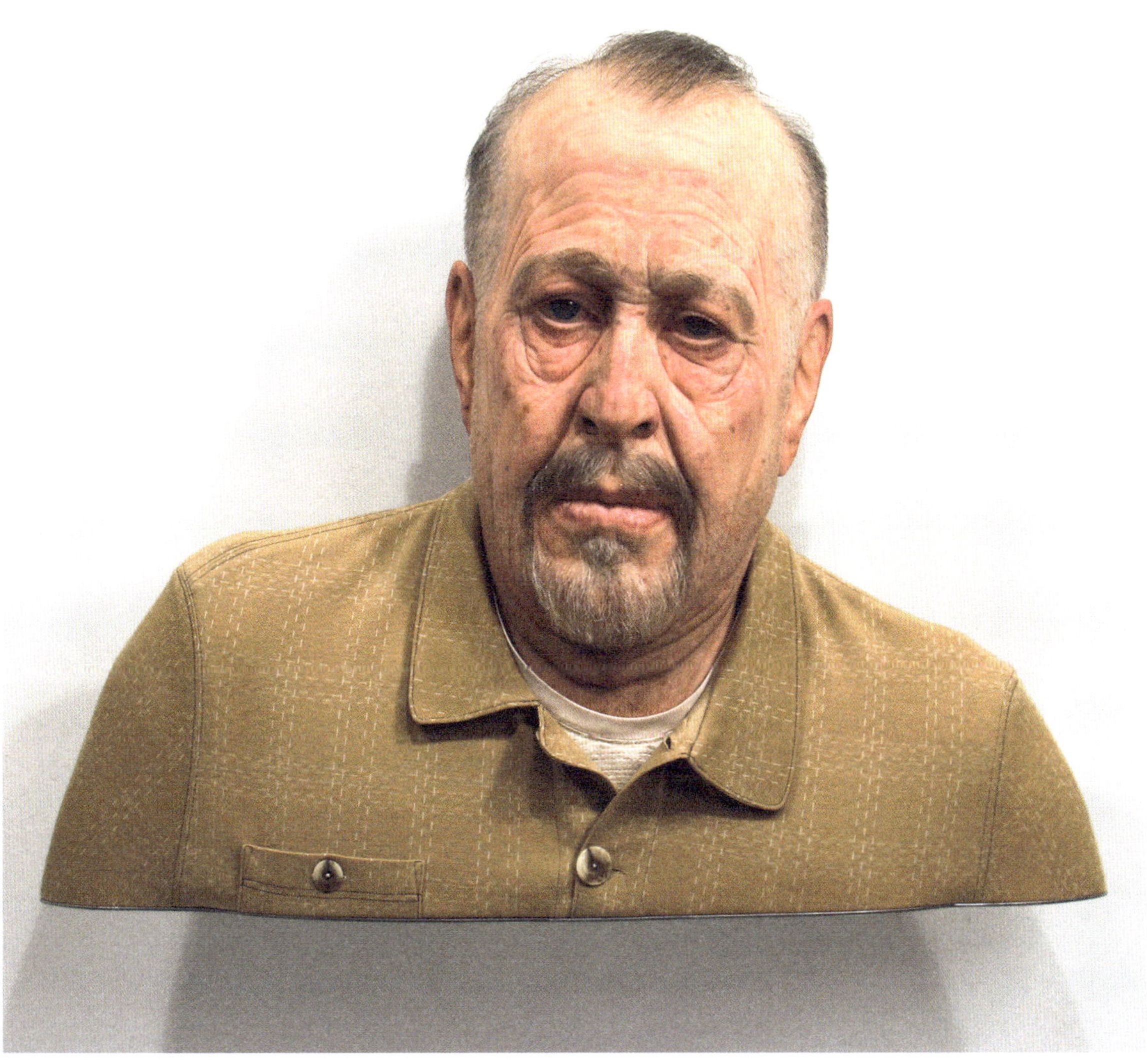

Plate 77. Evan Penny *(Old) No One—in Particular # 6, Series 2* 2005 silicone, pigment, hair, fabric, aluminum

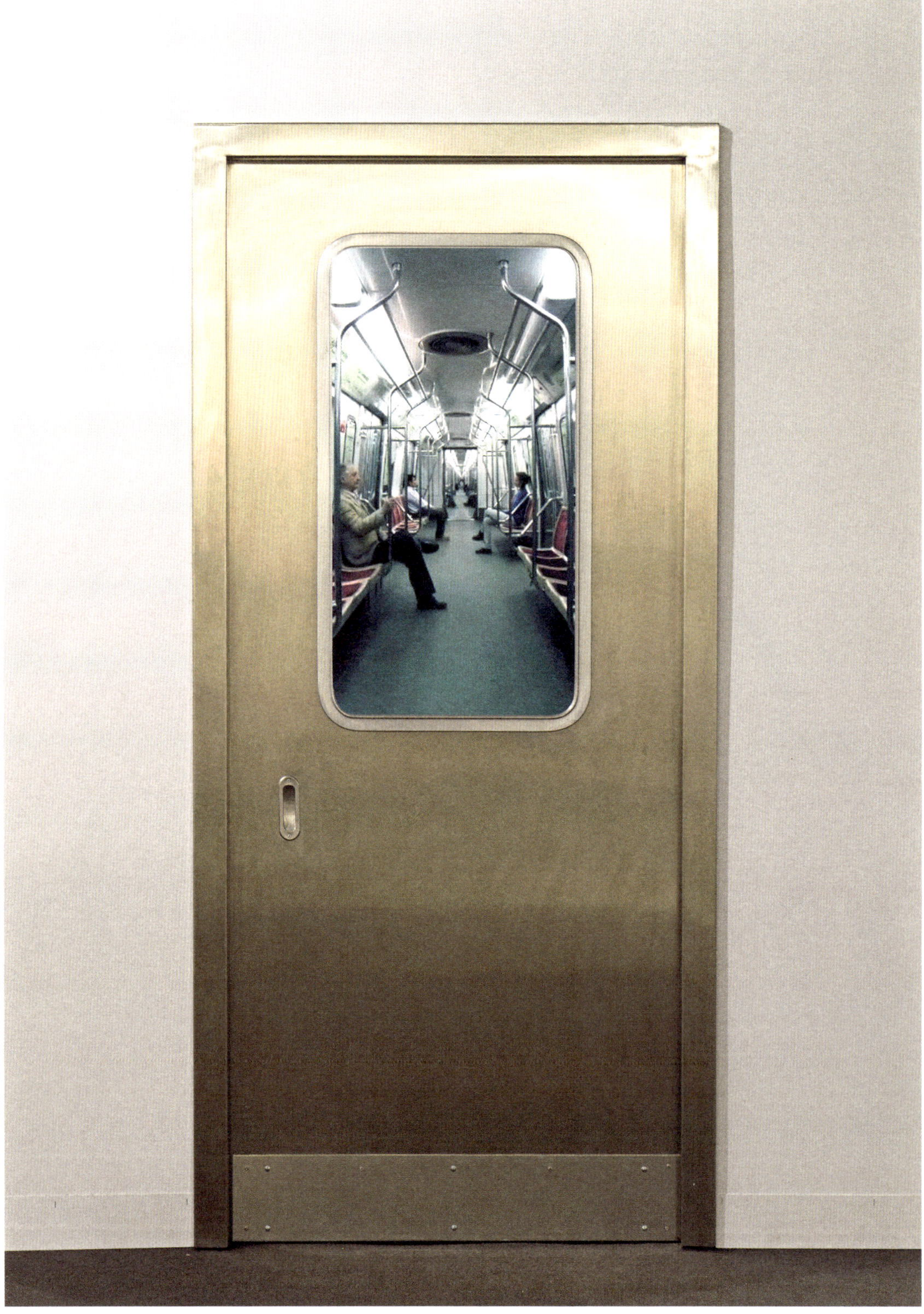

Plate 78. Leandro Erlich *Subway* 2010 Blu-ray disc (color, sound), stainless-steel structure, glass, certificate of authenticity

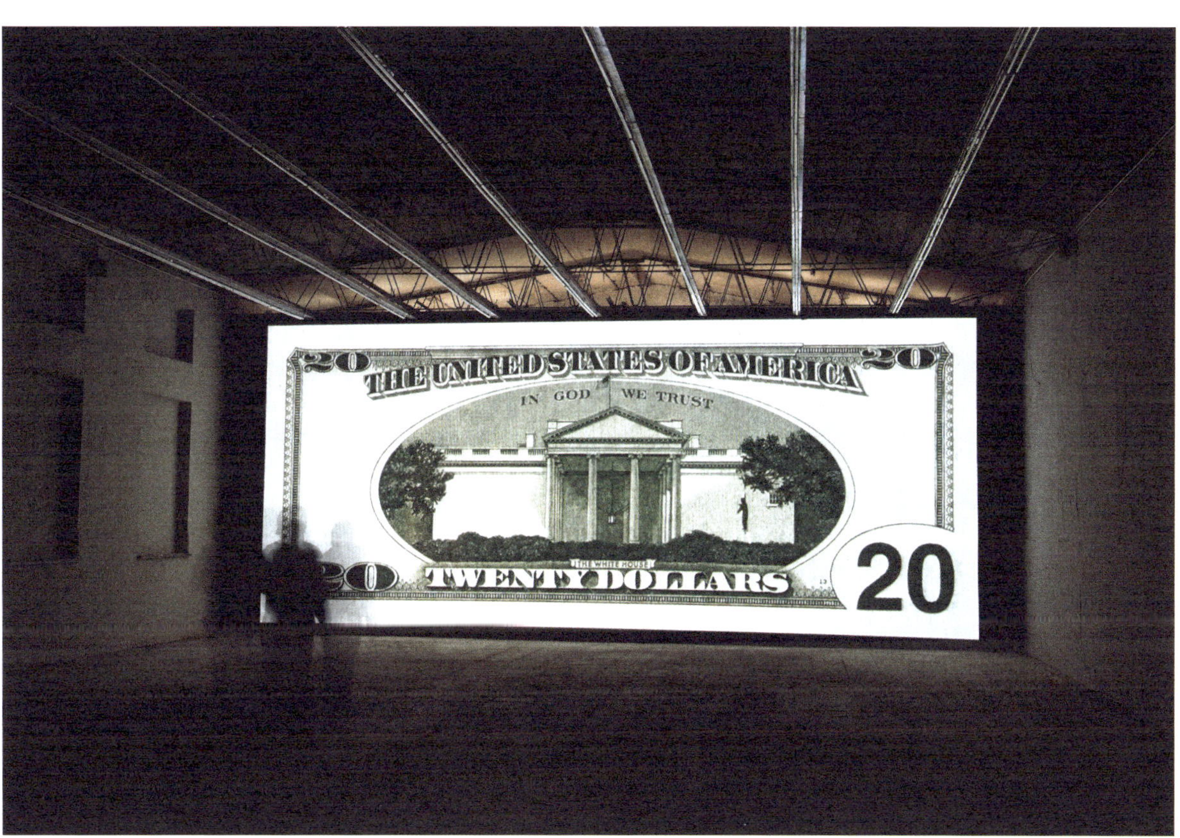

Plate 79. Jeon Joonho *The White House* 2005–2006 (installation view at Arario Beijing) digital animation

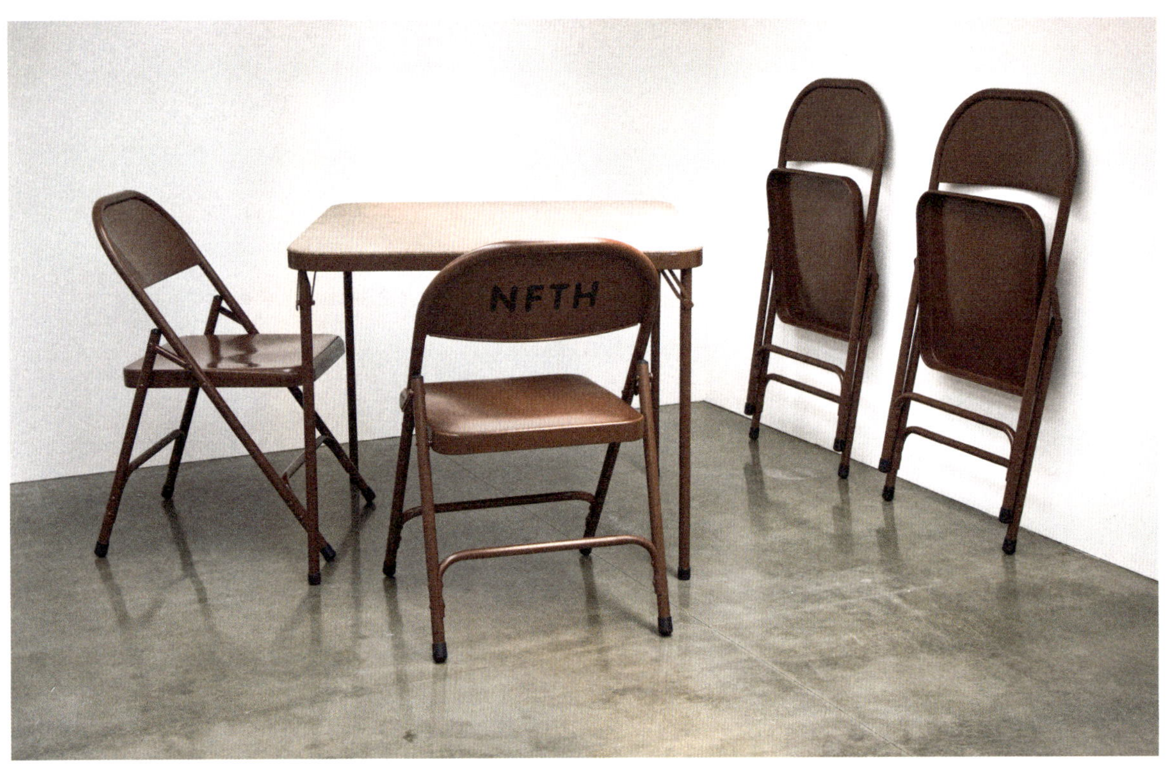

Plate 80. Robert Therrien *No title (Folding table and chairs, dark brown)* 2007 painted metal, fabric

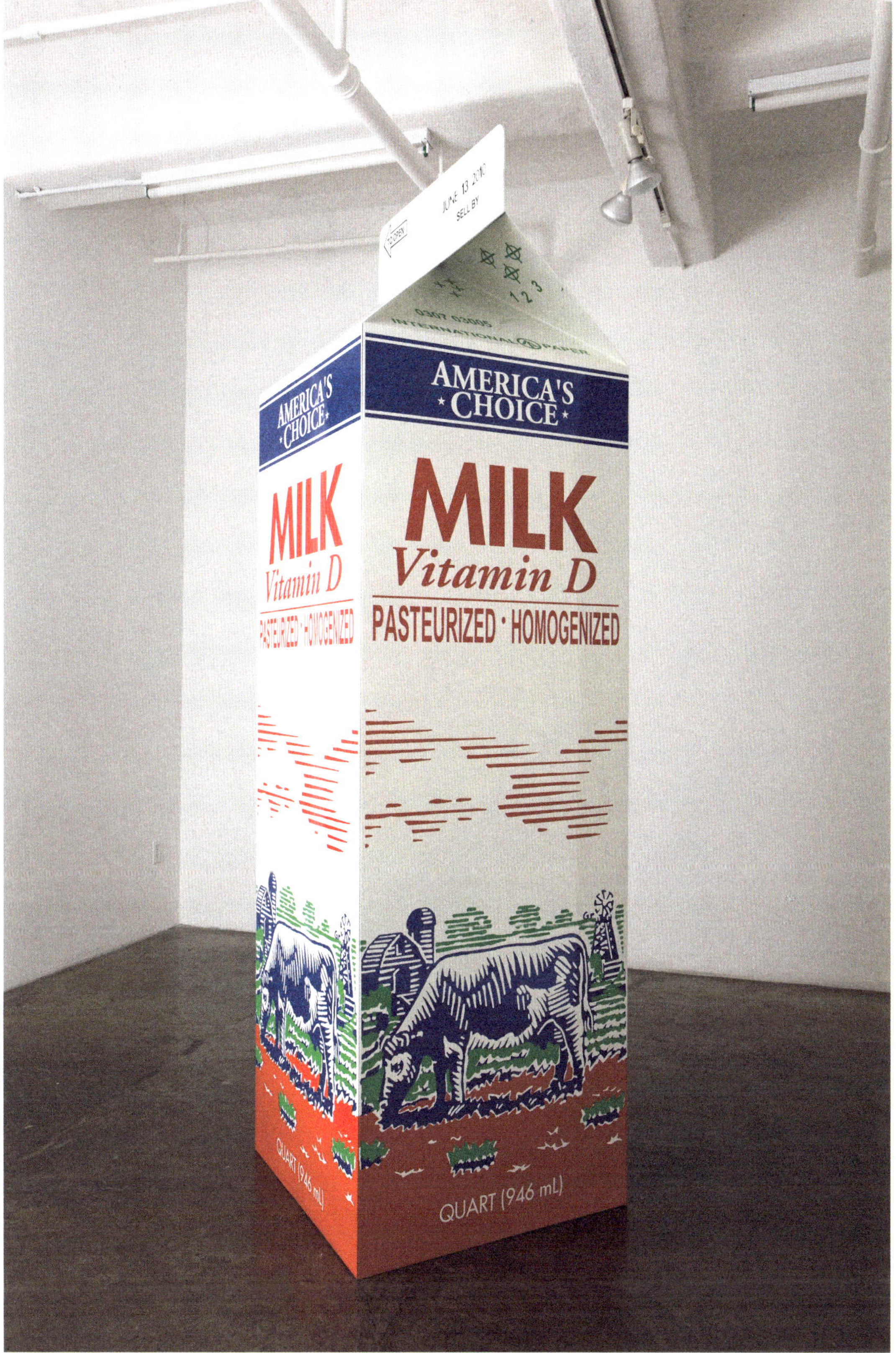

Plate 81. Jonathan Seliger *Heartland* 2010 enamel on bronze

F E A

II.–IV.

D T

TEXTS

Essays by
Michael Lobel, Rochelle Steiner,
and Josiah McElheny

E R U

L I F E L I K E

Fig. 1 Alex Hay *Legal Pad Sheet* 1967 spray lacquer and stencil on linen

II.
REALISM, CIRCA 1970

MICHAEL LOBEL

There are numerous historical precedents for an art of lifelike representation. These include the polychromed sculptures of ancient Greece, which put the lie to the popular belief that classical sculpture was all pristine, gleaming whiteness (fig. 2), the trompe l'oeil still lifes of nineteenth-century American painting, and even the famed twentieth-century avant-gardist Marcel Duchamp's final, posthumously revealed work, a disturbing tableau of a prone, nude female in a sylvan setting. Looking outside the field of fine art proper, there is also a long tradition of realistic wax sculpture, its most famous incarnation being the popular displays of Madame Tussauds. In the field of contemporary art, one of the more noteworthy manifestations of this impulse can be located in the artistic and critical discourses on realism that flourished right around 1970.

Even those having some familiarity with recent art might take pause at the claim that there was an efflorescence of realism circa 1970. That period, following on the emergence of Pop and Minimalism in the early 1960s, witnessed a veritable explosion of groundbreaking, so-called dematerialized practices in art, from conceptualism to body art, from performance to video. One doesn't, then, ordinarily think of realist, figurative art—particularly in the traditional mediums of painting and sculpture—as particularly relevant to that moment. Nevertheless, in line with the broader expansion of artistic possibilities, realism had its day as well. Art historians have not given it a great deal of attention, but it certainly played a lively role at the time in museums and galleries, in newspaper columns, and on magazine pages. An investigation of realist art around 1970, then, offers the opportunity to revisit certain practices and episodes that may not have received substantial historical scrutiny, while providing a backdrop for impulses that continue to play a major role in contemporary art-making.

Upon reflection, realist modes and notions of the "real" had profound currency in the visual arts of the sixties decade. In 1960, French art critic Pierre Restany coined the term Nouveau Réalisme to describe the efforts of a group of artists devoted to radical experiments in their practice, from Yves Klein's performative actions to Niki de Saint Phalle's gunshot-activated paintings. When the first stirrings of what would come to be called Pop Art appeared on the New York art scene soon after, they also were categorized early on as a form of new realism, thus connecting them to the artistic experiments already taking place across the Atlantic. Later in the decade, the Museum of Modern Art (MoMA) in New York dedicated an exhibition to showcasing *The Art of the Real*.(1) Soon after, in a discussion of the historical category of Realism and its ambiguous relationship to the "highly problematical concept of reality," scholar Linda Nochlin pointed out that the MoMA show "consisted not—as the uninitiated might have expected—of recognizable views of people, things or places, but of large striped or stained canvases and mammoth constructions of plywood, plastic or metal."(2) Nochlin's point was that even Minimalist sculptures could come to be lodged under the rubric of "the real," though in their case that term implied not the traditional workings of illusionistic art but rather the brute facticity

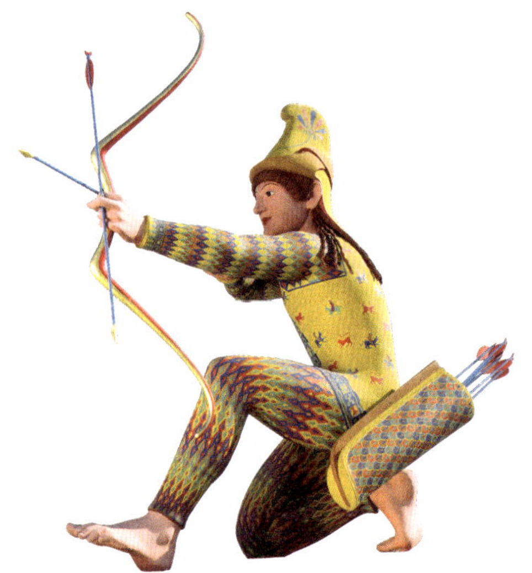

Fig. 2 Ulrike and Vinzenz Brinkmann in cooperation with Hermann Pflug and Ina Kleiss *Colour reconstruction of the Archer* (West pediment, Aphaia temple Aigina) 2006

(1) E. C. Goossen, *The Art of the Real: USA 1948-1968*, exh. cat. (New York: Museum of Modern Art, 1968).

(2) Linda Nochlin, *Realism* (Harmondsworth, England: Penguin Books, 1971), 13.

of the materials and processes involved in their production.

Although now better known as the veritable founder of the field of feminist art history, Nochlin was, at the time, deeply engaged in the scholarly analysis of realism, both as a broader category and, more specifically, within the context of the nineteenth-century Realist movement in art and literature. She was also interested in relating her historical research to contemporary practices. That was made evident in a substantive two-part article, "The Realist Criminal and the Abstract Law," published in successive issues of *Art in America* in late 1973.(3) The relationship between the historical and the contemporary was staged on the opening spread of the first installment, which featured a Jan van Eyck portrait of a man facing off against a signature frontal, photo-based portrait by contemporary painter Chuck Close. In her piece, Nochlin covered expansive terrain, ranging from broader analytic reflections on the workings of realism to a consideration of specific historical variants of realist art from antiquity to the present. In the course of her analysis, she shared some valuable insights of use in the context of the present exhibition, chief among them that:

> while realism may be a perennial phenomenon, one might do better to talk about "realisms" rather than a single unitary "realism." A wide range and variety of stylistic possibilities are subsumed under the general category. Indeed, it might be fruitful to think of realism as a country on a map, surrounded by other countries whose borders often merge imperceptibly with it.(4)

While addressing herself to a longer historical trajectory, Nochlin's scholarly investigations were clearly informed by current circumstances. Her article was in part a defense of contemporary realism, after a long period during which mainstream modernism had largely discredited it. A sense of the marginalized position of contemporary realist art is conveyed by the title of her piece; the triumphant successes of New York School painters such as Jackson Pollock, Mark Rothko, and Barnett Newman had, by mid-century, installed abstraction as the law of the land, with realism as its outlaw counterpart. Nochlin laid a good share of the blame for this set of circumstances on critic Clement Greenberg, whose influential model proposed that the developmental logic of modernist painting demanded that it rid itself of the ostensible impurity of narrative figuration. In so doing, Greenberg had set up an absolute opposition between realism and abstraction.

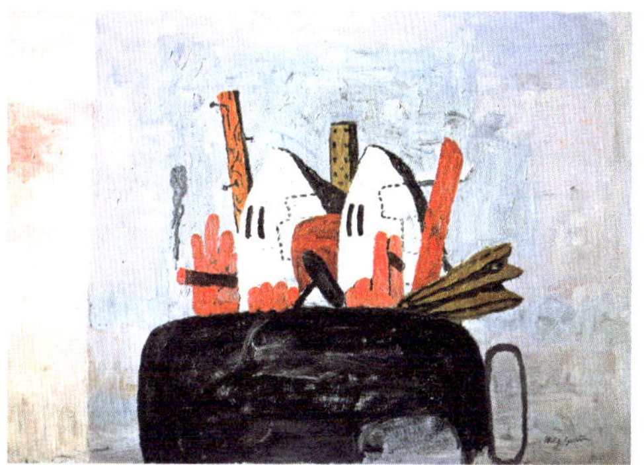

Fig. 3 Philip Guston *Edge of Town* 1969 oil on canvas

In spite of the categorical pronouncements, it's not as if figuration had somehow been completely banished, even from within the storied ranks of the New York School. It maintained a presence at the very center of that group, most conspicuously in Willem de Kooning's continued back-and-forth between abstraction and figuration (as evidenced by his legendary *Woman* series), and it persisted in the work of respected practitioners such as Larry Rivers, Grace Hartigan, and Fairfield Porter. It was also a key feature of what can be identified as second-generation New York School work, most notably the neo-Dada experiments of Robert Rauschenberg and Jasper Johns, as in the consistent play in Johns' work between the real object and its symbolic representation. Nonetheless, even as late as 1970 there were signs that figuration was still a no-go for members of the Abstract Expressionist generation. This was made apparent by the notoriously negative reactions to Philip Guston's exhibition, in the fall of that year, of a body of paintings that featured crudely rendered, cartoonlike imagery (fig. 3).

The harsh reception that Guston's show received probably had less to do with his embrace of figuration per se than with his seemingly ham-handed approach and his

(3) Linda Nochlin, "The Realist Criminal and the Abstract Law," *Art in America* 61, no. 5 (September-October 1973): 54-61; and "The Realist Criminal and the Abstract Law II," *Art in America* 61, no. 6 (November-December 1973): 97-103.

(4) Nochlin, "The Realist Criminal and the Abstract Law," 55.

perceived rejection of abstract painting, with which he had long been identified.(5) There was clearly significant interest from other quarters in taking stock of the figurative impulse in contemporary painting, as exemplified by the Whitney Museum of American Art's exhibition *22 Realists*, which had opened in the first months of 1970. In his essay for the show's catalogue, curator James Monte separated the exhibiting artists into two camps: those dedicated to the more traditional aims of pictorial illusionism (a group that included William Bailey, Alfred Leslie, Philip Pearlstein, and Sidney Tillim), and those whom he categorized as Post-Pop realists, among them Robert Bechtle, John Clem Clarke, Richard Estes (fig. 4), Audrey Flack, and Malcolm Morley.(6)

It is instructive to revisit the term "Post-Pop realism." Although now largely forgotten, it was widely used at the time to refer to a range of approaches that took photographic images as their jumping-off point.(7) Sixties Pop, in both Europe and America, had vigorously imported modes of photomechanical production into painting, whether in Andy Warhol's use of the photographic silkscreen technique or Gerhard Richter's signature blurred imagery. These experiments had opened the door for artists to take the photograph as the primary subject of their work. And that wasn't the only shift that Pop had set in motion. As James Mellow pointed out in a 1970 *New York Times* piece on contemporary representational painting, "...one of the odd services of Pop Art, when it was introduced in the early Sixties, was that it raised the old issue of content, or subject matter, in art. The recognizable subject in painting became fashionable—even avant-garde."(8) A reconsideration of the term Post-Pop realism helps return us to a moment when observers were still trying to figure out what the resurgence of realism after the reign of modernist abstraction meant, and how best to identify and categorize it.

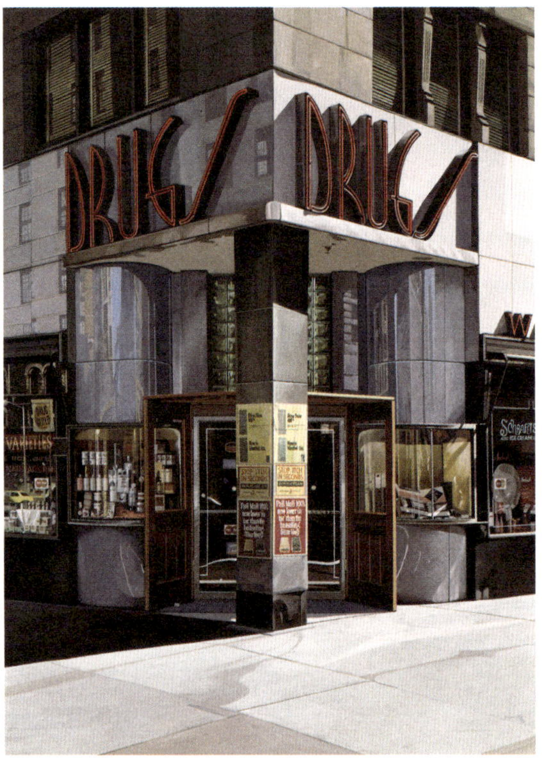

Fig. 4 Richard Estes *Drugs* 1970 oil on canvas

Eventually, that term, like other, alternative labels that were floated at the time ("Radical Realism" and "Sharp-Focus Realism among them),"(9) ceded ground to the name by which these impulses have generally come to be identified: Photorealism. This is usually how art history works, with one term winning out over others. Still, the present exhibition, in seeking to revisit the tradition of carefully wrought, lifelike representation in contemporary art, may prompt

(5)
Hilton Kramer penned a legendarily withering attack on Guston titled "A Mandarin Pretending to Be a Stumblebum," *New York Times*, October 25, 1970, B27.

(6)
James Monte, *22 Realists*, exh. cat. (New York: Whitney Museum of American Art, 1970).

(7)
In addition to Monte in his catalogue essay, the term was used by Douglas Davis in a 1972 *Newsweek* article on the appearance of various strains of photorealism and super realism on the contemporary art scene and by Carter Ratcliff in *Art International* in an extended critical reflection on the *22 Realists* show and related instances of realist painting in New York. See Douglas Davis, "Nosing Out Reality," *Newsweek* 70, August 14, 1972: 58; and Carter Ratcliff, "New York," *Art International* 14, no. 4 (April 1970): 69.

(8)
James R. Mellow, "When 'What' Is as Important as 'How,' " *New York Times*, March 1, 1970, sec. 2, 25.

(9)
Radical Realism was the name of a 1971 exhibition at the Museum of Contemporary Art, Chicago, that included work by Malcolm Morley, Ralph Goings, Duane Hanson, John Clem Clarke, and John DeAndrea. *Sharp-Focus Realism* was the title of a 1972 show at the Sidney Janis Gallery in New York that included the work of Goings, Morley, Hanson, DeAndrea, Robert Cottingham, Richard Estes, Jann Haworth, and Marilyn Levine. For a contemporary critical piece that comments on the surfeit of potential names for the emerging movement, see Paul Richard, "Post-Pop: Radical Realism," *Washington Post*, January 15, 1972, D6.

us to scrutinize the ways in which the category of Photorealism came to be defined in the first place. Most of the impetus to do so, in recent years, has come from European scholars and curators, particularly in the form of exhibitions such as *Hyperréalismes, USA 1965-1975* at the Musée d'Art moderne et contemporain in Strasbourg and *Picturing America: Fotorealismus der 70er Jahre* at the Deutsche Guggenheim in Berlin.[10] No doubt Photorealism, like Pop before it, is appealing to European audiences for the profound sense of Americanness it conveys, particularly in its presentation of an American landscape of advertising signage, automobiles, and consumer goods. On another front, we still lack a substantive account of how that movement was shaped by savvy art dealers such as Ivan Karp and Louis Meisel, who were surely influenced by the legendary gallerist Leo Castelli's earlier role in defining Pop Art. How might the dealers' views of the proper subject matter of Photorealism have led to the marginalization of such artists as Harold Bruder and Howard Kanovitz, who were both included in early shows such as *22 Realists* but whose chosen subjects were not as readily assimilable to the category as it came to be defined? And how did the Photorealist label likely incline the artists so identified to focus on certain types of subject matter at the expense of others?

Vija Celmins offers an illuminating test case, since her work bears all the hallmarks of a Photorealist approach. She has long based her pictures on photographic sources. This feature of her work was already present by the mid-1960s, when she was foregrounding her dependence on mass-media imagery, as in her 1965 painted rendering of a cover of *Time* magazine (fig. 5). Her subject matter also intersected with that of the Photorealist painters. The windshield view in her 1966 canvas *Freeway* (see page 26), along with her contemporaneous renderings of airplanes, resonate with the vehicular preoccupations of artists such as Ralph Goings and Don Eddy. More broadly, her early interest in common objects (lamps, hot plates, fans) aligned her with a post-Pop sensibility. In spite of these connections, however, Celmins was never categorized as a Photorealist.[11] This could be chalked up to any number of factors. Perhaps it was because she was based in Southern California (although that didn't stop Eddy from joining the club) or because of her gender (the central members of the group were all men, save for Audrey Flack and Janet Fish).

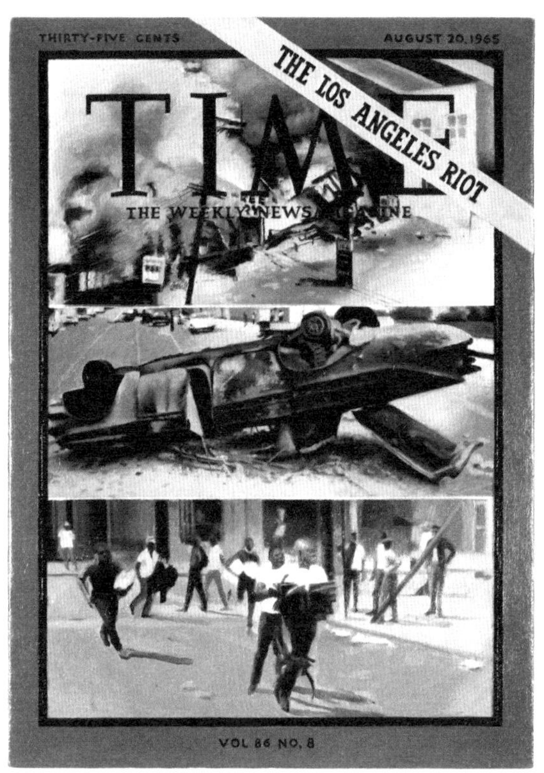

Fig. 5 Vija Celmins *Time Magazine Cover* 1965 oil on canvas

Or perhaps it is that Celmins' approach bears distinctive features that placed it outside the bounds of the category as it was largely defined. By the late 1960s, she already displayed an idiosyncratic choice of subjects (the surface of the moon, an unbroken expanse of ocean) that marked her work as quietly contemplative, at least in relation to the shiny modern surfaces on which such painters as Goings, Eddy, and Richard Estes were focusing. Her sixties work was also pointedly political. For instance, in rendering the aforementioned *Time* magazine cover, she selected an image that depicted vignettes from the recent Los Angeles riots. Similarly, the aircraft she portrayed were fighter planes—vehicles of

(10) For the publications accompanying these exhibitions, see Jean-Claude Lebensztejn and Patrick Javault, *Hyperréalismes, USA 1965-1975* (Strasbourg: Les Musées de Strasbourg, 2003) and Valerie L. Hillings, *Picturing America: Photorealism in the 1970s* (Berlin: Deutsche Guggenheim, 2009).

(11) Not only did she not exhibit with these artists or at the galleries that showcased their work, but there is only one passing mention of Celmins in Gregory Battcock's *Super Realism: A Critical Anthology* (New York: E. P. Dutton, 1975). That mention is made, not surprisingly, by Nochlin in her essay "Some Women Realists," 77.

militarized destruction and death. Celmins shared an early interest in political imagery with Flack, who began her own painterly engagement with photography by rendering documentary news pictures of subjects such as John F. Kennedy in Dallas and a Vietnam War protest march. It is worth noting that Nochlin, too, was engaged with exploring the contemporary connections between realist art and (feminist) politics.(12)

There is another aspect of Celmins' practice worthy of attention: early on, she experimented with making sculptures, including a group of oversized replicas of common objects. Several of these, particularly a pencil and a pink eraser, underscore her interest in process, in that they give monumental form to the humble tools she used to create her work. Another piece, *Untitled (Comb)* of 1970 (plate 13), while not a representation of an art-making implement per se, nonetheless constitutes a self-reflexive gesture.(13) Although one would ordinarily expect a common comb to be a mass-produced item, Celmins chose as her subject a handmade one, which is made clear by the text she dutifully re-created on the object's surface.(14) Her decision to craft a careful (if enlarged) replica of a handmade consumer product represents a complex and clever comment on some of Pop's basic principles. She may have also intended this as a response to the art being made around her. Based in Southern California, she was no doubt familiar with so-called Finish Fetish sculptors such as Craig Kauffman and Larry Bell, who were making sleek objects in such cutting-edge materials as vacuum-formed plastic and vacuum-coated glass.(15) While the glossy surface of *Untitled (Comb)* connects it to the general Finish Fetish look, Celmins' commitment to detailed verism puts her at a remove from the simplified geometric forms generally favored by those artists.

Celmins had a compatriot of sorts in Alex Hay (fig. 1), who was similarly rendering gargantuan versions of such humble objects as a paper bag (plate 3) and a paper airplane. Like Celmins, he didn't limit himself to sculpture, as he also enlarged items in painted form. While Hay's lack of notoriety is no doubt due in part to his subsequent departure from the New York art world, his and Celmins' practice of working across mediums points to another limitation of Photorealism as a category. That label came to be associated primarily if not exclusively with painting; the term's invocation of the essentially two-dimensional condition of the photograph implicitly excludes three-dimensional works (even if sculptors such as Duane Hanson and John DeAndrea did show alongside the Photorealist painters). The impact of realism at the time, however, was in no way confined to the medium of painting. The Walker Art Center had a hand in examining that very issue when, in 1970, it mounted an exhibition that focused on the figurative impulse in recent three-dimensional work. If that show, titled *Figures/Environments*, offers further evidence for the widespread interest in realist art circa 1970, it also attests to the sweeping transformations in artistic practice that had occurred in the preceding decade.

Figures/Environments included the work of eight contemporary artists, each of them working, in one fashion or another, with the human figure. The exhibited works all took the form of sculptural installations or environments. Alex Katz supplied tableaux assembled from flat, painted cutouts (fig. 6); Red Grooms constructed a walk-through re-creation of a discount department store in madcap, cartoonish form; Jann Haworth, George Segal, Hanson, and Paul Thek all offered up sculptural simulacra of the human figure; Lynton Wells contributed stuffed-cloth forms imprinted with photographic transfers; and Robert Whitman produced a disturbing mixed-media installation, with scenes of eating and regurgitation projected onto a mirrored tabletop. In the show's catalogue, the Walker's director at the time,

(12)
As noted, Nochlin's other major critical investment at this time was in developing a feminist approach to art history and criticism. In a 1974 article for *Arts Magazine*, "Some Women Realists," she brought together her two major fields of interest, surveying the myriad ways that women artists had made use of realist idioms from the nineteenth century to the present. See "Some Women Realists," reprinted in Linda Nochlin, *Women, Art, and Power and Other Essays* (New York: Harper & Row, 1988), 86-108.

(13)
However, it does recall the comblike implements that decorative painters often used to create faux wood graining, with a patterning much like that on the surface of Celmins' piece.

(14)
The writing on the comb not only includes the words "Handmade," but also "Balloid," which was the name of an imported brand from Switzerland. Could this constitute another self-reflexive reference, in this case to Celmins' status as a European immigrant to the United States?

(15)
The usual installation of Celmins' *Untitled (Comb)*, with the more than six-foot-tall object leaning up against a wall, gives it a strong resemblance to the contemporaneous plank pieces of John McCracken, another sculptor identified with the Finish Fetish group.

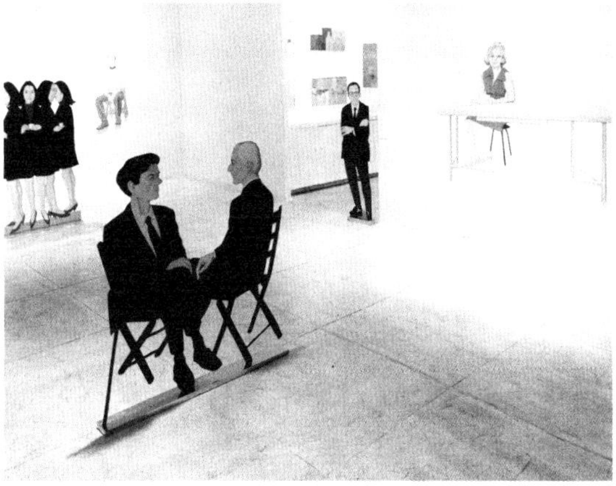

Fig. 6 Installation view of work by Alex Katz in the exhibition *Figures/ Environments* at the Walker Art Center, 1970

Martin Friedman, conceded that the exhibiting artists represented an "eccentric" range of approaches, adding that "no case can be made for a single style or philosophy."(16) He chalked this up to the generally "idiosyncratic" status of figurative art in the United States, but one could also view this as an early sign of the decentered, pluralistic condition that would increasingly come to characterize the state of contemporary art.

In his catalogue essay, Friedman linked the contemporary figurative impulse not to the American art of the preceding decades but to European avant-garde idioms of the early twentieth century—to Cubism, Expressionism, and Surrealism. He contrasts these European precedents with sixties Pop Art:

> Pop in the 1960s focused new interest on the human figure—Warhol's blurred, repeated images of headline personalities; Lichtenstein's comic strip heroes; Wesselmann's and Rosenquist's generic types derived from TV and the billboards. Advertising media promoting the American dream helped to reestablish the figure theme, but as a packaged element of popular culture.... The Pop artist regarded the figure as another commodity but, unlike his expressionist European predecessors, he did not employ it as a means of generating psychological insights about either his subject or himself.(17)

Friedman's mention of "psychological insights" gestures to his larger point. While Pop may have revived the figure as a worthy subject, post-Pop figuration was not necessarily confined to the distanced, mediated, largely affectless stance that was the earlier movement's hallmark. So much is evident from the sculptures of Segal and Hanson, which, if influenced by (or even at times categorized as) Pop, nonetheless invoke more affective and empathetic responses in their presentation of figures frozen in states of contemplation, enervation, and, at times, even physical degradation (as was the case with Hanson's earliest work).

Partisans of a more reductive approach to art, particularly the Minimalists and Conceptualists who had taken the art world by storm in the previous decade, would likely have viewed these various returns to the sculptural representation of the human form as overly sentimental and retrograde in their concession to the demands of figurative representation. The means that a number of these artists employed, however, spoke of their alignment with contemporary approaches. For one, there was an impressive array of new materials and techniques on view: painted aluminum, cast latex, molded fiberglass, photosensitized linen. Further, Segal, Hanson, and Thek all employed various types of casting to produce their figures, even if the materials each one used achieved very different formal effects. Their shared interest in direct casting evinces the factualist move in post-1960s art, the commitment to a "just the facts, ma'am" approach. There were a number of important precedents for the casting of body parts in the work of the postwar avant-garde, particularly that of Jasper Johns, Robert Morris, and Bruce Nauman, and in Duchamp's late work. This was not conventional sculpting, with its emphasis on skill and on the expressive possibilities of the artist's hand. Rather, casting signified a more direct, unmediated approach, a willingness to present things much as the artist had found them.

It is not coincidental that a number of artists in this show, not only Whitman but also Segal and Grooms, had earlier been involved with the theatrical experiments connected to the Happenings movement of the 1950s and 1960s. The performative and interactive nature of those activities underscored the degree to which realism could no longer be taken merely as a pictorial or illusionistic effect but was in equal measure a component of the heightened, participatory reality that the post-1960s avant-garde often strove to induce. *New York Times* critic John Canaday touched

(16)
Martin Friedman, introduction in *Figures/ Environments*, exh. cat. (Minneapolis, MN: Walker Art Center, 1970), 6.

(17)
Ibid.

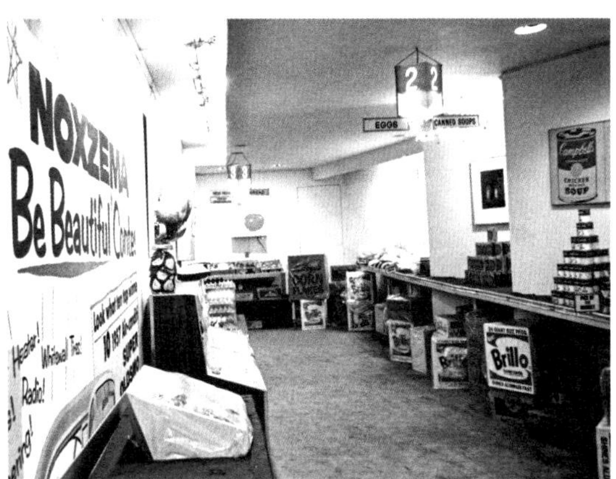

Fig. 7 Installation view of *The American Supermarket* at the Bianchini Gallery, 1964

on this tendency when, in a review of *Figures/Environments*, he declared it "extraordinary" that:

> in this century when figurative art has taken such a beating (and has usually deserved it) there should be so strong a movement in figurative sculpture not among the diehards but among young experimental artists, and that it should so often take the form of close allegiance to nature. Even when the reproduction is not close, the effort is to create a physical presence that competes with the visual world very much on its own terms.[18]

By focusing on the distinctive look of consumer goods, Pop Art had played a major role in blurring the distinction between the work of art and the larger "visual world," as Canaday put it. For instance, sculptor Claes Oldenburg's memorable *Store* had him selling painted plaster replicas of common objects from his storefront studio, while, in a similar vein, the Bianchini Gallery's 1964 *The American Supermarket* show (fig. 7) featured a gallery interior outfitted to resemble a supermarket, complete with display cases and aisle signage. Among the works on view were a number of Andy Warhol's recent box sculptures, painted and silkscreened wooden forms that replicated mundane packing boxes for products such as Kellogg's Corn Flakes, Del Monte peach halves, and, most memorably, Brillo soap pads (plate 1). On the occasion of a 1968 retrospective exhibition of Warhol's work at the Moderna Museet in Stockholm, the artist's sculptures were replaced by several hundred actual—that is to say, cardboard—Brillo packing cartons.[19] The actual and the facsimile, it seems, were largely interchangeable.

It would appear that nothing could be further from the spirit of Warhol's box sculptures than the major work that Thek showed in *Figures/Environments*. In 1967, he had stunned the New York art world with *The Tomb—Death of a Hippie* (fig. 8), a piece comprising a pink ziggurat that housed a detailed, full-size wax effigy of the artist.[20] There are myriad points of connection between Thek and Warhol: Thek had been the subject of a couple of Warhol's short films, both exhibited their work at New York's Stable Gallery, and the ziggurat of *The Tomb* and the geometric forms of the box sculptures can be taken as riffs on the predominantly geometric shapes employed by Minimalist artists.[21] Not to mention that both were, each in his own way, working in a realist sculptural idiom. Yet, in tone, their approaches were far apart. The graphic styling and mute objecthood of Warhol's boxes stand in contrast to the ancient, funereal, ritualistic overtones of Thek's sculptural assembly.

By the time he executed *The Tomb*, Thek had already staged a compelling encounter between his work and Warhol's. Several years earlier, he had obtained one of Warhol's *Brillo Boxes*, turned it on its side, removed its bottom facing, inserted a highly detailed wax sculpture of a sickening chunk of flesh into its hollow interior, and sealed it all up behind plexiglass (fig. 9). The resulting work brilliantly harnesses the tensions between the two very different versions of the "real" and of realism that he and Warhol were offering. The enclosure of Warhol's

(18)
John Canaday, "Odd Thing to Worry About, Ethics," *New York Times*, June 7, 1970, sec. 2, 19.

(19)
For a discussion of this episode, see the *Andy Warhol Catalogue Raisonné, vol. 02A: Paintings and Sculptures 1964-1969*, ed. Georg Frei and Neil Printz (New York: Phaidon, 2004), 78.

(20)
In the catalogue for *Figures/Environments*, the title for the work is given as *Thek's Tomb*.

(21)
In a 1966 essay, critic Gregory Battcock linked the two artists, relating Thek's so-called technological reliquaries to Warhol's approach to filmmaking. Battcock wrote: "While Thek's works are distantly removed from the familiar images characteristic of all Warhol's inventions, both artists have a similar approach toward a rediscovery of our common environment and identification of its particular reality." Gregory Battcock, "Humanism and Reality—Thek and Warhol," in *The New Art: A Critical Anthology*, ed. Gregory Battcock (New York: E. P. Dutton, 1966), 238. Battcock opines that Thek's and Warhol's projects share a common "humanism," an idiosyncratic claim considering the distance and aloofness that are so often seen to characterize Warhol's approach.

box has been broken open, revealing its empty core and hence undermining its artifice. The world of standardized packaging, with all its associations of efficiency and cleanliness (this is, after all, a box for soap pads), has come face to face with the fugitive and decaying realm of the fleshly—even if Thek has encased the latter behind a transparent barrier. *Meat Piece with Warhol Brillo Box* brings incongruous impulses into startling interaction. By staging an encounter between divergent artistic visions, Thek produced an unforgettable work at the same time that he demonstrated the potential that such realist idioms still held for contemporary art-making.

Thek's piece reflects on the very human impulse to contain an essential messiness (of the body, of the world, of human consciousness and experience) within circumscribed boundaries. History, and art history, often draw on that selfsame impulse, as a limited set of categories and explanatory devices are put to use making sense of the unruly complexity of the past. His artistic gesture is also inspiring in the way that he was able to alter an existing work to reveal a level of meaning that would otherwise have remained largely, if not wholly, unexplored. If art-historical narratives—even those from the relatively recent past—come to us equally readymade and packaged, we are certainly capable, as was Thek, of reworking them into something new, as long as we're willing to look at things with a fresh set of eyes.

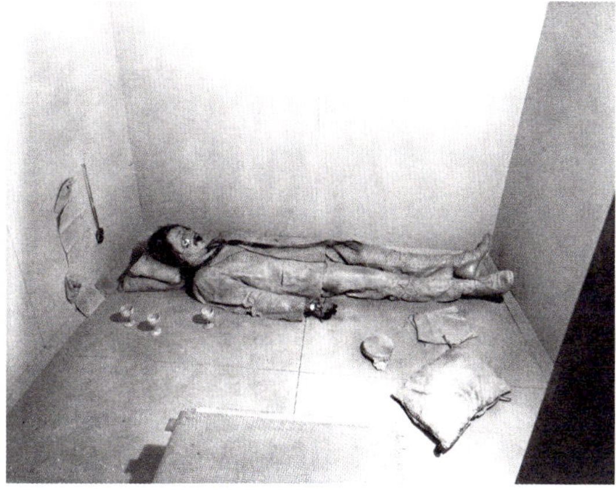

Fig. 8 Installation view of Paul Thek's *The Tomb—Death of a Hippie* at Stable Gallery, New York, 1967

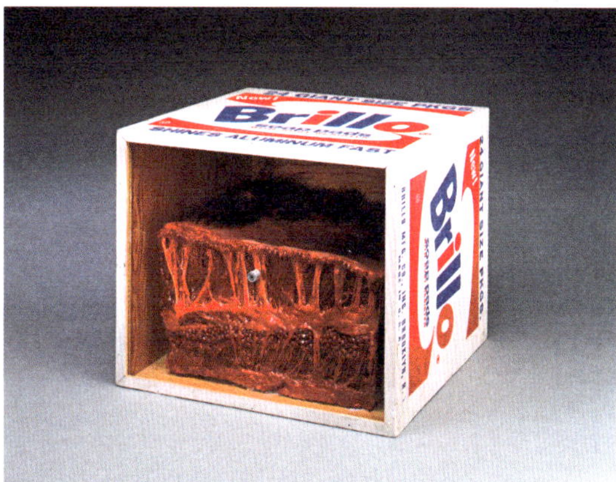

Fig. 9 Paul Thek *Meat Piece with Warhol Brillo Box* from the series *Technological Reliquaries* 1965 wax, painted wood, plexiglass

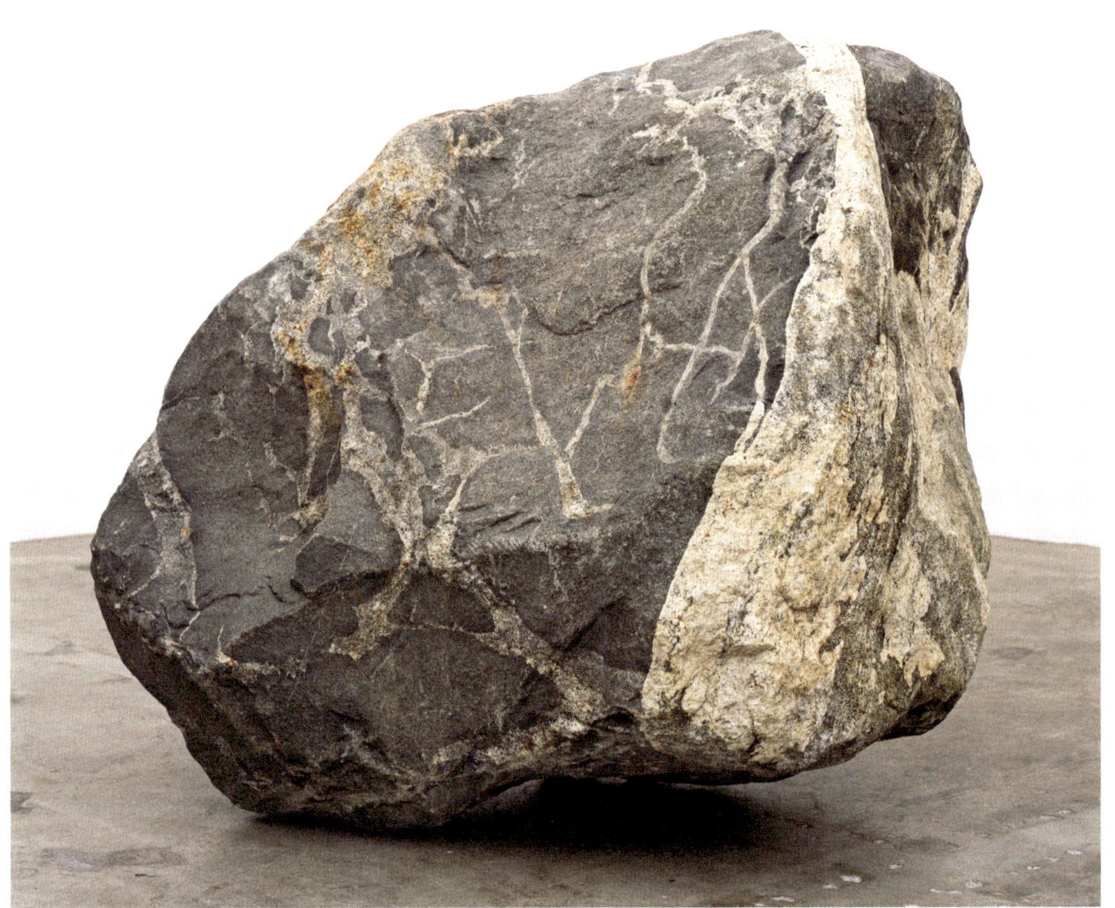

Fig. 1 Matt Johnson *4 EVA* 2006 granite with inlay

III.

SEEING MAY BE BELIEVING

ROCHELLE STEINER

For artists whose practices have emerged since the 1960s, the role of everyday objects in art is widely accepted as commonplace. Such items have been plucked from their functional realms and in turn considered, studied, replicated, recontextualized, and critiqued in and as art forms. With some materials found and some fabricated, some actual and some re-created, contemporary artists engaged with these common articles challenge our perceptions of truth and fiction, reality and simulation. "Is it real?" is a question that typically arises when viewing such works of art: has a found object been presented as is, has a replica been created, or are we looking at a photograph or a drawing that closely resembles an indexical image? Is a site authentic or a carefully crafted simulation? Embedded in such works are layers of ambiguity between reality, representation, and artifice. Ultimately, they take on the limits of perception and illusion, and may convince us that they are something they're not.

This practice is exemplified by Matt Johnson's *4EVA* (2006; fig. 1), a 3,500-pound boulder of ancient pre-Cambrian granite, flecked with what appears to be quartz veins. Upon close inspection, the marks seem to spell out the number "4" and the letters "EVA," shorthand for the word "FOREVER." Merging the age-old impulse to make marks with what appears to be the abbreviated language of text messaging, Johnson calls into question how and where he has intervened with this object, and strikes an unsettling balance between what might be considered real versus fake, found versus fabricated. Ultimately, this object begs the question, "Is it real?"

Likewise, Christian Jankowski's *Living Sculptures* (2006-2007; fig. 2) call upon our fascination with representation and complicate our perception of reality. Here he plays off the tradition of street performers in Barcelona and elsewhere who outfit and model themselves after statues of famous people and stand static for hours on end. But whereas these performers trick viewers into believing they are bronze, Jankowski's sculptures trick viewers into believing they are human. People frequently poke these works of art, which take the forms of Che, Caesar, and a surrealistic blue woman who seems to have stepped out of a Salvador Dalí painting, to see if they are metal or flesh. Many cannot resist leaving money as tips to congratulate good performances. Jankowski's *Living Sculptures* challenge passersby to consider whether they are "real," whereby real might be human or monument, depending on what one sees as the "original" source.

These artists are particularly indebted to the lineage that emerged from early twentieth-century Dada and Surrealist artworks that feature everyday objects, first and foremost Marcel Duchamp's readymades. His mundane domestic articles, including a hat rack, a bottle rack (fig. 3), a urinal, and a comb, were established as works of art. It is significant to note, however, that in the 1960s his bottle rack and urinal, among other readymades, were reproduced to look just like the originals, with "the replicas...laboriously crafted by Italian artisans whose work was subject to Duchamp's approval."[1] Art historian and curator Helen Molesworth points out that when Duchamp first arrived in New York, he simply purchased new items to replace the original *Bicycle Wheel* he had left in Paris and other pieces that had been lost or destroyed earlier. Ironically, however, his early objects of inspiration, which were no longer available in their original forms, needed to be re-created to retain their authenticity. "Making the readymades by hand to the specifications of the photographs was a means to keep them looking as much like the originals as possible."[2] How else could something that was manufactured more than half a century ago have been reproduced?

Such fabricated objects have come to be known as "reverse readymades" or "remade readymades," artistic representations that closely resemble "real" items, meticulously handcrafted versions of things that already existed, ironically created to pass for the found articles. Artists such as Robert Gober and Charles Ray, as well as those of a younger generation, including Johnson and Yoshihiro Suda, are more closely tied to Duchamp's later remade readymades than to his earlier Dada-inspired objects found in the world at large. They have each fabri-

(1)
Helen Molesworth, introduction in *Part Object Part Sculpture* (University Park, PA: Pennsylvania State University Press, 2005), 19.

(2)
Molesworth, "Duchamp: By Hand, Even," in *Part Object Part Sculpture*, 189.

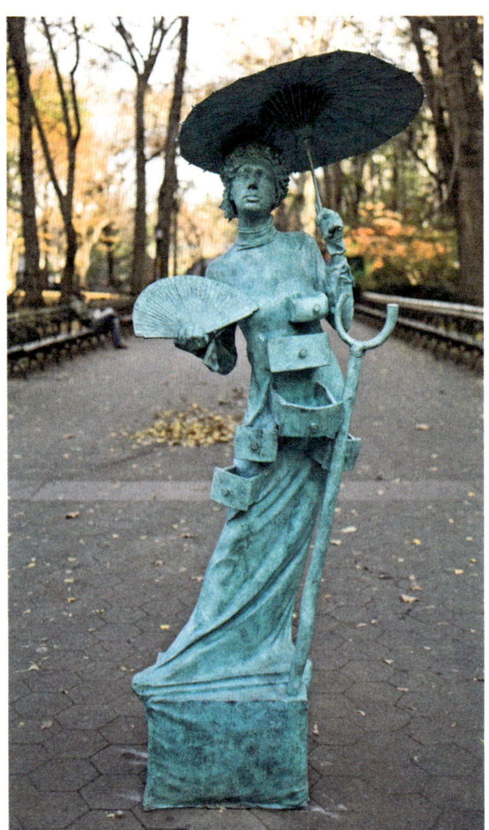

Fig. 2 Christian Jankowski *Dali Woman* from the *Living Sculptures* series 2006–2007 bronze

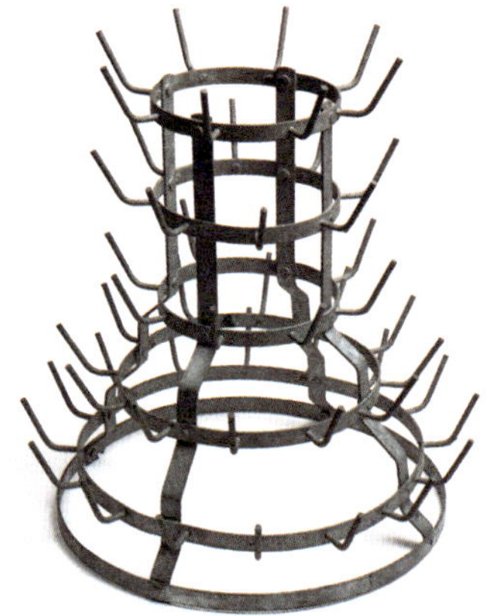

Fig. 3 Marcel Duchamp *Bottlerack* 1961 (replica of 1914 original) galvanized iron

cated elements as part of their artworks with an eye toward uncanny verisimilitude, rather than incorporating actual materials. These exceptionally lifelike objects are typically injected with personal narratives, social commentary, and/or humor, often resulting in powerfully charged and cunning works of art. Johnson's *American Spirit*, for example, replicates the cigarette pack out of paper, plastic, foam, and paint: an everyday element re-created physically, then presented in an unexpected and playful way, so that it appears to levitate (plate 29).

After realizing that a work is not real but a construction, a viewer question that often follows is: "How did the artist do that?" Onlookers may find themselves awestruck by the realistic nature of a representation and preoccupied in trying to determine the process by which verisimilitude was achieved. This typically comes to mind upon encountering the iconic work of Tom Friedman, such as *Untitled* (1995; fig 4), an actual-size pill capsule filled with minuscule handmade balls of Play-Doh, and *Untitled* (plate 56), a life-size replica of an insect poised on a white pedestal, as if it has landed on the side of a minimalist cube. Viewers become captivated by the artist's skill and the craftsmanship involved in making things so small, so complex, and so realistic.

In addition to following in the footsteps of Duchamp's readymades and reverse readymades, contemporary artists engaged with everyday items are also indebted to American Pop Art, a movement in which elements from daily life took center stage in both two- and three-dimensional works. Mid-twentieth-century artists highlighted and reflected upon the commodity aesthetics of this country's growing consumer culture, in particular through the display of popular icons such as Campbell's Soup cans, Coca Cola bottles, and the like. However, artists working in this vein and featuring objects at the center of their works are also aligned with the lineage of Photorealism developed in the 1960s and 1970s—perhaps even more so than with the commonly known Pop sensibility.[3] Where the Pop artists focused on the appeal of commercially recognizable consumer brands, the Photorealists emphasized ordinary, quintessentially American subjects. This tendency can be seen in Richard Estes' paintings of street scenes that present signs, window displays, phone booths, and other aspects of average life with incredible visual clarity and exactitude. A line from the Photorealists can be traced through Robert Bechtle's diner interior in *Fosters Freeze* (1970; plate 21) and patio exterior in *Watsonville Chairs* (1976) as well as Vija Celmins' series of paintings of the night

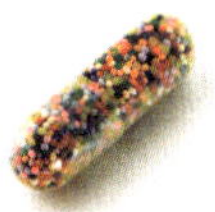

Fig. 4 Tom Friedman *Untitled* 1995
gelatin pill capsule, Play-Doh

sky (plate 38). The same is true of the utter ordinariness of Duane Hansen's stereotypical Americans, depicted in his highly figurative sculptures.

Another vital aspect of Photorealism that has influenced contemporary art-making is its handmade quality. The Photorealists utilized low-tech, though often labor-intensive processes to paint and draw images found in casual snapshots, rather than the mechanical forms of production associated with Pop Art, such as silkscreen printing.(4) Contemporary artists in subsequent decades have continued to value a handmade quality in their work; such intensity of production is exemplified by Chuck Close's precise process of transposing a simple snapshot of himself or others into a supersized, hyperreal portraits. In his later paintings, the meticulous method of gridding a canvas and transferring a photographic image quadrant by quadrant and detail by detail is not only incorporated into the final work of art, but visually foregrounded (fig. 5).

In what is perhaps one of the most obsessive applications of "reverse readymades" trained on an ordinary American

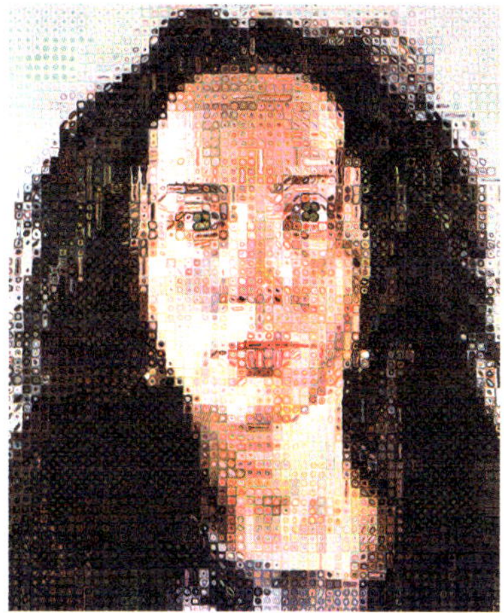

Fig. 5 Chuck Close *Kiki* 1993 oil on canvas

scene and executed by hand, Keith Edmier's 2008 installation entitled *Bremen Towne* (plate 65) is a full-scale sculptural replica of the interior of the 1970s Midwestern suburban home in which he grew up. Not unlike Photorealist painters who turned to photos as source materials, Edmier began this work with family snapshots from the period. From there he stretched the Photorealist tradition into three dimensions by re-creating the space of his past and everything in it, including appliances, curtains, flooring, ceiling, and so on. He obtained examples of some of these items with relative ease through such sources as eBay, but he re-created most of the pieces for *Bremen Towne* not out of necessity, but out of a commitment to the process of making them, and perhaps as a comment against the ease of turning to readymades as artistic solutions. The resulting work of art is a physical manifestation of Edmier's own childhood nostalgia associated with this location, as much as it is a still life and portrait of the era evoked.

Equally complex and layered are Thomas Demand's photographs that employ Photorealistic approaches to explore what can be known through images and our perceptions of representation. He likewise begins with pictures as the basis from which to construct his own imagery. Many of the "sites" in his shots are drawn from German history, and some may seem familiar because they derive from the media-saturated visual vocabulary prevalent at the beginning of the twenty-first century. From there he transposes his selections into three-dimensional paper and cardboard models that appear, when pho-

(3)
See Hal Foster, "The Return of the Real," in *The Return of the Real: The Avant-Garde at the End of the Century*, An October Book (Cambridge, MA: MIT Press, 1996), 127-170.

(4)
Pop Art first developed in relation to Abstract Expressionism, which was dominant in the 1950s. The first Pop works had a hand-painted quality, rather than the slickly or mechanically produced look they would later have. This was the subject of the exhibition *Hand-Painted Pop: American Art in Transition 1955-62*, curated by Paul Schimmel and Donna di Salvo, organized by the Whitney Museum of American Art, New York; the Museum of Contemporary Art, Los Angeles; and the Museum of Contemporary Art, Chicago, in 1992. See *Hand-Painted Pop: American Art in Transition 1955-62*, exh. cat. (New York: Rizzoli International Publications, 1992).

tographed, to be architectural settings. Like film sets that serve as temporary backdrops, his facsimiles look highly realistic when reproduced.

Demand is able to convince viewers that his subjects are actual sites filled with objects, yet at the same time his works are deliberately embedded with subtle clues to his subjects' production and artificiality, such as a crease or a pencil mark.[5] After they are photographed, his models are destroyed, and the artist relies on the final works to carry and convey the labor of their production. At least three of Demand's pieces, *Studio* (1997), *Barn* (1997; plate 36), and *Stable* (2000), particularly depict "distinct, yet interrelated, sites of production: a television studio, an artist's studio, and a shed with mechanized equipment" that, taken together as subjects, "refer back to the process of image-making"[6] and to production itself as a process within Demand's work.

One experiences a sense of amazement when viewing Edmier's and Demand's art, as well as that of others who take on such labor-intensive production. The onlooker's question "How did they do that?" stems not only from the precision of the re-creations, but also the sheer scale and complexity of such productions. Another case in point is Ai Weiwei's mind-boggling installation at London's Tate Modern in 2009 of one hundred million fabricated sunflower seeds, which covered the floor of the vast Turbine Hall with an endless sea of unidentifiable gray upon which viewers were invited to walk (fig. 6).

But perhaps the more relevant question to pose about the creative process employed by artists who take this approach toward verisimilitude is "*Why* did they do that?" Why would an artist choose to create a handcrafted version of something that is ubiquitous in everyday life, such as a prescription capsule, or kitchen appliances, or sunflower seeds? Why would an artist go to such lengths to produce something so exact that it can pass for a readymade object, be it a cigarette pack or an entire suburban home from a different era, at a time when the actual found objects are readily accepted as artistic material and easy to source? Likewise, why painstakingly produce a meticulous drawing or painting by hand that appears to be a mechani-

(5)
Roxana Marcoci, "Paper Moon," in *Thomas Demand* (New York: Museum of Modern Art, 2005), 10.

(6)
Ibid., 18.

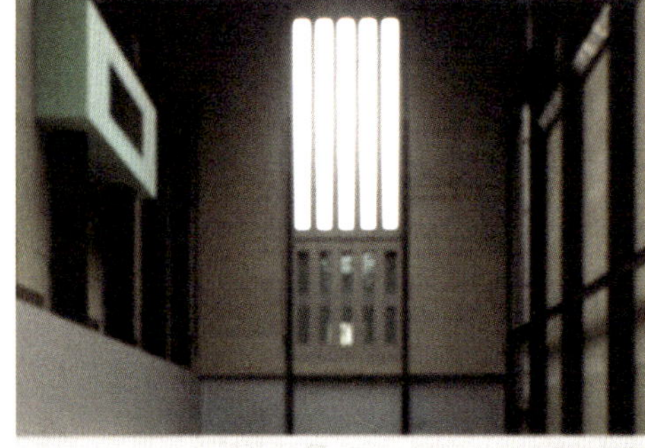
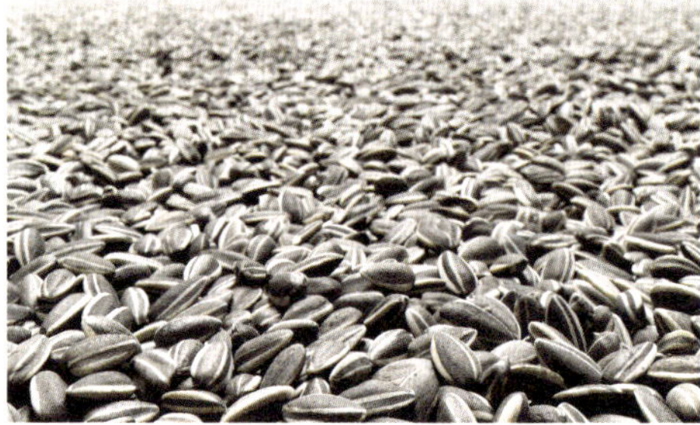

Fig. 6 Installation view of Ai Weiwei's *Sunflower Seeds* at Tate Modern, London, 2010

cally reproduced photograph, or construct a three-dimensional replica of a site only so that it can be photographed and pass for an image of an actual location before being destroyed?

The reason is exemplified by the work of Peter Fischli and David Weiss, the collaborative Swiss duo whose practice calls attention to aspects of the everyday that would otherwise likely be overlooked. The artists have been fascinated throughout their career by the unassuming, the workaday, and the banal, which they reveal and explore in a wide variety of forms. In the installation *Empty Room* (1995-1996; fig. 7; plate 26), viewers encounter a seemingly unfinished portion of a museum installation, a space filled with what appear to be boxes, buckets, tools, and leftover construction materials—the common bits and pieces that comprise a worksite-in-progress. It is as if we have stumbled upon a segment of the exhibition that has yet to be completed, a behind-the-scenes area of the museum filled with remnants not intended to be revealed to the public. This so-called "empty room" is more accurately a site of production, an example of labor as an artistic subject.

The topic of artistic labor in contemporary art is reinforced by the discovery that the *Empty Room* is filled with "reverse readymades" modeled after items from the artists' studio in Zürich as well as materials found in the Walker Art Center's basement during their 1996 retrospective exhibition there. Each object is carefully handcrafted, carved by the artists from polyurethane, painted, and then precisely arranged to look like a casual worksite. Although seemingly random, the installation follows the trompe l'oeil tradition, with meticulously handcrafted elements posed as "real" objects. The display serves as a portrait of the artists' working process—a glimpse into the effort that goes into and is embedded within the making of a work of art, particularly one that strives for verisimilitude.

Fischli and Weiss' artworks are not only depictions and simulations of common objects, but also signs of their own making. Artists working in this way honor and celebrate things from everyday life by making them anew and with precision—and in doing so they highlight the creative process as much as the things themselves. Each of these examples demonstrates the importance of the gesture of making at a time when everything imaginable seems to already exist. The meticulous handiwork and painstaking toil that goes into creating these pieces interrupts the dominant idea-based practices of the past century—as seen in Duchamp's found objects, in conceptual artists' dematerialization of objects, and in the appropriation of preexisting still and moving images. By utilizing handcrafted fabrication to re-create the ordinary through extraordinary means, these artists assert that craftsmanship and production remain valued in contemporary art, even—and especially—when it seems no longer necessary.

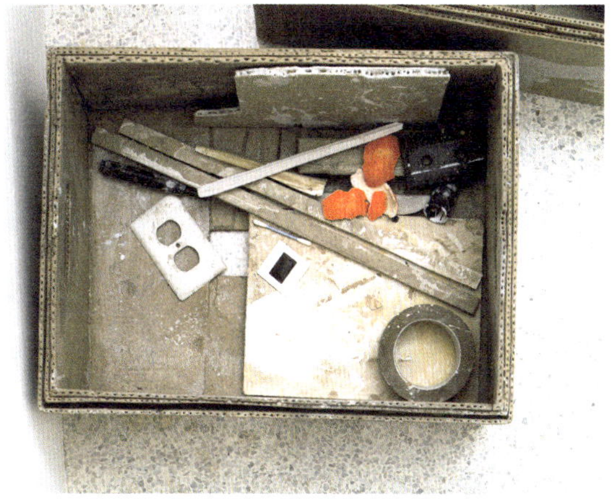

Fig. 7 Peter Fischli and David Weiss *Empty Room* 1995–1996 (detail) polyurethane, paint

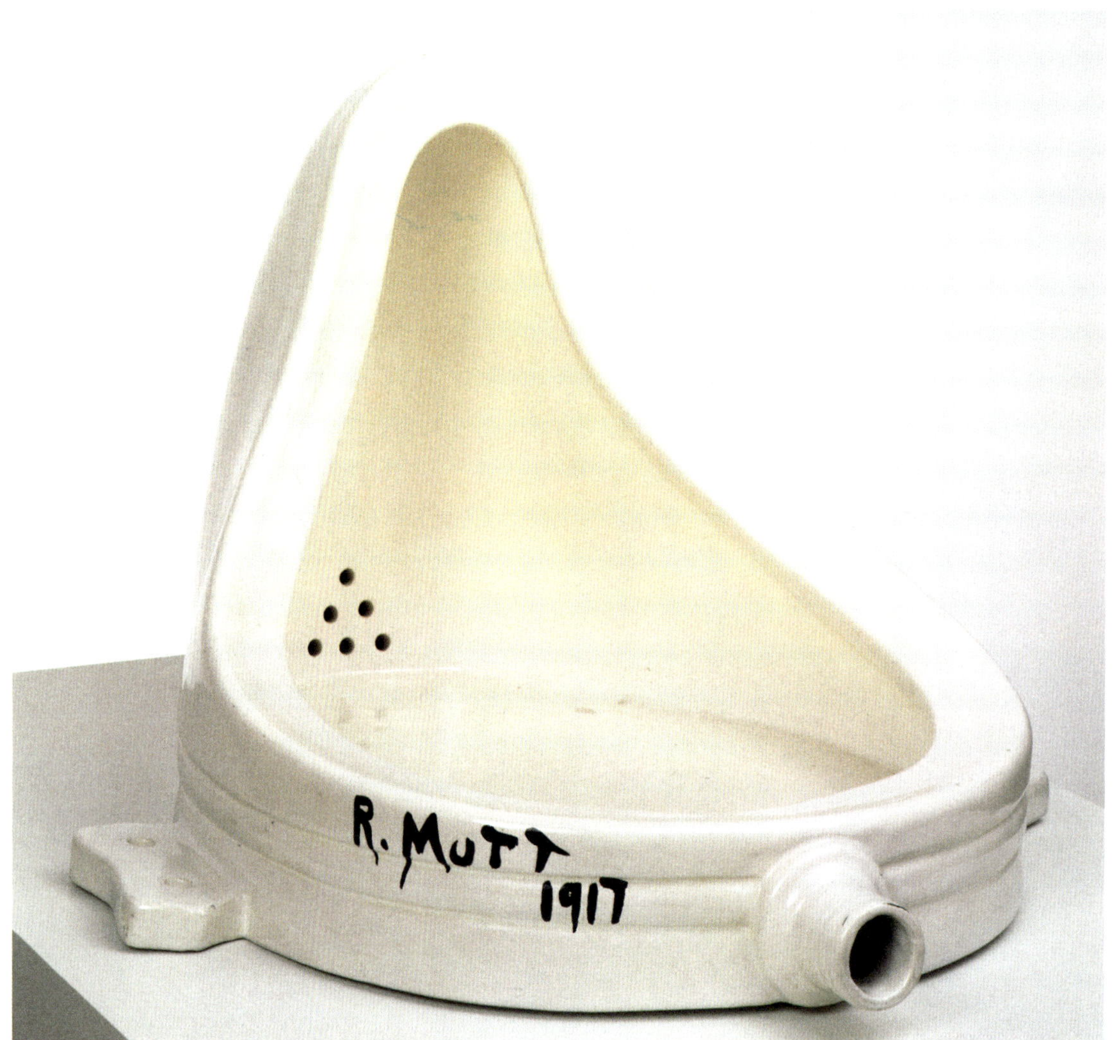

Fig. 1 Marcel Duchamp *Fountain* 1917/1964 glazed ceramic urinal, black paint

IV.
READYMADE RESISTANCE

JOSIAH McELHENY

Whether by faking, borrowing, or stealing, artists today commonly produce works of art that employ the vocabulary of industry. This is not surprising if one considers the extent to which the broader contemporary language of form derives from the global corporate system. Unlike earlier eras, nearly all products now draw on the collective labor of large numbers of people. We are supposed to be contented consumers of the factory-made wares of our brothers, sisters, and distant unheralded cousins in Asia. The message is that the individual can no longer be a producer of things except in highly circumscribed situations, and so artists must continually attempt to reclaim the territory of production or invent new relationships to it.

Critical discussions of works in this vein often make reference to Marcel Duchamp's early readymade sculptures, asserting that his precedent grants artists the authority to designate any object as their own artistic production and, accordingly, redefines the artwork as anything an artist deems. Yet one could also interpret Duchamp's signing of a urinal in 1917 (fig. 1) as an act of resistance to the forces of economic and industrial development surrounding him. The urinal he employed was produced by an elaborate industrial process; its economic origins make it an emblem of the structural changes occurring throughout the West at that time. Many of the things that people used were still made at home or nearby—a mix of industrial, artisanal, and personal production. But the remnants of preindustrial life were being swept away, the labor of the individual replaced more and more by that of groups functioning within factories, corporations, unions, and conglomerates. How does the individual artist-worker compete with this new context? Perhaps by doing as little—or as much—as possible. Duchamp's first readymades were industrial objects produced in great quantities. The difference between any two examples of mass production was "infra-slim," as he described it. Significantly, he didn't sign a custom-fit shoe or a hand-forged pitchfork, nonindustrial objects that display their non-standardized idiosyncrasy proudly. His choice might be seen as an early protest against the determined shrinking of society's space for individual production.

In the ninety years since Duchamp's *Fountain*, the process of industrial development has continued with ever-increasing force and speed to the point where virtually everything we use (or consume) is produced by corporations in a linked series of manufacturing processes and trade. And so the question remains: How can the individual artist produce works of art that effectively employ the commonly understood language of capitalist industry? Duchamp's attempt at an answer to this question only made it more pointed. He proposed something serious but also absurd, a change in authorship by fiat. This deceptively simple proposal seems not to be an option for artists, now that Western society promotes the idea of consumer choice itself as a kind of de facto authorship. What are other tactics or procedures?

By examining recently exhibited artworks and their antecedents, one could begin to write a manual of numerous approaches, but three stand out: One option is to "fake" the product by making an imitation or reconstruction of it. This often requires that an artist transmute or reconstitute the form in another material, since industrial materials typically require industrial processing. Another is to "borrow" preexisting objects and use them in a more or less intact state. Or one could "steal" the methods of capitalist production itself, by accessing an industrial process and adapting it for one's own use. Often, artists move from one procedure to another, elaborating them or mixing them up. The common thread is that these gestures do not pretend to erase the economic origins and processes underlying these products (or to obscure or aestheticize them, as in more traditional modes of assemblage). They suggest that the ongoing recurrence of readymade-like objects in sculpture might be taken as evidence of a common struggle to resist the continuing loss of individual creative autonomy in relation to production. Many strategies could work—anything except giving in, anything but simply buying and consuming.

From an art-historical perspective Jasper Johns' ale cans, flashlights (fig. 2), and lightbulbs are obvious and important precedents for creating fake versions of mass-market products, but his questioning of sign and signification does not drive younger artists' uses of analogous procedures. In Johns' lineage we might also consider the hand-painted objects and installations of

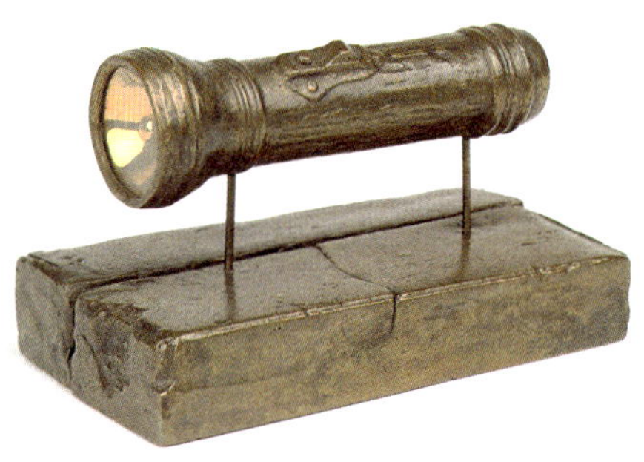

Fig. 2 Jasper Johns *Flashlight* 1960/1988 bronze, glass

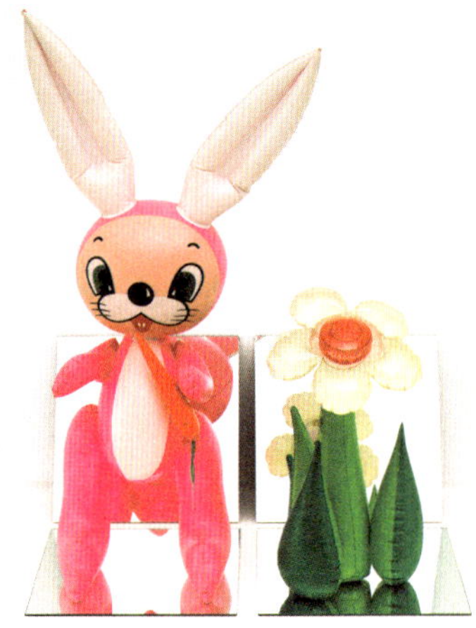

Fig. 3 Jeff Koons *Inflatable Flower and Bunny (Tall White and Pink Bunny)* 1979 vinyl, mirrors

Fischli & Weiss, though these may be more concerned with trompe l'oeil effects than with challenging industrial manufacture. More relevant are the groundbreaking examples of Robert Gober and Jeff Koons, artists who are well known for works that point to objects of mass production and who provide two diverging narratives in the struggle to engage commodity forms.

Koons' earliest work with preexisting industrial products includes *Inflatable Flower and Bunny (Tall White and Pink Bunny)* (1979; fig. 3), which consists of two store-bought blow-up toys displayed on inexpensive mirrors. Borrowing a mode of presentation that one might see in the window of a cheap gift shop, he puts these plastic products forward as art, via their transposition to the floor and to a different commercial/institutional context. In this sculpture Koons attempted to recast two childhood objects as adult ones, transforming them from transient to permanent, without altering the inflatables themselves. But we immediately intuit that these plastic products will inevitably fade and sag, even if hidden away in a box and exposed to light only for very short periods of time. The work does not exactly achieve Koons' oft-stated goal of giving us permission to perpetually indulge our most banal desires, existing instead as a historical placeholder in this line of thought. It is an example of "borrowing" from the world of capitalist production, but it does not represent Koons' most radical and extreme attempt to alter our perception of commodity culture.

Nearly three decades later, Koons' current work with ostensibly similar material stands in stark contrast with this early foray. He has moved on to creating his own wildly obsessive fake versions of industrial products. For the past decade, his studio (working in tandem with outside fabricators) has been busily producing his ongoing series of "Popeye" sculptures, begun in 2002 (fig. 4). In scale, texture, and small physical details, these objects appear to be common inflatable pool toys and dolls in the form of dolphins, monkeys, and lobsters, similar in kind to those Koons originally displayed on mirrors. But they are not. They are cast metal, typically aluminum, which is matte, painted to closely mimic the appearance of a plastic toy. Perfectly smooth castings, meticulous handwork, and sophisticated painting processes are used to achieve the appearance of cheap, disposable goods that are produced in large numbers with highly mechanized technology.

In these works Koons defies the original ethos of his models. Designed to be used at most for a couple of seasons, pool floats of this kind are intended to be lost, popped, or worn out so that they may be replaced with new ones. Yet Koons' sculptures are forever. They realize and permanently materialize his epiphany about the utter banality of our erotic imagination. The painstaking reconstruction of these objects is so radically different in its materials and processes that it fundamentally changes the nature of the forms—disregarding both their original use and, significantly, their planned obsolescence and inevitable failure. Koons's sculptures make the inexorable cycling of capitalism stand still. Styles may change, but these objects are monuments to another kind of permanence.

Robert Gober has long been engaged with a more perfunctory kind of faking than

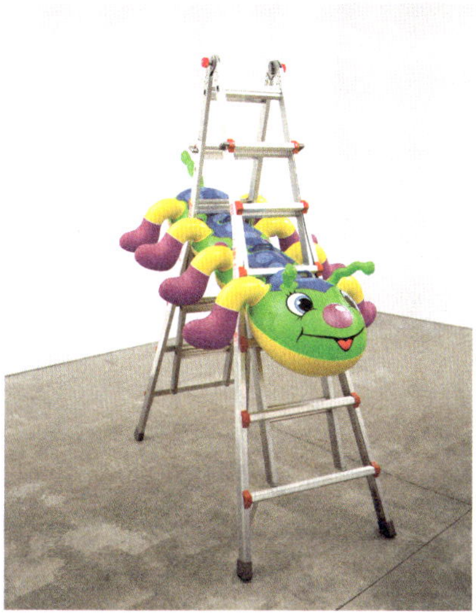

Fig. 4 Jeff Koons *Caterpillar Ladder* 2003 polychromed aluminum, aluminum, plastic

Koons, but in a relatively recent work he chose to "steal" the methods of industrial production. His diaper package, an element from his 2005 untitled installation at the Matthew Marks Gallery in New York (fig. 5), is an extremely convincing copy or double of a mass-market commodity, despite the fact that the contorted pose of the baby on its wrapper is unlikely to please a Luvs or Huggies CEO. There is a good reason why the sculpture is so believable as an actual mass-market object: the plastic packaging that wraps a stack of surrogate handmade plaster diapers was printed at a factory using the same materials and technology as those employed in the printing of "real" packages of disposable diapers. This mock consumable, made with such verisimilitude as to demolish the term itself, is an example of accessing industrial processes in order to convincingly adopt a vocabulary of production.

In this instance, however, it could be argued that the artist went too far. By stealing the original methods of production, Gober loses some of the subtle friction between individual and industrial labor that characterizes his best work. Sure, the image on the package strongly critiques the modern drive to normalize the functions of the body. But this critique plays itself out iconographically, at the level of image, rather than in the carefully calibrated making of the work. In its seamless imitation of every parameter of the original, the diaper package dissolves the tension between the individual's ability to resist the values promoted by commodity culture and the massive resources available to corporations to promote those values.

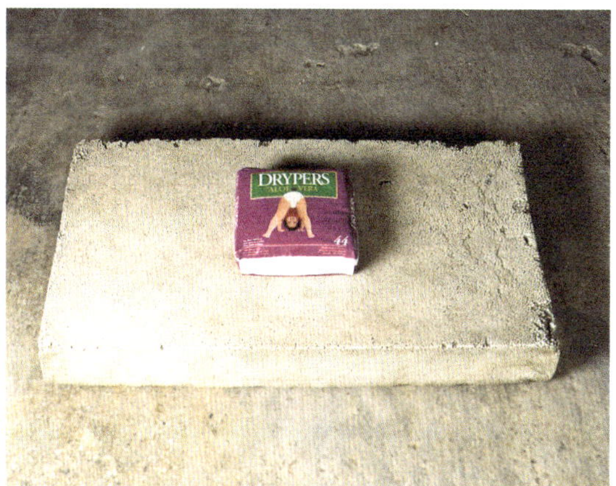

Fig. 5 Installation of Robert Gober's *Untitled* at Matthew Marks Gallery, New York, 2005

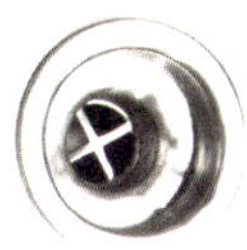

Fig. 6 Robert Gober *Drain* 1989 cast pewter

By contrast, Gober has often produced poignantly handmade, imperfect versions of products in order to transform them into metaphorical political protests. His early iconic work *Drain* (1989; fig. 6), is one of the most finely tuned examples of this approach. This small sculptural intervention appears to be a typical late-twentieth-century sink drain, improbably inserted into a wall literally at a ninety-degree angle to its original functionality. Yet a quick but careful look reveals what it is not. It is not an object from the plumbing store. It is not the result of a long line of decisions, beginning with complex negotiations over plumbing standards and cultural traditions concerning water use, followed by engineering calculations, and ending, after manufacture, with standardized tests measuring density, size, and tensile strength. It approximates the look of something like this, but it is not this. Small imperfections reveal it to be a hand-formed approximation, an individual's version of an economically efficient commodity, perfectly imperfect and customized. The material is changed from the usual cast iron or stain-

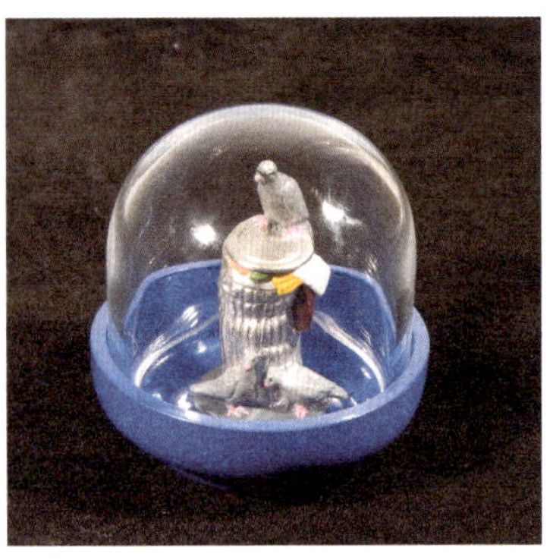
Fig. 7 Matt Johnson *50 cent* 2005 platinum, glass, enamel

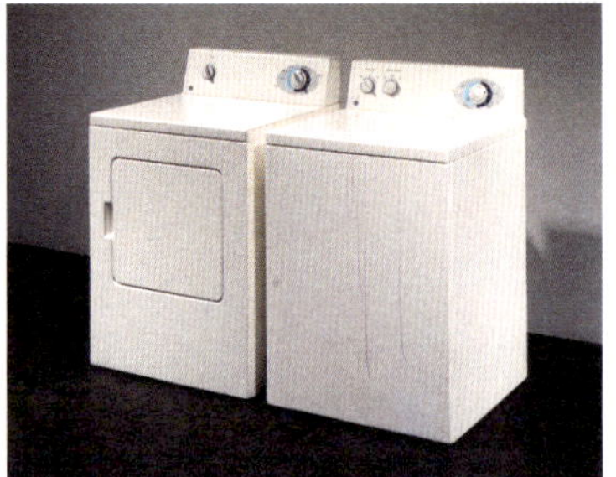
Fig. 8 Kaz Oshiro *Washer/Dryer #3* 2005 acrylic, Bondo on stretched canvas

less steel to pewter, which is infinitely easier to cast. *Drain* resists our impotence as independent makers. Anyone could make it in his or her garage.

Koons and Gober cast long shadows, but they do not mark an end to the tradition of faking the industrial, "readymade" object, a strain of contemporary art that continues in the work of several young artists, including Matt Johnson, Kris Martin, and Kaz Oshiro. Johnson's *50 cent* (2005; fig. 7), is a fake version of one of the lowest-end product lines, the gumball-machine toy, albeit his is partially platinum and holds a miniature trash can. Martin's *Golden Spike* (2005), is an open-ended edition in the form of a common framing nail cast not in steel but in gold; he hammers it into architecture as he sees fit. In both cases it is the change in material that represents the strongest element of resistance toward the power of industry. The original objects are by nature cheap and commonplace. By reconstructing them in expensive materials, Johnson and Martin propose a simple restructuring of monetary value, implying a value for the valueless. Oshiro's *Sony Bookshelf Speakers* (2003-2004; plate 42), along with his more recent sculpture-painting hybrids of fridges, washer/dryers (fig. 8), and tailgates, illustrate convincing reconstructions of the originals, made, oddly enough, from stretched canvas and Bondo. His transmutation of materials, like Johnson's and Martin's, suggests another notion of inherent value, though instead of rare metals he uses paint on canvas, which might be considered both more and less precious. Together the gestures of these three artists could be viewed as an irreverent joke about our ability as consumers to determine value. But the relative thinness of these pranks may also point to how hard it really is to meaningfully challenge the economic laws governing industrial objects.

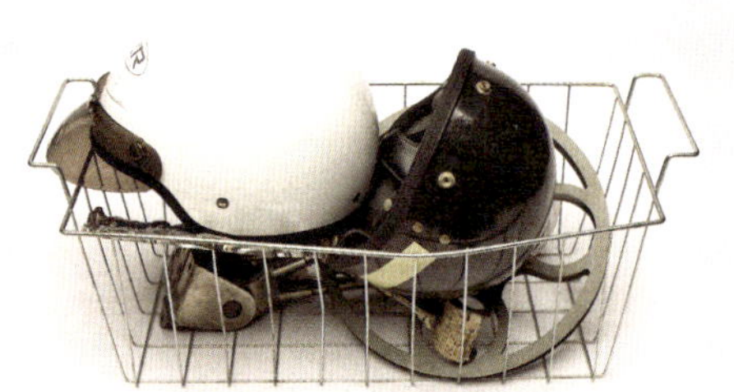
Fig. 9 Cady Noland *Untitled* 2008 1 metal basket, 2 motorcycle helmets, 1 film reel, 3 subway straps, metal

Turning to "borrowing," it is worth mentioning the rich current of sculptures and installations constructed as assemblages, works that consume and repurpose the products of industry for use in the artist's expressive palette. Many crucial pieces by figures from Jessica Stockholder to the late Jason Rhoades have involved this approach. Yet the process of subsuming these objects within an aesthetic scheme tends to obscure their economic and material origins. The resultant artworks are less legible as texts formed of a shared material language, and in them the tension between collective industrial labor and that of the individual subsides.

How, instead, might an artist use the actual products of our economic regime without either pictorializing them or simply claiming them like Duchamp? We may purchase these products in order to use them for our own artistic ends, but can they still remain just themselves in our hands? If they are included within the context of a larger work and visibly retain the traces of their material history, perhaps they can preserve their autonomy as something yet to be consumed. Artists have played with this idea for a while, whether in Cady Noland's deadpan accumulations (fig. 9), Mike Kelley's theatrical stagings, or Haim Steinbach's pared-down displays, which laugh at the lack of labor that consumption requires. Josephine Meckseper has recently co-opted the structure of store windows to deploy her own politically pointed rearrangement of products and images. Even Gabriel Orozco's sectioned Citroën (*La DS*, 1993) could be said to have been "borrowed" and then "returned" to us, looking functional at approximately half its original size. Can we do something new with preexisting manufactured objects without using them up? The recent work of Isa Genzken, Rachel Harrison, and Carol Bove suggests this is possible.

In various constructions that Genzken has presented, she slaps together a disparate variety of cheaply purchased and salvaged objects and materials. One gets the sense that she is perpetrating violence not just on the objects but on capital itself. Whether in Al *Dente* (2003), a plate of toy dinosaurs and cows, or in her *Vampire/Empire III* series of 2004, objects are doused in layers of paint, as if she has just finished pouring on gasoline and is about to light them on fire. The paint does not mask, consume, or dissolve the original object in a carefully balanced composition. *Hula Hoop* (2006), consists of a tangle of materials sitting opposite an untouched Mies van der Rohe Barcelona chair—a tasteful viewing platform in sharp contrast with the indecipherable agglomeration it faces. Genzken's is an antiaesthetic that leaves objects, with all their attendant information, intact so that we might contemplate their history as they meet her protest. By smashing, tying, dousing, sticking, gluing, and taping together everyday objects in a specific but thoroughly illogical manner, Genzken protests the modern power structures that create the manufactured objects of global culture. She does to the objects what she would likely do to the power players behind them: she tortures them but lets them live.

Rachel Harrison's sculptures highlight the differences between what an individual can create and what the media and industry create for us. A common mode of hers is a construction modeled from cheap materials, slathered with a frostinglike layer of mucky paint. These elements seem to imply that we can only make rough and messily biological modernisms; they are a celebration of the de-skilled. To these she adds small (and larger) bits of the world: stuck onto edges, backs, ledges, and niches are toys, pictures of movie stars, thermostats, bicycles, and more. These objects are in general unal-

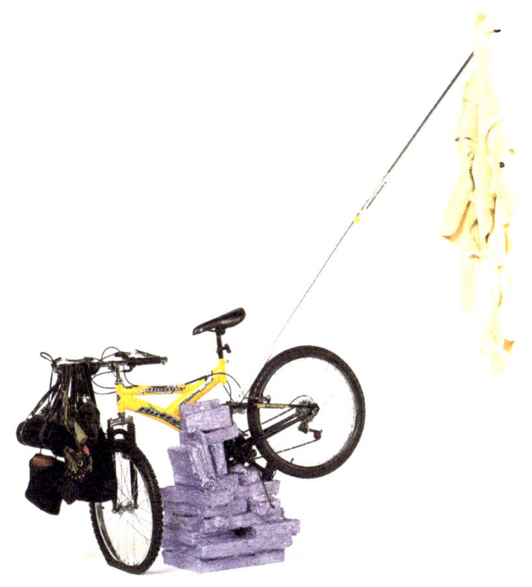

Fig. 10 Rachel Harrison *Huffy Howler* 2004 wood, polystyrene, cement, acrylic, Huffy Howler bicycle, handbags, rocks, brick, sheepskin, pole, wire, pigmented inkjet print, binder clips

tered, pristine, and fresh with the memory of their original commercial contexts and uses. Harrison's readymade additions highlight our plight: what we can do is so limited, so impoverished, yet they can do anything and everything. Her work offers an adaptive solution, a place where one can indulge the primordial imagination, even while assembling a toy from a Happy Meal. Or so, at least, it is to be hoped. *Huffy Howler* (2004; fig. 10) consists of a brand-new, Chinese manufactured bicycle, permanently entangled inside a sculpture, and yet it's as though you could still ride off on it. The bicycle doesn't read as an element in a perfectly composed still life; it looks instead as if it were somehow on loan to the sculpture. Harrison's gestures suggest that even if we can't compete with the power of industrial production, we can at least tangle it up in our own personal complexity. We can borrow these products for our own, sometimes meager, remade world, and perhaps this might render them impervious to the motives of their original production, advertisement, and sale.

In contrast, Bove provides a sublimated picture of our relationship to cultural production. In a number of her sculptures, used objects, especially 1960s books, records, driftwood, etc., are situated on furniture as permanently arranged

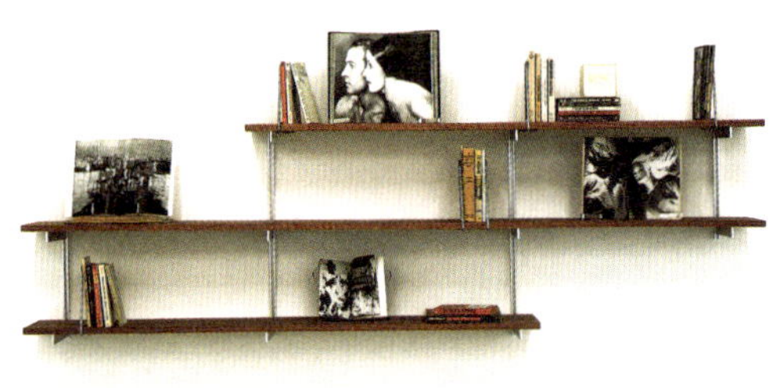

Fig. 11 Carol Bove *Adventures in Poetry* 2002 mixed media

moments. These works provide an apparently accurate picture of a completely superseded past. Strangely, we seem to be observing these objects not as antiques but in their original era, though this sense of time travel is tempered by our knowledge of what has taken place between then and now. If Bove's sculptures are a kind of time capsule or tomb, then they are extremely tenuous ones. For example, one could simply take a book off the shelf in *Adventures in Poetry* (2002; fig. 11), and the moment, as well as the sculpture, would disappear. And this is precisely what was supposed to have happened to these interrelated store-bought products, originally intended for college-educated sophisticates. Read a book; play a record; move on to the next style in furniture, music, and ideas. These products should have been—and maybe even were—discarded, donated, or dropped off at the Salvation Army. One feels this tension acutely, because each charged element of Bove's compositions retains its original form, with all its evidence of aging and use. Her arrangements resist the main thrust of capitalist production, its constant destructive renewal, its looming temporariness.

If these three sculptural modes could be termed cynical, accommodating, and nostalgic, respectively, there is always the option of trying to beat the industrialists at their own game. Someone like Takashi Murakami proves that the artist might actually be able to insert products into the mainstream marketplace, as he regularly does in Japan. There are also more nuanced options. Rather than literally becoming a kind of capitalist entrepreneur, one could steal time at the factory, creep into the closed-down company and grab the old equipment, or find a way to take over the whole product line.

One important forerunner in this regard is Rosemarie Trockel, who since the early 1980s has stolen time at the mill, so to speak, in order to make custom-knit fabrics that she attaches to rectangular wooden stretchers. The stitching in her woolen material looks like that of any commercially manufactured sweater, but the patterns are often quite different from those that one would ordinarily find for sale: Rorschach blots, hammers and sickles, scribbles, stains, and the wool logo, among other eccentric offerings (fig. 12). In the sense that these works are not painted and do not display any overt evidence of pictorial intervention, they seem like sculpture. Turning on its head Duchamp's notion that a painting is a readymade because you buy premanufactured canvas and tubes of paint, Trockel produces a feminist critique of painting by commissioning a fabric visibly knit, not woven, as if from a piece of a huge sweater or scarf. Instead of being knit at home (or at the studio) by an anonymous woman (artist), these works are stitched by an industrial-scale, automated machine. Rather than accept the necessity of using the products that industry provides (woven canvas), Trockel repurposed the textile-production line itself, which resulted in works that remind us of the economic powerlesssness of domestic manufacture in the West.

Trockel's knit works are grounded in the technologies of the industrial revolution, such as the automated Jacquard loom, which was revolutionary because of its punch-card-driven production of complex patterns; that fantastic contraption has now almost completely outlived its usefulness. What happens to these expensive machines when they no longer fit into the system? In another stab at disruption, Kris Martin custom-ordered an automated sign from a company that makes many of the mechanical arrival and departure boards found in European airports. His work *Mandi III* (2003) is just like any other such sign, except that it has no letters or text so that it displays only black on black as its panels flip by ominously. The sculpture is in many ways the original object, but it has been fundamentally reimagined. Martin did not commission the original manufacturer just for the sake of expediency. By realizing this sculpture not as a replica but as an effective product on its own twisted terms, he demonstrates that it is possible for the individual to idiosyncratically alter the course of industrial production.

If placing custom orders or buying up scrapped machines fall in line with typical corporate practice, how about something a bit more fraudulent? An effective example of this approach can be seen in Joe Scanlan's *DIY*, a repeatable work begun in 2002 and continuing today, in which the artist provides an instruction booklet explaining how to make a typical IKEA bookcase into a coffin. Additional information tells readers how to turn other IKEA products into sundry items for their own personal funeral homes. IKEA provides only the production and worldwide distribution of an identical form; Scanlan gives us the goods. *DIY* effectively deconstructs and physically repurposes the product, demonstrating that with nothing more than a hammer and a screwdriver one might be able to conceptually remake anything. This may or may not be a liberating idea.

Things are in transition. A new economic model that has been extensively discussed is one in which the consumer is given direct access to industrial production. In 2007, the *New York Times* editorial page trumpeted the imminent arrival of a domestic three-dimensional printer within "the next five years."(1) The idea is that a product may be "downloaded" and then produced at home. Digital customization of the product is intended to provide at least the semblance of personal influence beyond simple choice. When fully realized, this development will bring immensely sophisticated technologies for making things into the domestic environment. It's hard to imagine anything further from needle and thread, hammer and nail.

To some extent, these trends have already been adopted by artists. Kelley Walker and Liam Gillick, among many others, create e-mailable drawings that are translated into solid matter by ever-cheaper laser- and water-jet cutting. Thanks to computer-driven machines, it is becoming more and more economical to produce one-off versions of complex forms. Jorge Pardo has his own computer-controlled router in his studio, obviating the need for even e-mailing a drawing file. The definition of production itself is constantly evolving.

The potential freedom for individuals (or artists) supposedly provided by new developments in digitally driven, automated production is to some extent illusory—or, at the very least, temporary. Perhaps we think that the factory has arrived on our own doorsteps, providing us with infinite possibilities. But while most anything can be "hacked," the inherent structure of the tools and software still

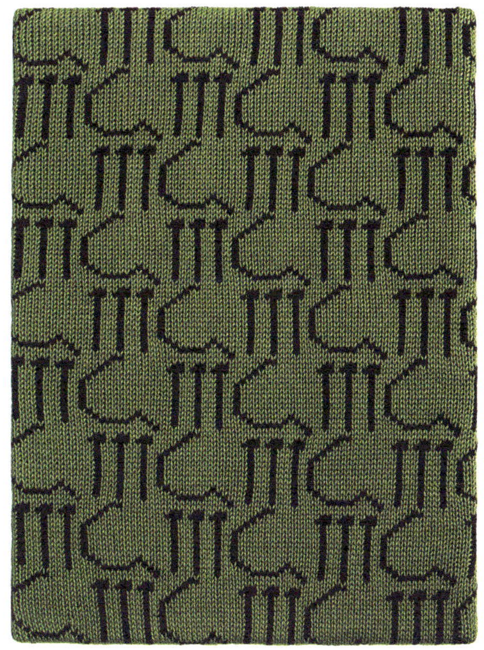

Fig. 12 Rosemarie Trockel *Untitled* 1986 wool

defines the field of possible forms that can be made. "Customization" will come to look more and more generic as the number of participants in its system increases. Our common understanding of production may move from the infinitely repeated, identical forms purchased off the shelf to one in which every industrial object is a unique commission, perfectly geared to our personal taste. It's not that technology is bad as far as opening up new conceptual space for artists is concerned. The question is, how does one produce idiosyncrasy in a future where everything that is made already looks idiosyncratic?

(1)
In March 2011, the paper featured Brooklynites' use of relatively cheap kits to build 3-D printers, though the capacities of these machines are at this writing still limited.

Exhibition Checklist

The works listed represent the Walker Art Center presentation of the exhibition; the checklist may vary with each tour venue. Numbers in bold before titles refer to plates in this catalogue.

Ai Weiwei
Chinese, b. 1957
58 Kui Hua Zi (Sunflower Seeds) 2009
1,000 porcelain sunflower seeds, sculpted and painted by hand, manufactured in Jingdezhen, China, in glass jar inscribed with title and artist's name; ed. 30/30
$6^{3/8}$ x $4^{3/8}$ x $4^{3/8}$ in. (16.2 x 11.1 x 11.1 cm)
Collection New Museum of Contemporary Art, New York

Akasegawa Genpei
Japanese, b. 1937
5 "Greater Japan Zero-Yen Notes" and Bottled Money from Exchange 1967
glass jar, printed material, envelopes, letters, currency
jar: 13 x $8^{1/2}$ x $8^{1/2}$ in. (33 x 21.6 x 21.6 cm)
Walker Art Center, Minneapolis;
T. B. Walker Acquisition Fund, 2009

Tauba Auerbach
American, b. 1981
51 Untitled (Fold) 2011
acrylic on canvas
63 x 48 in. (160 x 121.9 cm)
Courtesy the artist and Paula Cooper Gallery, New York

Robert Bechtle
American, b. 1932
17 '73 Malibu 1974
oil on canvas
48 x 69 in. (121.9 x 152.4 cm)
Courtesy Louis K. and Susan P. Meisel
21 Fosters Freeze 1970
oil on linen
48 x 60 in. (121.9 x 152.4 cm)
The Robert B. Mayer Family Collection, Chicago

Dike Blair
American, b. 1952
All works gouache on paper
43 Untitled 2008
15 x 20 in. (38.1 x 50.8 cm)
Collection Anna Gaskell and Scott Silver
44 Untitled 2010
18 x 24 in. (45.7 x 61 cm)
Courtesy Gagosian Gallery
45 Untitled 2008
18 x 24 in. (45.7 x 61 cm)
Courtesy Gagosian Gallery
46 Untitled 2008
15 x 20 in. (38.1 x 50.8 cm)
Collection Marie Abma, New York
47 Untitled 2009
24 x 18 in. (61 x 45.7 cm)
Mugrabi Collection
48 Untitled 2006
14 x 10 in. (35.6 x 25.4 cm)
Private collection, New York

James Casebere
American, b. 1953
63 Landscape with Houses (Dutchess County, NY) #8 2010
framed digital chromogenic print mounted to Dibond; ed. 1/5
$74^{1/8}$ x $90^{3/4}$ x 3 in.
(188.3 x 230.5 x 7.6 cm)
Courtesy the artist and Sean Kelly Gallery, New York

Maurizio Cattelan
Italian, b. 1960
76 Untitled 2001
mixed media/assemblage/collage; powered device, miniaturized elevator cabs with computer chips, working mechanical doors and lights; ed. 2/10
elevator: $33^{5/8}$ x $33^{3/4}$ x $18^{1/2}$ in.
(85.4 x 85.7 x 47 cm)
door frame: $12^{1/2}$ x 8 x $1^{1/2}$ in.
(31.8 x 20.3 x 3.8 cm)
Collection Ralph and Peggy Burnet, Minneapolis

Vija Celmins
American, b. Latvia, 1938
2 Eggs 1964
oil on canvas
$24^{1/4}$ x $35^{1/4}$ in. (61.6 x 89.5 cm)
Collection Museum of Contemporary Art San Diego; Museum purchase with funds from George Wick and Ansley I. Graham Trust, Los Angeles, in memory of Hope Wick
14 Eraser 1967
acrylic on balsa wood
$6^{5/8}$ x 20 x $3^{1/8}$ in. (16.8 x 50.8 x 7.9 cm)
Collection Orange County Museum of Art, Newport Beach, California; Gift of Avco Financial Services, Newport Beach, California
13 Untitled (Comb) 1970
enamel on wood
77 x 24 in. (195.6 x 61 cm)
Collection Los Angeles County Museum of Art; Contemporary Art Council Fund/Contemporary Art Department
38 Night Sky #6 1993
oil on linen mounted on wood
$19^{1/8}$ x $22^{3/8}$ x $1^{3/16}$ in. (48.6 x 56.8 x 3 cm)
Walker Art Center, Minneapolis;
Purchased with the aid of funds from Harriet and Edson W. Spencer and the T. B. Walker Acquisition Fund, 1995

John Clem Clarke
American, b. 1937
16 Plywood with Roller Marks, #3 1974
oil on canvas
86 x 58 in. (218.4 x 147.3 cm)
Hallmark Art Collection, Kansas City, Missouri

Chuck Close
American, b. 1940
4 Big Self-Portrait 1967–1968
acrylic on canvas
$107^{1/2}$ x $83^{1/2}$ x 2 in. (273.1 x 212.1 x 5.1 cm)
Walker Art Center; Minneapolis Art Center Acquisition Fund, 1969

Susan Collis
British, b. 1956
57 Forever Young 2009
pine plank, ebony, white holly, walnut, birds-eye maple and walnut sapwood veneers, silver, platinum, laminated chipboard, garnets, cedar of Lebanon wood, smoky quartz, black diamonds, oxidized silver, mother of pearl, white gold, smoky topaz, amber, mahogany, tulipwood, embroidery linen, thread
dimensions variable
Courtesy the artist and Tony Shafrazi Gallery, New York
61 Refugee 2007
ballpoint pen, pencil and glue on paper
20 x 11 x 24 in. (50.8 x 27.9 x 61 cm)
Courtesy Tony Shafrazi Gallery, New York

Thomas Demand
German, b. 1964
36 Barn 1997
color chromogenic print
$72^{1/4}$ x $99^{3/4}$ x $1^{1/2}$ in.
(183.5 x 253.4 x 3.8 cm)
Walker Art Center, Minneapolis;
Butler Family Fund, 1998
41 Rain/Regen 2008
35mm film (color, sound) transferred to HD video; 4 minutes
Courtesy the artist and Matthew Marks Gallery

Esteban Pastorino Diaz
Argentinian, b. 1972
34 Cuatro Vientos 2006
digital chromogenic print
$38^{3/16}$ x $46^{1/16}$ in. (97 x 117 cm)
Private collection

Daniel Douke
American, b. 1943
20 Ace 1979
acrylic on Masonite
8 x 8 x 12 1/4 in. (20.3 x 20.3 x 31.1 cm)
Collection Minnesota Museum of American Art; Gift of Mr. Arthur Cohen

Keith Edmier
American, b. 1967
65 Bremen Towne (detail) 2006–2007
building materials, reproduction and vintage fabrics, furnishings, fixtures, finishes
dimensions variable
Courtesy the artist and Friedrich Petzel Gallery, New York

Leandro Erlich
Argentinian, b. 1973
78 Subway 2010
Blu-ray disc (color, sound), stainless-steel structure, glass, certificate of authenticity; 1:30 minutes looped; ed. of 5, 2 AP
82 5/8 x 43 3/8 x 10 in.
(209.9 x 110.2 x 25.4 cm)
Private collection; Courtesy Sean Kelly Gallery, New York

Dan Fischer
American, b. 1977
All works graphite on paper
71 Charles Ray 2001
23 1/2 x 16 1/2 in. (59.7 x 41.9 cm)
Collection A. G. Rosen
70 Tom Friedman 2001
14 1/8 x 11 in. (35.9 x 27.9 cm)
Collection Brett Shaheen; Courtesy Shaheen Modern and Contemporary Art, Cleveland
68 Gerhard Richter 2002
22 1/4 x 15 in. (56.5 x 38.1 cm)
Collection Glenn and Amanda Fuhrman, New York; Courtesy FLAG Art Foundation
69 Robert Gober 2003
22 3/8 x 17 1/2 in. (56.8 x 44.5 cm)
Collection Glenn and Amanda Fuhrman, New York; Courtesy FLAG Art Foundation
72 Thomas Demand 2005
15 x 11 in. (38.1 x 27.9 cm)
Collection Glenn and Amanda Fuhrman, New York; Courtesy FLAG Art Foundation
67 Warhol Brillo Box 2009
17 1/8 x 14 1/2 in. (43.5 x 36.8 cm)
Courtesy the Collection of Ann and Steven Ames, New York

Peter Fischli and David Weiss
Swiss, b. 1952/b. 1946
26 Empty Room 1995–1996
polyurethane, paint
dimensions variable
Walker Art Center, Minneapolis; T. B. Walker Acquisition Fund, 1996

Tom Friedman
American, b. 1965
56 Untitled 2001
clay, wire, fuzz, hair, plastic, paint
7/8 x 5/8 x 1/2 in. (2.2 x 1.6 x 1.3 cm)
Private collection

Robert Gober
American, b. 1954
25 Newspaper 1992
photolithograph on paper, twine; ed. 2/10
6 x 16 3/4 x 13 1/4 in. (15.2 x 42.5 x 33.7 cm)
Walker Art Center, Minneapolis; T. B. Walker Acquisition Fund, 1994
24 Untitled 1997
cast plastic, painted bronze, paper, silver-plated steel, wood; AP 1/1
17 1/4 x 13 x 13 in. (43.8 x 33 x 33 cm)
Courtesy the artist, New York

Duane Hanson
American, 1925-1996
15 Janitor 1973
polyester, fiberglass, mixed media
65 1/2 x 28 x 22 in. (166.4 x 71.1 x 55.9 cm)
Milwaukee Art Museum; Gift of Friends of Art, 1973

Alex Hay
American, b. 1930
10 Cash Register Slip 1966
spray lacquer and stencil on linen
80 5/8 x 37 7/8 in. (204.8 x 96.2 cm)
Private collection
Courtesy Peter Freeman, Inc., New York
3 Paper Bag 1968
fiberglass, epoxy, spray lacquer and stencil on paper
59 3/8 x 29 1/4 x 18 in.
(150.8 x 74.3 x 45.7 cm)
Whitney Museum of American Art, New York; Purchase with funds from the Friends of the Whitney Museum of American Art, 1969

Jasper Johns
American, b. 1930
11 Bread 1969
embossed lead, oil paint, paper; ed. of 61
20 5/8 x 17 11/16 in. (52.4 x 44.9 cm)
Walker Art Center, Minneapolis; Gift of Kenneth E. Tyler, 1985

Matt Johnson
American, b. 1978
29 American Spirit 2010
paper, plastic, foam, paint, magnets; ed. 3/3
object: 1 x 3 1/2 x 2 1/4 in. (2.5 x 8.9 x 5.7 cm)
pedestal: 36 1/2 x 18 1/2 x 18 1/2 in. (92.7 x 47 x 47 cm)
Courtesy the artist and Blum & Poe, Los Angeles

Jeon Joonho
Korean, b. 1969
79 The White House 2005–2006
digital animation; 32:16 minutes
Courtesy the artist and Gallery Hyundai, Seoul, Korea

Edward Kienholz
American, 1927–1944
8 Sawdy 1971
car door, mirrored window, automotive lacquer, polyester resin, screenprint, fluorescent light, galvanized sheet metal
39 x 37 1/2 x 8 in.
(99.1 x 95.3 x 20.3 cm)
Walker Art Center, Minneapolis; Gift of Kenneth E. Tyler, 1985

Isaac Layman
American, b. 1977
39 Oven 2010
archival inkjet print; AP 1/2
45 x 60 in. (114.3 x 152.4 cm)
Collection Ellen and Herbert Levitt

David Lefkowitz
American, b. 1962
55 Selections from Fixtures 1991–2011
oil on wood panels
dimensions vary
Courtesy the artist and Carrie Secrist Gallery, Chicago

Ron Mueck
Australian, b. 1958
28 Crouching Boy in Mirror 1999–2000
mixed media
figure: 17 x 18 x 11 in. (43.2 x 45.7 x 27.9 cm)
mirror: 18 x 22 x 1/4 in. (45.7 x 55.9 x 25.4 cm)
Broad Art Foundation, Santa Monica

Catherine Murphy
American, b. 1946
40 Moiré Chair 1991
oil on canvas
40 x 46 in. (101.6 x 116.8 cm)
Courtesy the artist and Peter Freeman, Inc., New York

Jud Nelson
American, b. 1943
54 Hefty 2-Ply 1979–1981
marble
$26^{3/4}$ x $26^{1/2}$ x 18 in.
(67.9 x 67.3 x 45.7 cm)
Walker Art Center, Minneapolis; Purchased with the aid of funds from Mr. and Mrs. James K. Wittenberg, the National Endowment for the Arts, and the Art Center Acquisition Fund, 1979

Ruben Nusz
American, b. 1978
73 Nothing good happens after midnight/everything good happens after midnight 2008
acrylic, oil, tea, walnut ink on wax and resin with incense and cremation ashes
dimensions vary
Courtesy the artist

Kaz Oshiro
Japanese, b. 1967
42 Sony Bookshelf Speakers 2003–2004
acrylic, Bondo on stretched canvas
$108^{1/2}$ x $19^{5/8}$ x $9^{7/8}$ in. (275.6 x 49.8 x 25.1 cm) installed
Collection Frederick R. Weisman Art Foundation, Beverly Hills, California
66 Dumpster (Flesh with Turquoise Swoosh) 2011
acrylic on stretched canvas, caster wheels
$47^{3/4}$ x $75^{1/2}$ x 34 in. overall
(121.3 x 191.8 x 86.4 cm)
Private collection Family Hunting, the Netherlands; Courtesy galerie frank elbaz, Paris
74 Zero Case Spinner (gun metal—torn FRAGILE stickers) 2011
acrylic, Bondo on stretched canvas, caster wheels
$31^{1/4}$ x $20^{1/4}$ x 10 in.
(79.4 x 51.4 x 25.4 cm)
Private collection Family Hunting, the Netherlands; Courtesy galerie frank elbaz, Paris

Roxy Paine
American, b. 1966
75 Untitled 2002
polymer, lacquer, oil on wood frame
$60^{1/2}$ x $90^{3/8}$ x $9^{1/2}$ in.
(153.7 x 229.6 x 24.1 cm)
Private collection, New York

Evan Penny
South African, b. 1953
77 (Old) No One—in Particular # 6, Series 2 2005
silicone, pigment, hair, fabric, aluminum
40 x 32 x $7^{1/2}$ in. (101.6 x 81.3 x 19.1 cm)
Collection Ralph and Peggy Burnet, Minneapolis

Sylvia Plimack Mangold
American, b. 1938
18 August 1974
acrylic on canvas
78 x 65 in. (198.1 x 165.1 cm)
Minneapolis Institute of Arts; Gift of funds from Alida Messinger
19 In Memory of My Father 1976
acrylic on canvas
$30^{1/8}$ x $72^{1/16}$ in. (76.5 x 183 cm)
Art Institute of Chicago; Through prior gift of Adeline Yates

Robert Rauschenberg
American, 1925–2008
7 Cardbird Box II 1971
offset printed paper, cardboard, wood; ed. 1/20
16 x $15^{7/8}$ x $3^{1/2}$ in. (40.6 x 40.3 x 8.9 cm)
Walker Art Center, Minneapolis; Gift of Kenneth E. Tyler, 1985

Charles Ray
American, b. 1953
23 Bath 1989
porcelain bathtub, brass, aluminum, water
60 x $29^{1/2}$ x 21 in. (152.4 x 74.9 x 53.3 cm)
Museum of Contemporary Art, Los Angeles; El Paso Natural Gas Company Fund for California Art, 1989
22 No 1991
color photograph in artist's frame; ed. of 4
39 x 31 x 2 in. (99.1 x 78.7 x 5.1 cm)
Museum of Contemporary Art, Los Angeles; Gift of Lannan Foundation, 1997

Gerhard Richter
German, b. 1932
31 9 Objekte (9 Objects) 1969
portfolio of 9 photolithographs with cover sheet and portfolio folder; ed. of 26
$17^{1/2}$ x $17^{1/2}$ in. (44.5 x 44.5 cm) each
Walker Art Center, Minneapolis; T. B. Walker Acquisition Fund, 1991
12 Candle (Kerze) 1982
oil on canvas
$27^{1/2}$ x $21^{1/2}$ in. (69.8 x 54.6 cm)
Art Institute of Chicago; Through prior gift of Mr. and Mrs. Lewis Larned Coburn; Gift of Lannan Foundation, 1997.172
30 Betty 1991
offset print on cardboard with nitrocellulose varnish, mounted on plastic, framed behind glass; ed. of 75
$38^{1/4}$ x $26^{1/16}$ in. (97.1 x 66.2 cm)
Collection Ralph and Peggy Burnet, Minneapolis
37 Lake Shore Drive, Chicago 1992
oil on canvas
48 x 32 in. (121.9 x 81.3 cm)
Walker Art Center, Minneapolis; Promised gift of Martha and Bruce Atwater, Minneapolis

Ugo Rondinone
Swiss, b. 1964
59 still.life. (cardboard leaning on the wall) 2009
bronze cast, lead, paint; ed of 1, AP
$46^{1/4}$ x $46^{1/8}$ x 9 in.
(117.5 x 117.2 x 22.9 cm)
Courtesy Sadie Coles HQ, London

Peter Rostovsky
Russian, b. 1970
49 Curtain 2010
oil on linen
48 x 72 in. (121.9 x 182.9 cm)
Collection Michael Peterman and David Wilson

Edward Ruscha
American, b. 1937
9 I'm Amazed 1971
screenprint on paper; AP, ed. of 100
40 x $59^{13/16}$ in. (101.6 x 151.9 cm)
Walker Art Center, Minneapolis; T. B. Walker Acquisition Fund, McKnight Acquisition Fund, 2002

Jonathan Seliger
American, b. 1955
81 Heartland 2010
enamel on bronze
103 x 29 x 29 in. installed
(261.6 x 73.7 x 73.7 cm)
Courtesy the artist and Jack Shainman Gallery, New York

Paul Sietsema
American, b. 1968
64 Untitled ink drawing 2009
ink on paper in artist's frame
$28^{7/8}$ x $21^{3/8}$ in. (73.3 x 54.3 cm)

Private collection, New York
Courtesy Matthew Marks Gallery

Rudolf Stingel
Italian, b. 1956
50 Untitled (after Sam) 2006
oil on canvas
132 x 180 in. (335.3 x 457.2 cm)
Collection Museum of Contemporary Art, Chicago; Gift of Katherine S. Schamberg by exchange

Yoshihiro Suda
Japanese, b. 1969
62 Weeds 2008
painted wood
dimensions vary
Courtesy the artist and Gallery Koyanagi, Tokyo

Sam Taylor-Wood
British, b. 1967
32 Still Life 2001
35mm film (color, sound) transferred to video; 3:44 minutes
Fisher Collection, San Francisco

Paul Thek
American, 1933–1988
6 Untitled (Foot) circa 1968
latex
$6\frac{3}{4}$ x $9\frac{3}{4}$ x 4 in. (17.1 x 24.8 x 10.2 cm)
Walker Art Center, Minneapolis; Anonymous gift, 2005

Robert Therrien
American. b. 1947
80 No title (Folding table and chairs, dark brown) 2007
painted metal, fabric
approximately 104 x 180 x 180 in. (264.2 x 457.2 x 457.2 cm)
Courtesy the artist and Gagosian Gallery

Mungo Thomson
American, b. 1969
53 Between Projects 2001
handmade pencils
$7\frac{1}{2}$ x $\frac{1}{4}$ in. (19.1 x .6 cm) each
Courtesy of di Rosa, Napa
33 New York, New York, New York, New York 2004
4-channel video installation (color, sound)
running times/dimensions variable
Courtesy the artist

Rirkrit Tiravanija
Thai, b. Argentina, 1961
35 Young man, if my wife makes it ... 2000
wooden chopsticks, plastic, metal bowl; ed. 12/27
$7\frac{1}{4}$ x 12 x $9\frac{1}{2}$ in. (18.4 x 30.5 x 24.1 cm)
Walker Art Center, Minneapolis; T. B. Walker Acquisition Fund, 2001

Gavin Turk
British, b. 1967
27 Nomad 2001
painted bronze
$16\frac{1}{2}$ x $41\frac{1}{4}$ x $66\frac{1}{2}$ in. (41.9 x 104.8 x 168.9 cm)
Collection Ralph and Peggy Burnet, Minneapolis

Andy Warhol
American, 1928–1987
1 White Brillo Box 1964
17 x $16\frac{7}{8}$ x 14 in. (43.2 x 42.9 x 35.6 cm)
1 Yellow Brillo Box 1964
13 x 16 x $11\frac{1}{2}$ in. (33 x 40.6 x 29.2 cm)
synthetic polymer paint, screenprint on wood
Walker Art Center, Minneapolis; Gifts of Kate Butler Peterson, 2002

Paul Winstanley
British, b. 1954
52 Utopia 1 2005
oil on linen
$74\frac{13}{16}$ x $92\frac{15}{16}$ in. (190 x 236 cm)
Collection Ralph and Peggy Burnet, Minneapolis

Steve Wolfe
American, b. Italy, 1955
60 Untitled (Are You Experienced?) 1993
oil, enamel, lithography, modeling paste on board
$20\frac{3}{4}$ x $20\frac{1}{4}$ x 1 in. (52.7 x 51.4 x 2.5 cm) framed
Collection Lawrence Luhring; Courtesy Luhring Augustine, New York

Lenders to the Exhibition

Marie Abma, New York
Ann and Steven Ames, New York
Art Institute of Chicago
Bruce and Martha Atwater
Blum & Poe, Los Angeles
Broad Art Foundation, Santa Monica
Ralph and Peggy Burnet, Minneapolis
Sadie Coles HQ, London
Paula Cooper Gallery, New York
di Rosa, Napa, California
galerie frank elbaz, Paris
Fisher Collection, San Francisco
Peter Freeman, Inc., New York
Glenn and Amanda Furhman/FLAG Art Foundation, New York
Gagosian Gallery
Anna Gaskell and Scott Silver
Robert Gober, New York
Gallery Hyundai, Seoul, Korea
Gallery Koyanagi, Tokyo
Hallmark Art Collection, Kansas City
Family Hunting, the Netherlands
Sean Kelly Gallery, New York
David Lefkowitz, Minneapolis
Ellen and Herbert Levitt
Los Angeles County Museum of Art
Lawrence Luhring/Luhring Augustine, New York
Matthew Marks Gallery
Robert B. Mayer Family Collection, Chicago
Louis K. and Susan P. Meisel
Milwaukee Art Museum
Minneapolis Institute of Arts
Minnesota Museum of American Art
Mugrabi Collection
Museum of Contemporary Art, Chicago
Museum of Contemporary Art, Los Angeles
Museum of Contemporary Art San Diego
New Museum of Contemporary Art, New York
Ruben Nusz
Orange County Museum of Art, Newport Beach
Michael Peterman and David Wilson
Friedrich Petzel Gallery, New York
Collection A. G. Rosen
Carrie Secrist Gallery, Chicago
Tony Shafrazi Gallery, New York
Brett Shaheen/Shaheen Modern and Contemporary Art, Cleveland
Jack Shainman Gallery, New York
Mungo Thomson
Walker Art Center, Minneapolis
Frederick R. Weisman Art Foundation, Beverly Hills
Whitney Museum of American Art, New York
Private collections

Walker Art Center Board of Trustees 2011–2012

Reproduction Credits

Inside cover

Charles Ray, from caption contributions to Bruce Ferguson's essay "The Sculpture of Charles Ray," in *Charles Ray* (Malmö, Sweden: Rooseum Center for Contemporary Art, 1990), 15.
Page 10: Private collection. Photo: Cameron Wittig

Engberg, "Previous Lives"

Fig. 1: ©Duane Hanson/VG Bild-Kunst. Brigitte Hellgoth/ ©documenta Archiv. Courtesy Documenta Archiv

Fig. 2: Courtesy Seventeen Gallery, London

Fig. 3: Collection the artist

Fig. 4: Metropolitan Museum of Art, New York; George A. Hearn Fund, 1977. Photo ©Metropolitan Museum of Art/ Art Resource, NY

Fig. 5: Collection Nancy and Mark Gorrell, Berkeley. ©Robert Bechtle

Fig. 6: Courtesy Louis K. Meisel Gallery, New York

Fig. 7: ©Ed Ruscha. Courtesy Gagosian Gallery, New York

Fig. 8: ©2012 Chuck Close. Courtesy the Pace Gallery. Photo courtesy the artist and the Pace Gallery

Fig. 9: ©Vija Celmins. Courtesy McKee Gallery, New York

Fig. 10: Museum of Fine Arts, Boston; Henry H. and Zoe Oliver Sherman Fund, 1984

Fig. 11: Orange County Museum of Art, Newport Beach, CA. ©Charles Ray

Fig. 12: Courtesy the artist

Fig. 13: Hirshhorn Museum and Sculpture Garden, Smithsonian Institution, Washington, DC; Joseph H. Hirshhorn Bequest and Purchase Funds, Holenia Purchase Fund, in memory of Joseph H. Hirshhorn, and Museum Purchase, 2003. Photo: Lee Stalsworth

Fig. 14: Nelson-Atkins Museum of Art, Kansas City, MO; Gift of Mr. and Mrs. Adam Aronson ©Idelle Weber. Photo: John Lamberton

Fig. 15: ©Hiroshi Sugimoto. Courtesy the artist and the Pace Gallery

Fig. 16: Courtesy Seventeen Gallery, London

Fig. 17: Private collection. Courtesy Mitchell-Innes & Nash, New York

Fig. 18: ©Franz Gertsch. Courtesy Gagosian Gallery. Photo: Robert McKeever

Fig. 19: ©Felix Gonzalez-Torres Foundation. Courtesy Andrea Rosen Gallery, New York, and the Museum of Modern Art, New York. Photo: Peter Muscato

Fig. 20: Art Institute of Chicago; Through prior gifts of Mary and Leigh Block, Mr. and Mrs. Joel Starrels, Mrs. Gilbert W. Chapman, and Mr. and Mrs. Roy J. Friedman; restricted gift of Donna and Howard Stone, 2007. Courtesy the artist and Matthew Marks Gallery, New York

Fig. 21: Courtesy Peter Mendenhall Gallery, Los Angeles

Fig. 22: Courtesy the artist and Luhring Augustine, New York

Fig. 23: Private Collection Family Hunting, the Netherlands. Courtesy the artist and galerie frank elbaz, Paris. Photo: Kaz Oshiro

Fig. 24: Courtesy the artist

Fig. 25: Albright-Knox Art Gallery, Buffalo, NY; Sarah Norton Goodyear Fund, 2007. ©Robert Therrien. Courtesy Gagosian Gallery, New York. Photo: Joshua White

Fig. 26: Hirshhorn Museum and Sculpture Garden, Smithsonian Institution, Washington, DC. Photo: Anthony d'Offay, London

Fig. 27: Courtesy Leandro Erlich Studio, Buenos Aires

Fig. 28: Courtesy Gavin Brown's enterprise

Fig. 29: Courtesy the artist

Lobel, "Realism, circa 1970"

Fig. 1: Stiftung Archaeologie, University of Heidelberg, Germany. Photo: Dieter Rehm

Fig. 2: Museum of Modern Art, New York; Gift of Edward R. Broida. ©2011 Estate of Philip Guston. Courtesy McKee Gallery, New York

Fig. 3: Art Institute of Chicago; Restricted Gift of Edgar Kaufmann, Jr.; Twentieth-Century Purchase Fund, 1970. Photo ©Art Institute of Chicago

Fig. 4: ©Vija Celmins. Courtesy McKee Gallery, New York

Fig 5: Dallas Museum of Art; Ruth and Clarence Roy Fund and DMA/amfAR Benefit Auction Fund

Fig. 6: ©2012 Walker Art Center, Minneapolis. Photo: Eric Sutherland

Fig. 7: Lucy R. Lippard Papers, Archives of American Art, Smithsonian Institution. Courtesy Archives of American Art, Smithsonian Institution

Fig. 8: Courtesy the Leo Baeck Institute, New York. Photo: John D. Schiff

Fig. 9: Philadelphia Museum of Art; Purchased with funds contributed by the Daniel W. Dietrich Foundation, 1990. ©Estate of George Paul Thek. Courtesy Alexander and Bonin, New York

Steiner, "Seeing May Be Believing"

Fig. 1: Courtesy the artist and Blum & Poe, Los Angeles. Photo: Joshua White

Fig. 2: Courtesy Regen Projects, Los Angeles, and Public Art Fund, New York. Photo: Seong Kwan

Fig. 3: Philadelphia Museum of Art; Gift of Jacqueline, Paul, and Peter Matisse in memory of their mother, Alexina Duchamp, 1998. ©2011 Artists Rights Society (ARS), New York / ADAGP, Paris / Succession Marcel Duchamp

Fig. 4: Courtesy the artist; Luhring Augustine, New York; and Stephen Friedman Gallery, London

Fig. 5: Walker Art Center, Minneapolis; Gift of Judy and Kenneth Dayton, 1994. ©2012 Chuck Close

Fig. 6: ©Ai Weiwei. Photo ©2012 Tate, London

Fig. 7: Courtesy Walker Art Center, Minneapolis

McElheny, "Readymade Resistance"

The essay "Readymade Resistance: Art and the Forms of Industrial Production" by Josiah McElheny originally appeared in *Artforum* (October 2007). ©*Artforum*

Fig. 1: San Francisco Museum of Modern Art; Purchase through a gift of Phyllis Wattis. ©2012 Artists Rights Society (ARS), New York / ADAGP, Paris / Succession Marcel Duchamp

Fig. 2: Walker Art Center, Minneapolis; Gift of Judy and Kenneth Dayton, 1998. ©Jasper Johns/ Licensed by VAGA, New York, NY

Figs. 3–4: ©Jeff Koons. Courtesy the artist

Fig. 5: ©2012 Robert Gober. Courtesy Matthew Marks Gallery, New York

Fig. 6: Astrup Fearnley Collection, Oslo; Collection S.M.A.K. (Stedelijk Museum voor Actuele Kunst), Gent (4/8), Carnegie Museum of Art, Pittsburgh; Robert S. Waters Charitable Trust Fund, Patrons Art Fund, Second Century Acquisition Fund, and Oxford Development Acquisition Fund, 93.4 (AP 1/2); Private collections. Courtesy Matthew Marks Gallery, New York

Fig. 7: Courtesy the artist and Blum & Poe, Los Angeles

Fig. 8: Courtesy the artist and galerie frank elbaz, Paris. Photo: Kaz Oshiro

Fig. 9: Walker Art Center, Minneapolis; Gift of the artist and Helen van der Meij-Tcheng, by exchange, 2009

Fig. 10: Walker Art Center, Minneapolis; T. B. Walker Acquisition Fund, 2008

Fig. 11: ©Carol Bove. Courtesy the artist; Maccarone, New York; and David Zwirner, New York

Fig. 12: ©2012 Artists Rights Society (ARS), New York / VG Bild-Kunst, Bonn

Plates

Plates 1–2: Courtesy Walker Art Center, Minneapolis

Plate 3: Whitney Museum of American Art, New York; Purchase with funds from the Friends of the Whitney Museum of American Art. ©Alex Hay. Courtesy the artist and Peter Freeman, Inc., New York. Photo: Jerry L. Thompson

Plate 4: ©2012 Chuck Close. Courtesy Walker Art Center, Minneapolis

Plates 5–6: Courtesy Walker Art Center, Minneapolis

Plate 7: Courtesy Walker Art Center, Minneapolis

Plate 8: ©Kienholz. Courtesy L. A. Louver, Venice, CA / Walker Art Center, Minneapolis

Plate 9: ©2012 Ed Ruscha. Courtesy Walker Art Center, Minneapolis

Plate 10: ©Alex Hay. Courtesy the artist and Peter Freeman, Inc., New York.

Plate 11: Museum of Contemporary Art San Diego; Museum purchase with funds from George Wick and Ansley I. Graham Trust, Los Angeles in memory of Hope Wick. ©Vija Celmins. Courtesy McKee Gallery, New York

Plate 12: Courtesy the artist and Marian Goodman Gallery, New York / Paris

Plate 13: ©Vija Celmins. Courtesy McKee Gallery, New York

Plate 14: Orange County Museum of Art, Newport Beach, CA; Gift of Avco Financial Services, Newport Beach. ©Vija Celmins

Plate 15: Milwaukee Art Museum; Gift of Friends of Art, 1973. Photo: John Nienhuis

Plate 16: Courtesy Hallmark Art Collection, Kansas City

Plate 17: ©Robert Bechtle. Courtesy Louis K. Meisel Gallery, New York

Plate 18: ©Sylvia Plimack Mangold

Plate 19: Art Institute of Chicago; Through prior gift of Adeline Yates, 2009. ©Sylvia Plimack Mangold. Photo ©Art Institute of Chicago

Plate 20: Courtesy Minnesota Museum of American Art, St. Paul

Plate 21: ©Robert Bechtle

Plates 22–23: ©Charles Ray. Courtesy Matthew Marks Gallery, New York

Plate 24: ©2012 Robert Gober. Courtesy the artist. Photo: Erma Estwick

Plate 25: ©2012 Robert Gober. Courtesy Walker Art Center, Minneapolis

Plate 26: Courtesy Walker Art Center, Minneapolis

Plate 27: Gavin Turk. Courtesy Gavin Turk/ Livestock Market, Ltd.

Plate 28: Broad Art Foundation, Santa Monica. ©Ron Mueck. Courtesy the artist and Anthony d'Offay, Ltd.

Plate 29: ©Matt Johnson. Courtesy the artist and Blum & Poe, Los Angeles. Photo: Joshua White

Plate 30: Courtesy the artist and Marian Goodman Gallery, New York/Paris

Plate 31: Courtesy Walker Art Center, Minneapolis

Plate 32: ©Sam Taylor-Wood. Courtesy White Cube, London

Plate 33: Courtesy the artist

Plate 34: ©Esteban Pastorino Diaz. Courtesy the artist and Photographs Do Not Bend Gallery, Dallas

Plate 35: Courtesy Walker Art Center, Minneapolis

Plate 36: ©2012 Thomas Demand, Artists Rights Society (ARS), New York / VG Bild-Kunst, Bonn. Courtesy Walker Art Center, Minneapolis

Plate 37: Courtesy the artist and Marian Goodman Gallery, New York/Paris

Plate 38: ©Vija Celmins. Courtesy Walker Art Center, Minneapolis

Plate 39: Courtesy the artist and Lawrimore Projects, Seattle

Plate 40: ©Catherine Murphy. Courtesy Knoedler & Company, New York

Plate 41: ©2012 Thomas Demand, Artists Rights Society (ARS), New York / VG Bild-Kunst, Bonn. Courtesy Matthew Marks Gallery, New York

Plate 42: Courtesy Rosamund Felsen Gallery, Santa Monica. Photo ©Douglas M. Parker Studios

Plates 43–48: Courtesy the artist and Gagosian Gallery, New York

Plate 49: Courtesy the artist

Plate 50: Museum of Contemporary Art, Chicago; Gift of Katherine S. Schamberg by exchange, 2006. ©Rudolf Stingel. Photo: Michael David Rose, ©Museum of Contemporary Art, Chicago

Plate 51: ©Tauba Auerbach. Courtesy Paula Cooper Gallery, New York

Plate 52: Courtesy the artist and Mitchell-Innes & Nash, New York

Plate 53: Courtesy the artist

Plate 54: Courtesy Walker Art Center, Minneapolis

Plate 55: Courtesy the artist and Carrie Secrist Gallery, Chicago

Plate 56: Courtesy the artist; Luhring Augustine, New York; and Stephen Friedman Gallery, London

Plate 57: Courtesy Seventeen Gallery, London

Plate 58: Published by Carolina Nitsch for the New Museum of Contemporary Art, New York. Courtesy Carolina Nitsch

Plate 59: Courtesy Sadie Coles HQ, London

Plate 60: Courtesy the artist and Luhring Augustine, New York

Plate 61: Courtesy Seventeen Gallery, London

Plate 62: ©Yoshihiro Suda. Courtesy Gallery Koyanagi, Tokyo

Plate 63: Courtesy the artist and Sean Kelly Gallery, New York

Plate 64: ©Paul Sietsema. Courtesy Matthew Marks Gallery, New York

Plate 65: Courtesy the artist and Friedrich Petzel Gallery, New York

Plate 66: Courtesy the artist and galerie frank elbaz, Paris. Photo: Kaz Oshiro

Plates 67–72: Courtesy Derek Eller Gallery, New York

Plate 73: Courtesy the artist

Plate 74: Courtesy the artist and galerie frank elbaz, Paris. Photo: Kaz Oshiro

Plate 75: ©Roxy Paine. Courtesy James Cohan Gallery, New York/Shanghai

Plate 76: Courtesy the artist and Marian Goodman Gallery, New York

Plate 77: ©Evan Penny. Courtesy Sperone Westwater, New York

Plate 78: ©Leandro Erlich. Courtesy Sean Kelly Gallery, New York

Plate 79: Courtesy the artist and Gallery Hyundai, Seoul

Plate 80: ©Robert Therrien. Courtesy Gagosian Gallery. Photo: Robert McKeever

Plate 81: Courtesy the artist and Jack Shainman Gallery, New York

Object Lessons

Page 66: Excerpt from *Robert Gober: Sculptures and Installations 1979–2007*, ed. Theodora Vischer, exh. cat. (Göttingen, Germany: Steidl, 2009), 386.

Page 92: Excerpt from interview with Vija Celmins in *Art21: Art in the Twenty-First Century*, season 2, "Time" episode (2003), http://video.pbs.org/video/1237794459. ©2003–2007 Art21, Inc. All rights reserved.

Page 103: Excerpt from Peter Rostovsky, "The Heart of the Tin Man: Painting and Photography" (lecture presented at the seminar Image Capture: Photo-based Painting in a Digital Culture, Bonniers Konsthall, Stockholm, Sweden, March 23, 2011).

Page 118: Excerpt from an e-mail conversation between Mungo Thomson and Siri Engberg, November 2011.

Page 125: Excerpt from an interview with the artist, in *The Unilever Series: Ai Weiwei Sunflower Seeds* (Tate Modern: London, 2010), http://www.tate.org.uk/modern/exhibitions/unileverseries2010/room3.shtm. Translation ©2010 Tate.

Page 128: Excerpt from a conversation between Susan Collis, Mackay Butcher, and Cylena Simonds in the gallery brochure for Collis' solo presentation *For all the things we thought we'd love forever* at Frieze Art Fair, London, October 15–18, 2009.

Page 132: Excerpt from an e-mail interview with Paul Sietsema by Yesomi Umolu, October 2011.

Page 136: Excerpt from an interview with Keith Edmier by Siri Engberg, New York, October 2011.

Page 139: Excerpt from a Skype interview with Kaz Oshiro by Yesomi Umolu, October 2011.

Published on the occasion of the exhibition Lifelike, curated by Siri Engberg and organized by the Walker Art Center, Minneapolis.

Lifelike is made possible by major support from John L. Thomson and the Andy Warhol Foundation for the Visual Arts. Additional support is generously provided by Peggy and Ralph Burnet, Ellie and Tom Crosby, Jr., and Michael J. Peterman and David A. Wilson.

The exhibition catalogue is made possible by a grant from the Andrew W. Mellon Foundation in support of Walker Art Center publications. Additional support for the Keith Edmier insert is provided by Friedrich Petzel Gallery, New York.

Walker Art Center, Minneapolis
February 25–May 27, 2012

New Orleans Museum of Art, Louisiana
November 10, 2012–January 27, 2013

Museum of Contemporary Art San Diego
February 24–May 26, 2013

Blanton Museum of Art, University of Texas at Austin
June 23–September 29, 2013

Library of Congress Cataloging-in-Publication Data

Engberg, Siri.
Lifelike / Siri Engberg ; with contributions from Michael Lobel, Josiah McElheny, and Rochelle Steiner. -- First edition.
pages cm
Published on the occasion of the exhibition Lifelike, organized by Siri Engberg for the Walker Art Center, Minneapolis.
Includes bibliographical references.
ISBN 978-0-935640-68-7
1. Realism in art--Exhibitions. 2. Material culture in art--Exhibitions. 3. Art, Modern--20th century--Exhibitions. 4. Art, Modern--21st century--Exhibitions. I. Lobel, Michael. II. McElheny, Josiah, 1966- III. Steiner, Rochelle. IV. Walker Art Center. V. Title.
N6494.R4E39 2012
709.05'1074776579--dc23

2011052843

First Edition

Available through D.A.P./Distributed Art Publishers, 155 Sixth Avenue, New York, NY 10013 www.artbook.com

Curatorial Fellow
Yesomi Umolu

Design Director
Emmet Byrne

Designer
Andrea Hyde

Editors
Kathleen McLean and Pamela Johnson

Design Studio Coordinator
Dylan Cole

Senior Imaging Specialist
Greg Beckel

Printed in the United States by The Avery Group at Shapco Printing, Inc., Minneapolis, Minnesota